Named Entities Workshop 2010

(NEWS 2010)

Held at ACL 2010

Uppsala, Sweden
16 July 2010

ISBN: 978-1-61738-818-7

Printed from e-media with permission by:

Curran Associates, Inc.
57 Morehouse Lane
Red Hook, NY 12571

CURRAN ASSOCIATES INC.
proceedings.com

Some format issues inherent in the e-media version may also appear in this print version.

Printed by Curran Associates, Inc. (2010)

Association for Computational Linguistics
209 N. Eighth Street
Stroudsburg, Pennsylvania 18360

Phone: 1-570-476-8006
Fax: 1-570-476-0860

acl@aclweb.org

Additional copies of this publication are available from:

Curran Associates, Inc.
57 Morehouse Lane
Red Hook, NY 12571 USA
Phone: 845-758-0400
Fax: 845-758-2634
Email: curran@proceedings.com
Web: www.proceedings.com

Preface

Named Entities play a significant role in Natural Language Processing and Information Retrieval. While identifying and analyzing named entities in a given natural language is a challenging research problem by itself, the phenomenal growth in the Internet user population, especially among the non-English speaking parts of the world, has extended this problem to the crosslingual arena. We specifically focus on research on all aspects of the Named Entities in our workshop series, Named Entities WorkShop (NEWS). The first of the NEWS workshops (NEWS 2009) was held as a part of ACL-IJCNLP 2009 conference in Singapore, and the current edition (NEWS 2010) is being held as a part of ACL 2010, in Uppsala, Sweden.

The purpose of the NEWS workshop is to bring together researchers across the world interested in identification, analysis, extraction, mining and transformation of named entities in monolingual or multilingual natural language text. The workshop scope includes many interesting specific research areas pertaining to the named entities, such as, orthographic and phonetic characteristics, corpus analysis, unsupervised and supervised named entities extraction in monolingual or multilingual corpus, transliteration modelling, and evaluation methodologies, to name a few. For this years edition, 11 research papers were submitted, each of which was reviewed by at least 3 reviewers from the program committee. 7 papers were chosen for publication, covering main research areas, from named entities recognition, extraction and categorization, to distributional characteristics of named entities, and finally a novel evaluation metrics for co-reference resolution. All accepted research papers are published in the workshop proceedings.

This year, as parts of the NEWS workshop, we organized two shared tasks: one on Machine Transliteration Generation, and another on Machine Transliteration Mining, participated by research teams from around the world, including industry, government laboratories and academia.

The transliteration generation task was introduced in NEWS 2009. While the focus of the 2009 shared task was on establishing the quality metrics and on baselining the transliteration quality based on those metrics, the 2010 shared task expanded the scope of the transliteration generation task to about dozen languages, and explored the quality depending on the direction of transliteration, between the languages. We collected significantly large, hand-crafted parallel named entities corpora in dozen different languages from 8 language families, and made available as common dataset for the shared task. We published the details of the shared task and the training and development data six months ahead of the conference that attracted an overwhelming response from the research community. Totally 7 teams participated in the transliteration generation task. The approaches ranged from traditional unsupervised learning methods (such as, Phrasal SMT-based, Conditional Random Fields, etc.) to somewhat unique approaches (such as, DirectTL approach), combined with several model combinations for results re-ranking. A report of the shared task that summarizes all submissions and the original whitepaper are also included in the proceedings, and will be presented in the workshop. The participants in the shared task were asked to submit short system papers (4 pages each) describing their approach, and each of such papers was reviewed by at least two members of the program committee to help improve the quality of the content and presentation of the papers. 6 of them were finally accepted to be published in the workshop proceedings (one participating team did not submit their system paper in time).

NEWS 2010 also featured a second shared task this year, on Transliteration Mining; in this shared task we focus specifically on mining transliterations from the commonly available resource Wikipedia titles. The objective of this shared task is to identify transliterations from linked Wikipedia titles between English and another language in a non-Latin script. 5 teams participated in the mining task, each participating in multiple languages. The shared task was conducted in 5 language pairs, and the paired

Wikipedia titles between English and each of the languages was provided to the participants. The participating systems output was measured using three specific metrics. All the results are reported in the shared task report.

We hope that NEWS 2010 would provide an exciting and productive forum for researchers working in this research area. The technical programme includes 7 research papers and 9 system papers (3 as oral papers, and 6 as poster papers) to be presented in the workshop. Further, we are pleased to have Dr Dan Roth, Professor at University of Illinois and The Beckman Institute, delivering the keynote speech at the workshop.

We wish to thank all the researchers for their research submission and the enthusiastic participation in the transliteration shared tasks. We wish to express our gratitude to CJK Institute, Institute for Infocomm Research, Microsoft Research India, Cairo Microsoft Innovation Centre and Thailand National Electronics and Computer Technology Centre for preparing the data released as a part of the shared tasks. Finally, we thank all the programme committee members for reviewing the submissions in spite of the tight schedule.

Workshop Chairs

Haizhou Li, Institute for Infocomm Research, Singapore
A Kumaran, Microsoft Research, India

16 July 2010
Uppsala, Sweden

Organizers:

Haizhou Li, Institute for Infocomm Research (Singapore)
A Kumaran, Microsoft Research (India)

Workshop Organizing Committee:

Haizhou Li, Institute for Infocomm Research (Singapore)
A Kumaran, Microsoft Research (India)
Kevin Knight, ISI (USA)
Grzegorz Kondrak, University of Alberta (Canada)
Min Zhang, Institute for Infocomm Research (Singapore)

Shared Task Organizing Committee - Transliteration Generation:

Haizhou Li, Institute for Infocomm Research (Singapore)
A Kumaran, Microsoft Research (India)
Min Zhang, Institute for Infocomm Research (Singapore)
Vladimir Pervouchine, Institute for Infocomm Research (Singapore)

Shared Task Organizing Committee - Transliteration Mining:

A Kumaran, Microsoft Research (India)
Haizhou Li, Institute for Infocomm Research (Singapore)
Mitesh M. Khapra, Indian Institute of Technology Bombay (India)

Program Committee:

Kalika Bali, Microsoft Research (India)
Rafael Banchs, BarcelonaMedia (Spain)
Sivaji Bandyopadhyay, University of Jadavpur (India)
Pushpak Bhattacharyya, IIT-Bombay (India)
Monojit Choudhury, Microsoft Research (India)
Marta Ruiz Costa-jussa, UPC (Spain)
Gregory Grefenstette, Exalead (France)
Mitesh M. Khapra, Indian Institute of Technology Bombay, (India)
Sanjeev Khudanpur, Johns Hopkins University (USA)
Kevin Knight, ISI (USA)
Grzegorz Kondrak, University of Alberta (Canada)
A Kumaran, Microsoft Research (India)
Olivia Kwong, City University (Hong Kong)
Gina-Anne Levow, University of Manchester (UK)
Haizhou Li, Institute for Infocomm Research (Singapore)
Andrew McCallum, University of Massachusetts Amherst (USA)
Arul Menezes, Microsoft Research (USA)
Jong-Hoon Oh, NICT (Japan)
Vladimir Pervouchine, Institute for Infocomm Research (Singapore)
Yan Qu, Advertising.com (USA)
Satoshi Sekine, New York University (USA)
Sunita Sarawagi, IIT-Bombay (India)

Sudeshna Sarkar, IIT-Kharagpur (India)
Richard Sproat, University of Illinois at Urbana-Champaign (USA)
Keh-Yih Su, Behavior Design Corporation (Taiwan)
Raghavendra Udupa, Microsoft Research (India)
Vasudeva Varma, IIIT-Hyderabad (India)
Haifeng Wang, Baidu.com Inc. (China)
Shuly Wintner, University of Haifa (Israel)
Chai Wutiwiwatchai, NECTEC (Thailand)
Min Zhang, Institute for Infocomm Research (Singapore)

Table of Contents

Conference Program

Friday, 16 July 2010

Session 1: Oral

9:00–9:15 Opening Remarks
A. Kumaran and Haizhou Li

9:15–10:00 Keynote Speech
Dan Roth

10:00–10:30 *Transliteration Generation and Mining with Limited Training Resources*
Sittichai Jiampojamarn, Kenneth Dwyer, Shane Bergsma, Aditya Bhargava, Qing Dou, Mi-Young Kim and Grzegorz Kondrak

10:30–11:00 Morning Break

Session 2: Oral

11:00–11:20 *Transliteration Using a Phrase-Based Statistical Machine Translation System to Re-Score the Output of a Joint Multigram Model*
Andrew Finch and Eiichiro Sumita

11:20–11:40 *Transliteration Mining with Phonetic Conflation and Iterative Training*
Kareem Darwish

Friday, 16 July 2010 (continued)

Session 3: Poster

Session 4: Oral

Friday, 16 July 2010 (continued)

15:20–16:00 Lunch Break

Session 5: Oral

16:00–16:20 *Think Globally, Apply Locally: Using Distributional Characteristics for Hindi Named Entity Identification*
Shalini Gupta and Pushpak Bhattacharyya

16:20–16:40 *Rule-Based Named Entity Recognition in Urdu*
Kashif Riaz

16:40–17:00 *CONE: Metrics for Automatic Evaluation of Named Entity Co-Reference Resolution*
Bo Lin, Rushin Shah, Robert Frederking and Anatole Gershman

17:00–17:10 Closing

Report of NEWS 2010 Transliteration Generation Shared Task

Haizhou Li[†], A Kumaran[‡], Min Zhang[†] and Vladimir Pervouchine[†]

[†]Institute for Infocomm Research, A*STAR, Singapore 138632
{hli,mzhang,vpervouchine}@i2r.a-star.edu.sg

[‡]Multilingual Systems Research, Microsoft Research India
A.Kumaran@microsoft.com

Abstract

This report documents the Transliteration Generation Shared Task conducted as a part of the Named Entities Workshop (NEWS 2010), an ACL 2010 workshop. The shared task features machine transliteration of proper names from English to 9 languages and from 3 languages to English. In total, 12 tasks are provided. 7 teams from 5 different countries participated in the evaluations. Finally, 33 standard and 8 non-standard runs are submitted, where diverse transliteration methodologies are explored and reported on the evaluation data. We report the results with 4 performance metrics. We believe that the shared task has successfully achieved its objective by providing a common benchmarking platform for the research community to evaluate the state-of-the-art technologies that benefit the future research and development.

1 Introduction

Names play a significant role in many Natural Language Processing (NLP) and Information Retrieval (IR) systems. They are important in Cross Lingual Information Retrieval (CLIR) and Machine Translation (MT) as the system performance has been shown to positively correlate with the correct conversion of names between the languages in several studies (Demner-Fushman and Oard, 2002; Mandl and Womser-Hacker, 2005; Hermjakob et al., 2008; Udupa et al., 2009). The traditional source for name equivalence, the bilingual dictionaries — whether handcrafted or statistical — offer only limited support because new names always emerge.

All of the above point to the critical need for robust Machine Transliteration technology and systems. Much research effort has been made to address the transliteration issue in the research community (Knight and Graehl, 1998; Meng et al., 2001; Li et al., 2004; Zelenko and Aone, 2006; Sproat et al., 2006; Sherif and Kondrak, 2007; Hermjakob et al., 2008; Al-Onaizan and Knight, 2002; Goldwasser and Roth, 2008; Goldberg and Elhadad, 2008; Klementiev and Roth, 2006; Oh and Choi, 2002; Virga and Khudanpur, 2003; Wan and Verspoor, 1998; Kang and Choi, 2000; Gao et al., 2004; Zelenko and Aone, 2006; Li et al., 2009b; Li et al., 2009a). These previous work fall into three categories, i.e., grapheme-based, phoneme-based and hybrid methods. Grapheme-based method (Li et al., 2004) treats transliteration as a direct orthographic mapping and only uses orthography-related features while phoneme-based method (Knight and Graehl, 1998) makes use of phonetic correspondence to generate the transliteration. Hybrid method refers to the combination of several different models or knowledge sources to support the transliteration generation.

The first machine transliteration shared task (Li et al., 2009b; Li et al., 2009a) was held in NEWS 2009 at ACL-IJCNLP 2009. It was the first time to provide common benchmarking data in diverse language pairs for evaluation of state-of-the-art techniques. NEWS 2010 is a continued effort of NEWS 2009. It builds on the foundations established in the first transliteration shared task and extends the scope to include new language pairs.

The rest of the report is organised as follows. Section 2 outlines the machine transliteration task and the corpora used and Section 3 discusses the metrics chosen for evaluation, along with the rationale for choosing them. Sections 4 and 5 present the participation in the shared task and the results with their analysis, respectively. Section 6 concludes the report.

Proceedings of the 2010 Named Entities Workshop, ACL 2010, pages 1–11,
Uppsala, Sweden, 16 July 2010.

2 Transliteration Shared Task

In this section, we outline the definition and the description of the shared task.

2.1 "Transliteration": A definition

There exists several terms that are used interchangeably in the contemporary research literature for the conversion of names between two languages, such as, transliteration, transcription, and sometimes Romanisation, especially if Latin scripts are used for target strings (Halpern, 2007).

Our aim is not only at capturing the name conversion process from a source to a target language, but also at its practical utility for downstream applications, such as CLIR and MT. Therefore, we adopted the same definition of transliteration as during the NEWS 2009 workshop (Li et al., 2009a) to narrow down "transliteration" to three specific requirements for the task, as follows: *"Transliteration is the conversion of a given name in the source language (a text string in the source writing system or orthography) to a name in the target language (another text string in the target writing system or orthography), such that the target language name is: (i) phonemically equivalent to the source name (ii) conforms to the phonology of the target language and (iii) matches the user intuition of the equivalent of the source language name in the target language, considering the culture and orthographic character usage in the target language."*

In NEWS 2010, we introduce three back-transliteration tasks. We define back-transliteration as a process of restoring transliterated words to their original languages. For example, NEWS 2010 offers the tasks to convert western names written in Chinese and Thai into their original English spellings, or romanized Japanese names into their original Kanji writings.

2.2 Shared Task Description

Following the tradition in NEWS 2009, the shared task at NEWS 2010 is specified as development of machine transliteration systems in one or more of the specified language pairs. Each language pair of the shared task consists of a source and a target language, implicitly specifying the transliteration direction. Training and development data in each of the language pairs have been made available to all registered participants for developing a transliteration system for that specific language pair using any approach that they find appropriate.

At the evaluation time, a standard hand-crafted test set consisting of between 1,000 and 3,000 source names (approximately 10% of the training data size) have been released, on which the participants are required to produce a ranked list of transliteration candidates in the target language for each source name. The system output is tested against a reference set (which may include multiple correct transliterations for some source names), and the performance of a system is captured in multiple metrics (defined in Section 3), each designed to capture a specific performance dimension.

For every language pair every participant is required to submit at least one run (designated as a "standard" run) that uses only the data provided by the NEWS workshop organisers in that language pair, and no other data or linguistic resources. This standard run ensures parity between systems and enables meaningful comparison of performance of various algorithmic approaches in a given language pair. Participants are allowed to submit more "standard" runs, up to 4 in total. If more than one "standard" runs is submitted, it is required to name one of them as a "primary" run, which is used to compare results across different systems. In addition, up to 4 "non-standard" runs could be submitted for every language pair using either data beyond that provided by the shared task organisers or linguistic resources in a specific language, or both. This essentially may enable any participant to demonstrate the limits of performance of their system in a given language pair.

The shared task timelines provide adequate time for development, testing (approximately 1 month after the release of the training data) and the final result submission (7 days after the release of the test data).

2.3 Shared Task Corpora

We considered two specific constraints in selecting languages for the shared task: language diversity and data availability. To make the shared task interesting and to attract wider participation, it is important to ensure a reasonable variety among the languages in terms of linguistic diversity, orthography and geography. Clearly, the ability of procuring and distributing a reasonably large (approximately 10K paired names for training and testing together) hand-crafted corpora consisting primarily of paired names is critical for this process. At the end of the planning stage and after discussion with the data providers, we have chosen the set of 12 tasks shown in Table 1 (Li et al., 2004; Kumaran and Kellner, 2007; MSRI, 2009; CJKI, 2010).

NEWS 2010 leverages on the success of NEWS 2009 by utilizing the training and dev data of NEWS 2009 as the training data of NEWS 2010 and the test data of NEWS 2009 as the dev data of NEWS 2010. NEWS 2010 provides totally new test data across all 12 tasks for evaluation. In addition to the 7 tasks inherited from NEWS 2009, NEWS 2010 is enhanced with 5 new tasks, three new languages (Arabic, Bangla and Thai) and two back-transliteration (Chinese to English and Thai to English).

The names given in the training sets for Chinese, Japanese, Korean and Thai languages are Western names and their respective transliterations; the Japanese Name (in English) $\rightarrow$ Japanese Kanji data set consists only of native Japanese names; the Arabic data set consists only of native Arabic names. The Indic data set (Hindi, Tamil, Kannada, Bangla) consists of a mix of Indian and Western names.

For all of the tasks chosen, we have been able to procure paired names data between the source and the target scripts and were able to make them available to the participants. For some language pairs, such as English-Chinese and English-Thai, there are both transliteration and back-transliteration tasks. Most of the task are just one-way transliteration, although Indian data sets contained mixture of names of both Indian and Western origins. The language of origin of the names for each task is indicated in the first column of Table 1.

Finally, it should be noted here that the corpora procured and released for NEWS 2010 represent perhaps the most diverse and largest corpora to be used for any common transliteration tasks today.

3 Evaluation Metrics and Rationale

The participants have been asked to submit results of up to four standard and four non-standard runs. One standard run must be named as the primary submission and is used for the performance summary. Each run contains a ranked list of up to 10 candidate transliterations for each source name. The submitted results are compared to the ground truth (reference transliterations) using 4 evaluation metrics capturing different aspects of transliteration performance. We have dropped two MAP metrics used in NEWS 2009 because they don't offer additional information to MAP_{ref}. Since a name may have multiple correct transliterations, all these alternatives are treated equally in the evaluation, that is, any of these alternatives is considered as a correct transliteration, and all candidates matching any of the reference transliterations are accepted as correct ones.

The following notation is further assumed:

- N : Total number of names (source words) in the test set
- n_i : Number of reference transliterations for i-th name in the test set ($n_i \geq 1$)
- $r_{i,j}$: j-th reference transliteration for i-th name in the test set
- $c_{i,k}$: k-th candidate transliteration (system output) for i-th name in the test set ($1 \leq k \leq 10$)
- K_i : Number of candidate transliterations produced by a transliteration system

3.1 Word Accuracy in Top-1 (ACC)

Also known as Word Error Rate, it measures correctness of the first transliteration candidate in the candidate list produced by a transliteration system. $ACC = 1$ means that all top candidates are correct transliterations i.e. they match one of the references, and $ACC = 0$ means that none of the top candidates are correct.

$$ACC = \frac{1}{N} \sum_{i=1}^{N} \left\{ \begin{array}{l} 1 \text{ if } \exists r_{i,j} : r_{i,j} = c_{i,1}; \\ 0 \text{ otherwise} \end{array} \right\} \quad (1)$$

3.2 Fuzziness in Top-1 (Mean F-score)

The mean F-score measures how different, on average, the top transliteration candidate is from its closest reference. F-score for each source word is a function of Precision and Recall and equals 1 when the top candidate matches one of the references, and 0 when there are no common characters between the candidate and any of the references.

Precision and Recall are calculated based on the length of the Longest Common Subsequence (LCS) between a candidate and a reference:

$$LCS(c, r) = \frac{1}{2} (|c| + |r| - ED(c, r)) \quad (2)$$

Name origin	Source script	Target script	Data Owner	Data Size			Task ID
				Train	Dev	Test	
Western	English	Chinese	Institute for Infocomm Research	32K	6K	2K	EnCh
Western	Chinese	English	Institute for Infocomm Research	25K	5K	2K	ChEn
Western	English	Korean Hangul	CJK Institute	5K	2K	2K	EnKo
Western	English	Japanese Katakana	CJK Institute	23K	3K	3K	EnJa
Japanese	English	Japanese Kanji	CJK Institute	7K	3K	3K	JnJk
Arabic	Arabic	English	CJK Institute	25K	2.5K	2.5K	ArAe
Mixed	English	Hindi	Microsoft Research India	10K	2K	2K	EnHi
Mixed	English	Tamil	Microsoft Research India	8K	2K	2K	EnTa
Mixed	English	Kannada	Microsoft Research India	8K	2K	2K	EnKa
Mixed	English	Bangla	Microsoft Research India	10K	2K	2K	EnBa
Western	English	Thai	NECTEC	26K	2K	2K	EnTh
Western	Thai	English	NECTEC	24K	2K	2K	ThEn

Table 1: Source and target languages for the shared task on transliteration.

where ED is the edit distance and $|x|$ is the length of x. For example, the longest common subsequence between "abcd" and "afcde" is "acd" and its length is 3. The best matching reference, that is, the reference for which the edit distance has the minimum, is taken for calculation. If the best matching reference is given by

$$r_{i,m} = \arg\min_j (ED(c_{i,1}, r_{i,j})) \quad (3)$$

then Recall, Precision and F-score for i-th word are calculated as

$$R_i = \frac{LCS(c_{i,1}, r_{i,m})}{|r_{i,m}|} \quad (4)$$

$$P_i = \frac{LCS(c_{i,1}, r_{i,m})}{|c_{i,1}|} \quad (5)$$

$$F_i = 2\frac{R_i \times P_i}{R_i + P_i} \quad (6)$$

- The length is computed in distinct Unicode characters.
- No distinction is made on different character types of a language (e.g., vowel vs. consonants vs. combining diereses etc.)

3.3 Mean Reciprocal Rank (MRR)

Measures traditional MRR *for any right answer* produced by the system, from among the candidates. $1/MRR$ tells approximately the average rank of the correct transliteration. MRR closer to 1 implies that the correct answer is mostly produced close to the top of the n-best lists.

$$RR_i = \left\{ \begin{array}{l} \min_j \frac{1}{j} \text{ if } \exists r_{i,j}, c_{i,k} : r_{i,j} = c_{i,k}; \\ 0 \text{ otherwise} \end{array} \right\} \quad (7)$$

$$MRR = \frac{1}{N} \sum_{i=1}^{N} RR_i \quad (8)$$

3.4 MAP$_{ref}$

Measures tightly the precision in the n-best candidates for i-th source name, for which reference transliterations are available. If all of the references are produced, then the MAP is 1. Let's denote the number of correct candidates for the i-th source word in k-best list as $num(i,k)$. MAP$_{ref}$ is then given by

$$MAP_{ref} = \frac{1}{N} \sum_{i}^{N} \frac{1}{n_i} \left(\sum_{k=1}^{n_i} num(i,k) \right) \quad (9)$$

4 Participation in Shared Task

7 teams from 5 countries and regions (Canada, Hong Kong, India, Japan, Thailand) submitted their transliteration results.

Two teams have participated in all or almost all tasks while others participated in 1 to 4 tasks. Each language pair has attracted on average around 4 teams. The details are shown in Table 3.

Teams are required to submit at least one standard run for every task they participated in. In total, we receive 33 standard and 8. Table 2 shows the number of standard and non-standard runs submitted for each task. It is clear that the most "popular" task is transliteration from English to Hindi attempted by 5 participants. The next most popular are other Indic scripts (Tamil, Kannada, Bangla) and Thai, attempted by 3 participants. This is somewhat different from NEWS 2009, where the two most popular tasks were English to Hindi and English to Chinese transliteration.

	English to Chinese	Chinese to English	English to Thai	Thai to English	English to Hindi	English to Tamil
Language pair code	EnCh	ChEn	EnTh	ThEn	EnHi	EnTa
Standard runs	5	2	2	2	7	3
Non-standard runs	0	0	1	1	2	1

	English to Kannada	English to Japanese Katakana	English to Korean Hangul	English to Japanese Kanji	Arabic to English	English to Bengali (Bangla)
Language pair code	EnKa	EnJa	EnKo	JnJk	ArAe	EnBa
Standard runs	3	2	1	1	2	3
Non-standard runs	1	0	0	0	0	2

Table 2: Number of runs submitted for each task. Number of participants coincides with the number of standard runs submitted.

Team ID	Organisation	EnCh	ChEn	EnTh	ThEn	EnHi	EnTa	EnKa	EnJa	EnKo	JnJk	ArAe	EnBa
1*	IIT, Bombay					x							
2	University of Alberta	x	x	x	x	x	x	x	x	x	x	x	x
3						x							
4	City University of Hong Kong	x	x										
5	NICT			x	x	x	x	x	x			x	x
6				x	x								
7	Jadavpur University					x	x	x					x

Table 3: Participation of teams in different tasks. *Participation without a system paper.

5 Task Results and Analysis

5.1 Standard runs

All the results are presented numerically in Tables 4–15, for all evaluation metrics. These are the official evaluation results published for this edition of the transliteration shared task.

Among the four submitted system papers[1], Song et al. (2010) and Finch and Sumita (2010) adopt the approach of phrase-based statistical machine transliteration (Finch and Sumita, 2008), an approach initially developed for machine translation (Koehn et al., 2003) while Das et al. (2010) adopts the approach of Conditional Random Fields (CRF) (Lafferty et al., 2001). Jiampojamarn et al. (2010) further develop DirectTL approach presented at the previous NEWS workshop (Jiampojamarn et al., 2009), achieving very good performance in the NEWS 2010.

An example of a completely language-independent approach is (Finch and Sumita, 2010). Other participants used language-independent approach but added language-specific pre- or post-processing (Jiampojamarn et al., 2010; Das et al., 2010; Song et al., 2010), including name origin recognition for English to Hindi task (Jiampojamarn et al., 2010).

Combination of different models via re-ranking of their outputs has been used in most of the systems (Das et al., 2010; Song et al., 2010; Finch and Sumita, 2010). In fact, one system (Song et al., 2010) is mostly devoted to re-ranking of the system output to achieve significant improvement of the ACC (accuracy in top-1) results compared to the same system in NEWS 2009 workshop (Song, 2009).

Compared the same seven tasks among the NEWS 2009 and the NEWS 2010 (almost same training sets, but different test sets), we can see that the performance in the NEWS 2010 drops except the English to Korean task. This could be due to the fact that NEWS 2010 introduces a entirely

[1]To maintain anonymity, papers of the teams that submitted anonymous results are not cited in this report.

new test set, which come from different sources than the train and dev sets, while NEWS 2009 have all train, dev and test sets from the same sources.

As far as back-transliteration is concerned, we can see that English-to-Thai and Thai-to-English have the similar performance. However, Chinese-to-English back transliteration performs much worse than English-to-Chinese forward transliteration. This could be due to the fact that Thai and English are alphabet languages in nature while Chinese is not. As a result, Chinese have much fewer transliteration units than English and Thai. In other words, Chinese to English transliteration is a one-to-many mapping while English-to-Chinese is a many-to-one mapping. The later one has fewer mapping ambiguities.

5.2 Non-standard runs

For the non-standard runs there exist no restrictions on the use of data or other linguistic resources. The purpose of non-standard runs is to see how best personal name transliteration can be, for a given language pair. In NEWS 2010, the approaches used in non-standard runs are typical and may be summarised as follows:

- Pronunciation dictionaries to convert words to their phonetic transcription (Jiampojamarn et al., 2010).
- Web search. First, transliteration candidates are generated. A Web search is then performed to re-affirm or re-rank the candidacy (Das et al., 2010).

Unfortunately, these additional knowledge used in the non-standard runs is not helpful since all non-standard runs perform worse than their corresponding standard runs. This would be an interesting issue to look into.

6 Conclusions and Future Plans

The Transliteration Generation Shared Task in NEWS 2010 shows that the community has a continued interest in this area. This report summarizes the results of the shared task. Again, we are pleased to report a comprehensive calibration and baselining of machine transliteration approaches as most state-of-the-art machine transliteration techniques are represented in the shared task. The most popular techniques such as Phrase-Based Machine Transliteration (Koehn et al., 2003), system combination and re-ranking, are inspired by recent progress in statistical machine translation. As the standard runs are limited by the use of corpus, most of the systems are implemented under the direct orthographic mapping (DOM) framework (Li et al., 2004). While the standard runs allow us to conduct meaningful comparison across different algorithms, we recognise that the non-standard runs open up more opportunities for exploiting larger linguistic corpora. It is also noted that two systems have reported significant performance improvement over their NEWS 2009 systems.

NEWS 2010 Shared Task represents a successful debut of a community effort in driving machine transliteration techniques forward. We would like to continue this event in the future conference to promote the machine transliteration research and development.

Acknowledgements

The organisers of the NEWS 2010 Shared Task would like to thank the Institute for Infocomm Research (Singapore), Microsoft Research India, CJK Institute (Japan) and National Electronics and Computer Technology Center (Thailand) for providing the corpora and technical support. Without those, the Shared Task would not be possible. We thank those participants who identified errors in the data and sent us the errata. We also want to thank the members of programme committee for their invaluable comments that improve the quality of the shared task papers. Finally, we wish to thank all the participants for their active participation that have made this first machine transliteration shared task a comprehensive one.

References

Yaser Al-Onaizan and Kevin Knight. 2002. Machine transliteration of names in arabic text. In *Proc. ACL-2002 Workshop: Computational Apporaches to Semitic Languages*, Philadelphia, PA, USA.

CJKI. 2010. CJK Institute. http://www.cjk.org/.

Amitava Das, Tanik Saikh, Tapabrata Mondal, Asif Ekbal, and Sivaji Bandyopadhyay. 2010. English to Indian languages machine transliteration system at NEWS 2010. In *Proc. ACL Named Entities Workshop Shared Task.*

D. Demner-Fushman and D. W. Oard. 2002. The effect of bilingual term list size on dictionary-based cross-language information retrieval. In *Proc. 36-th Hawaii Int'l. Conf. System Sciences*, volume 4, page 108.2.

Andrew Finch and Eiichiro Sumita. 2008. Phrase-based machine transliteration. In *Proc. 3rd Int'l. Joint Conf NLP*, volume 1, Hyderabad, India, January.

Andrew Finch and Eiichiro Sumita. 2010. Transliteration using a phrase-based statistical machine translation system to re-score the output of a joint multigram model. In *Proc. ACL Named Entities Workshop Shared Task.*

Wei Gao, Kam-Fai Wong, and Wai Lam. 2004. Phoneme-based transliteration of foreign names for OOV problem. In *Proc. IJCNLP*, pages 374–381, Sanya, Hainan, China.

Yoav Goldberg and Michael Elhadad. 2008. Identification of transliterated foreign words in Hebrew script. In *Proc. CICLing*, volume LNCS 4919, pages 466–477.

Dan Goldwasser and Dan Roth. 2008. Transliteration as constrained optimization. In *Proc. EMNLP*, pages 353–362.

Jack Halpern. 2007. The challenges and pitfalls of Arabic romanization and arabization. In *Proc. Workshop on Comp. Approaches to Arabic Script-based Lang.*

Ulf Hermjakob, Kevin Knight, and Hal Daumé. 2008. Name translation in statistical machine translation: Learning when to transliterate. In *Proc. ACL*, Columbus, OH, USA, June.

Sittichai Jiampojamarn, Aditya Bhargava, Qing Dou, Kenneth Dwyer, and Grzegorz Kondrak. 2009. DirecTL: a language-independent approach to transliteration. In *Proc. ACL/IJCNLP Named Entities Workshop Shared Task.*

Sittichai Jiampojamarn, Kenneth Dwyer, Shane Bergsma, Aditya Bhargava, Qing Dou, Mi-Young Kim, and Grzegorz Kondrak. 2010. Transliteration generation and mining with limited training resources. In *Proc. ACL Named Entities Workshop Shared Task.*

Byung-Ju Kang and Key-Sun Choi. 2000. English-Korean automatic transliteration/back-transliteration system and character alignment. In *Proc. ACL*, pages 17–18, Hong Kong.

Alexandre Klementiev and Dan Roth. 2006. Weakly supervised named entity transliteration and discovery from multilingual comparable corpora. In *Proc. 21st Int'l Conf Computational Linguistics and 44th Annual Meeting of ACL*, pages 817–824, Sydney, Australia, July.

Kevin Knight and Jonathan Graehl. 1998. Machine transliteration. *Computational Linguistics*, 24(4).

P. Koehn, F. J. Och, and D. Marcu. 2003. Statistical phrase-based translation. In *Proc. HLT-NAACL.*

A Kumaran and T. Kellner. 2007. A generic framework for machine transliteration. In *Proc. SIGIR*, pages 721–722.

J. Lafferty, A. McCallum, and F. Pereira. 2001. Conditional random fields: Probabilistic models for segmenting and labeling sequence data. In *Proc. Int'l. Conf. Machine Learning*, pages 282–289.

Haizhou Li, Min Zhang, and Jian Su. 2004. A joint source-channel model for machine transliteration. In *Proc. 42nd ACL Annual Meeting*, pages 159–166, Barcelona, Spain.

Haizhou Li, A Kumaran, Vladimir Pervouchine, and Min Zhang. 2009a. Report of NEWS 2009 machine transliteration shared task. In *Proc. Named Entities Workshop at ACL 2009.*

Haizhou Li, A Kumaran, Min Zhang, and Vladimir Pervouchine. 2009b. ACL-IJCNLP 2009 Named Entities Workshop — Shared Task on Transliteration. In *Proc. Named Entities Workshop at ACL 2009.*

T. Mandl and C. Womser-Hacker. 2005. The effect of named entities on effectiveness in cross-language information retrieval evaluation. In *Proc. ACM Symp. Applied Comp.*, pages 1059–1064.

Helen M. Meng, Wai-Kit Lo, Berlin Chen, and Karen Tang. 2001. Generate phonetic cognates to handle name entities in English-Chinese cross-language spoken document retrieval. In *Proc. ASRU.*

MSRI. 2009. Microsoft Research India. http://research.microsoft.com/india.

Jong-Hoon Oh and Key-Sun Choi. 2002. An English-Korean transliteration model using pronunciation and contextual rules. In *Proc. COLING 2002*, Taipei, Taiwan.

Tarek Sherif and Grzegorz Kondrak. 2007. Substring-based transliteration. In *Proc. 45th Annual Meeting of the ACL*, pages 944–951, Prague, Czech Republic, June.

Yan Song, Chunyu Kit, and Hai Zhao. 2010. Reranking with multiple features for better transliteration. In *Proc. ACL Named Entities Workshop Shared Task*.

Yan Song. 2009. Name entities transliteration via improved statistical translation on character-level chunks. In *Proc. ACL/IJCNLP Named Entities Workshop Shared Task*.

Richard Sproat, Tao Tao, and ChengXiang Zhai. 2006. Named entity transliteration with comparable corpora. In *Proc. 21st Int'l Conf Computational Linguistics and 44th Annual Meeting of ACL*, pages 73–80, Sydney, Australia.

Raghavendra Udupa, K. Saravanan, Anton Bakalov, and Abhijit Bhole. 2009. "They are out there, if you know where to look": Mining transliterations of OOV query terms for cross-language information retrieval. In *LNCS: Advances in Information Retrieval*, volume 5478, pages 437–448. Springer Berlin / Heidelberg.

Paola Virga and Sanjeev Khudanpur. 2003. Transliteration of proper names in cross-lingual information retrieval. In *Proc. ACL MLNER*, Sapporo, Japan.

Stephen Wan and Cornelia Maria Verspoor. 1998. Automatic English-Chinese name transliteration for development of multilingual resources. In *Proc. COLING*, pages 1352–1356.

Dmitry Zelenko and Chinatsu Aone. 2006. Discriminative methods for transliteration. In *Proc. EMNLP*, pages 612–617, Sydney, Australia, July.

Team ID	ACC	F-score	MRR	MAP_{ref}	Organisation
			Primary runs		
4	0.477333	0.740494	0.506209	0.455491	City University of Hong Kong
2	0.363333	0.707435	0.430168	0.347701	University of Alberta
			Non-primary standard runs		
2	0.362667	0.704284	0.428854	0.347500	University of Alberta
2	0.360333	0.706765	0.428990	0.345215	University of Alberta
2	0.357000	0.702902	0.419415	0.341567	University of Alberta

Table 4: Runs submitted for English to Chinese task.

Team ID	ACC	F-score	MRR	MAP_{ref}	Organisation
			Primary runs		
4	0.226766	0.749237	0.268557	0.226090	City University of Hong Kong
2	0.137209	0.740364	0.197665	0.136702	University of Alberta

Table 5: Runs submitted for Chinese to English back-transliteration task.

Team ID	ACC	F-score	MRR	MAP_{ref}	Organisation
			Primary runs		
5	0.391000	0.872526	0.505264	0.391000	NICT
2	0.377500	0.866254	0.467328	0.377500	University of Alberta
			Non-standard runs		
6	0.247000	0.842063	0.366959	0.247000	

Table 6: Runs submitted for English to Thai task.

Team ID	ACC	F-score	MRR	MAP_{ref}	Organisation
			Primary runs		
5	0.396690	0.872642	0.524511	0.396690	NICT
2	0.352056	0.861207	0.450472	0.352056	University of Alberta
			Non-standard runs		
6	0.092778	0.706995	0.131779	0.092778	

Table 7: Runs submitted for Thai to English back-transliteration task.

Team ID	ACC	F-score	MRR	MAP_{ref}	Organisation
			Primary runs		
2	0.456456	0.884199	0.559212	0.456456	University of Alberta
5	0.445445	0.883841	0.574195	0.445445	NICT
3	0.381381	0.860320	0.403172	0.381381	
1	0.158158	0.810309	0.231594	0.158158	IIT, Bombay
7	0.150150	0.714490	0.307674	0.150150	Jadavpur University
			Non-primary standard runs		
2	0.456456	0.885122	0.558203	0.456456	University of Alberta
1	0.142142	0.799092	0.205945	0.142142	IIT, Bombay
			Non-standard runs		
7	0.254254	0.751766	0.369072	0.254254	Jadavpur University
7	0.170170	0.738777	0.314335	0.170170	Jadavpur University

Table 8: Runs submitted for English to Hindi task.

Team ID	ACC	F-score	MRR	MAP_{ref}	Organisation
			Primary runs		
2	0.390000	0.890692	0.515298	0.390000	University of Alberta
5	0.390000	0.886560	0.522088	0.390000	NICT
7	0.013000	0.562917	0.121233	0.013000	Jadavpur University
			Non-standard runs		
7	0.082000	0.759856	0.142317	0.082000	Jadavpur University

Table 9: Runs submitted for English to Tamil task.

Team ID	ACC	F-score	MRR	MAP_{ref}	Organisation
			Primary runs		
5	0.371000	0.871131	0.506010	0.371000	NICT
2	0.341000	0.867133	0.460189	0.341000	University of Alberta
7	0.056000	0.663196	0.111500	0.056000	Jadavpur University
			Non-standard runs		
7	0.055000	0.662106	0.168750	0.055000	Jadavpur University

Table 10: Runs submitted for English to Kannada task.

Team ID	ACC	F-score	MRR	MAP_{ref}	Organisation
			Primary runs		
2	0.397933	0.791233	0.507828	0.398062	University of Alberta
5	0.378295	0.782682	0.510096	0.377778	NICT

Table 11: Runs submitted for English to Japanese Katakana task.

Team ID	ACC	F-score	MRR	MAP_{ref}	Organisation
			Primary runs		
2	0.553604	0.770168	0.672665	0.553835	University of Alberta

Table 12: Runs submitted for English to Korean task.

Team ID	ACC	F-score	MRR	MAP_{ref}	Organisation
			Primary runs		
2	0.125937	0.426349	0.201497	0.127339	University of Alberta

Table 13: Runs submitted for English to Japanese Kanji back-transliteration task.

Team ID	ACC	F-score	MRR	MAP_{ref}	Organisation
			Primary runs		
2	0.463679	0.923826	0.535097	0.265379	University of Alberta
5	0.403014	0.891443	0.512337	0.327418	NICT

Table 14: Runs submitted for Arabic to English task.

Team ID	ACC	F-score	MRR	MAP_{ref}	Organisation
			Primary runs		
5	0.411705	0.882858	0.549913	0.411705	NICT
2	0.394551	0.876947	0.511876	0.394551	University of Alberta
7	0.232089	0.818470	0.325345	0.232089	Jadavpur University
			Non-standard runs		
7	0.429869	0.875349	0.526152	0.429869	Jadavpur University
7	0.369324	0.845273	0.450589	0.369324	Jadavpur University

Table 15: Runs submitted for English to Bengali (Bangla) task.

Whitepaper of NEWS 2010 Shared Task on Transliteration Generation*

Haizhou Li†**, A Kumaran**‡**, Min Zhang**† **and Vladimir Pervouchine**†

†Institute for Infocomm Research, A*STAR, Singapore 138632
{hli,mzhang,vpervouchine}@i2r.a-star.edu.sg

‡Multilingual Systems Research, Microsoft Research India
A.Kumaran@microsoft.com

Abstract

Transliteration is defined as phonetic translation of names across languages. Transliteration of Named Entities (NEs) is necessary in many applications, such as machine translation, corpus alignment, cross-language IR, information extraction and automatic lexicon acquisition. All such systems call for high-performance transliteration, which is the focus of shared task in the NEWS 2010 workshop. The objective of the shared task is to promote machine transliteration research by providing a common benchmarking platform for the community to evaluate the state-of-the-art technologies.

1 Task Description

The task is to develop machine transliteration system in one or more of the specified language pairs being considered for the task. Each language pair consists of a source and a target language. The training and development data sets released for each language pair are to be used for developing a transliteration system in whatever way that the participants find appropriate. At the evaluation time, a test set of source names only would be released, on which the participants are expected to produce a ranked list of transliteration candidates in another language (i.e. n-best transliterations), and this will be evaluated using common metrics. For every language pair the participants must submit at least one run that uses only the data provided by the NEWS workshop organisers in a given language pair (designated as "standard" run, primary submission). Users may submit more "stanrard" runs. They may also submit several "non-standard" runs for each language pair that use other data than those provided by the NEWS 2010 workshop; such runs would be evaluated and reported separately.

*http://translit.i2r.a-star.edu.sg/news2010/

2 Important Dates

Research paper submission deadline	1 May 2010
Shared task	
Registration opens	1 Feb 2010
Registration closes	13 Mar 2010
Training/Development data release	19 Feb 2010
Test data release	13 Mar 2010
Results Submission Due	20 Mar 2010
Results Announcement	27 Mar 2010
Task (short) Papers Due	5 Apr 2010
For all submissions	
Acceptance Notification	6 May 2010
Workshop Date	16 Jul 2010

3 Participation

1. Registration (1 Feb 2010)
   (a) NEWS Shared Task opens for registration.
   (b) Prospective participants are to register to the NEWS Workshop homepage.
2. Training & Development Data (19 Feb 2010)
   (a) Registered participants are to obtain training and development data from the Shared Task organiser and/or the designated copyright owners of databases.
   (b) All registered participants are required to participate in the evaluation of at least one language pair, submit the results and a short paper and attend the workshop at ACL 2010.
3. Evaluation Script (19 Feb 2010)

Proceedings of the 2010 Named Entities Workshop, ACL 2010, pages 12–20,
Uppsala, Sweden, 16 July 2010.

(a) A sample test set and expected user output format are to be released.

(b) An evaluation script, which runs on the above two, is to be released.

(c) The participants must make sure that their output is produced in a way that the evaluation script may run and produce the expected output.

(d) The same script (with held out test data and the user outputs) would be used for final evaluation.

4. Test data (13 Mar 2010)

(a) The test data would be released on 13 March 2010, and the participants have a maximum of 7 days to submit their results in the expected format.

(b) One "standard" run must be submitted from every group on a given language pair. Additional "standard" runs may be submitted, up to 4 "standard" runs in total. However, the participants must indicate one of the submitted "standard" runs as the "primary submission". The primary submission will be used for the performance summary. In addition to the "standard" runs, more "non-standard" runs may be submitted. In total, maximum 8 runs (up to 4 "standard" runs plus up to 4 "non-standard" runs) can be submitted from each group on a registered language pair. The definition of "standard" and "non-standard" runs is in Section 5.

(c) Any runs that are "non-standard" must be tagged as such.

(d) The test set is a list of names in source language only. Every group will produce and submit a ranked list of transliteration candidates in another language for each given name in the test set. Please note that this shared task is a "transliteration generation" task, i.e., given a name in a source language one is supposed to generate one or more transliterations in a target language. It is not the task of "transliteration discovery", i.e., given a name in the source language and a set of names in the target language evaluate how to find the appropriate names from the target set that are transliterations of the given source name.

5. Results (27 Mar 2010)

(a) On 27 March 2010, the evaluation results would be announced and will be made available on the Workshop website.

(b) Note that only the scores (in respective metrics) of the participating systems on each language pairs would be published, and no explicit ranking of the participating systems would be published.

(c) Note that this is a shared evaluation task and not a competition; the results are meant to be used to evaluate systems on common data set with common metrics, and not to rank the participating systems. While the participants can cite the performance of their systems (scores on metrics) from the workshop report, they should not use any ranking information in their publications.

(d) Furthermore, all participants should agree not to reveal identities of other participants in any of their publications unless you get permission from the other respective participants. By default, all participants remain anonymous in published results, unless they indicate otherwise at the time of uploading their results. Note that the results of all systems will be published, but the identities of those participants that choose not to disclose their identity to other participants will be masked. As a result, in this case, your organisation name will still appear in the web site as one of participants, but it will not be linked explicitly to your results.

6. Short Papers on Task (5 Apr 2010)

(a) Each submitting site is required to submit a 4-page system paper (short paper) for its submissions, including their approach, data used and the results on either test set or development set or by n-fold cross validation on training set.

(b) The review of the system papers will be done to improve paper quality and readability and make sure the authors' ideas and methods can be understood by the workshop participants. We are aiming at accepting all system papers, and selected ones will be presented orally in the NEWS 2010 workshop.

(c) All registered participants are required to register and attend the workshop to introduce your work.

(d) All paper submission and review will be managed electronically through https://www.softconf.com/acl2010/NEWS.

4 Language Pairs

The tasks are to transliterate personal names or place names from a source to a target language as summarised in Table 1. NEWS 2010 Shared Task offers 12 evaluation subtasks, among them ChEn and ThEn are the back-transliteration of EnCh and EnTh tasks respectively. NEWS 2010 releases training, development and testing data for each of the language pairs. NEWS 2010 continues some language pairs that were evaluated in NEWS 2009. In such cases, the training and development data in the release of NEWS 2010 may overlap with those in NEWS 2009. However, the test data in NEWS 2010 are entirely new.

The names given in the training sets for Chinese, Japanese, Korean and Thai languages are Western names and their respective transliterations; the Japanese Name (in English) → Japanese Kanji data set consists only of native Japanese names; the Arabic data set consists only of native Arabic names. The Indic data set (Hindi, Tamil, Kannada, Bangla) consists of a mix of Indian and Western names.

Examples of transliteration:

English → Chinese
Timothy → 蒂莫西

English → Japanese Katakana
Harrington → ハリントン

English → Korean Hangul
Bennett → 베넷

Japanese name in English → Japanese Kanji
Akihiro → 秋宏

English → Hindi
San Francisco → सैन फ्रान्सिस्को

English → Tamil
London → லண்டன்

English → Kannada
Tokyo → ಟೋಕ್ಯೋ

Arabic → Arabic name in English
خالد → Khalid

5 Standard Databases

Training Data (Parallel)
Paired names between source and target languages; size 5K – 32K.
Training Data is used for training a basic transliteration system.

Development Data (Parallel)
Paired names between source and target languages; size 2K – 6K.
Development Data is in addition to the Training data, which is used for system fine-tuning of parameters in case of need. Participants are allowed to use it as part of training data.

Testing Data
Source names only; size 2K – 3K.
This is a held-out set, which would be used for evaluating the quality of the transliterations.

1. Participants will need to obtain licenses from the respective copyright owners and/or agree to the terms and conditions of use that are given on the downloading website (Li et al., 2004; MSRI, 2010; CJKI, 2010). NEWS 2010 will provide the contact details of each individual database. The data would be provided in Unicode UTF-8 encoding, in XML format; the results are expected to be submitted in UTF-8 encoding in XML format. The XML formats details are available in Appendix A.

2. The data are provided in 3 sets as described above.

3. Name pairs are distributed as-is, as provided by the respective creators.

   (a) While the databases are mostly manually checked, there may be still inconsistency (that is, non-standard usage, region-specific usage, errors, etc.) or incompleteness (that is, not all right variations may be covered).

   (b) The participants may use any method to further clean up the data provided.

Name origin	Source script	Target script	Data Owner	Data Size			Task ID
				Train	Dev	Test	
Western	English	Chinese	Institute for Infocomm Research	32K	6K	2K	EnCh
Western	Chinese	English	Institute for Infocomm Research	25K	5K	2K	ChEn
Western	English	Korean Hangul	CJK Institute	5K	2K	2K	EnKo
Western	English	Japanese Katakana	CJK Institute	23K	3K	3K	EnJa
Japanese	English	Japanese Kanji	CJK Institute	7K	3K	3K	JnJk
Arabic	Arabic	English	CJK Institute	25K	2.5K	2.5K	ArAe
Mixed	English	Hindi	Microsoft Research India	10K	2K	2K	EnHi
Mixed	English	Tamil	Microsoft Research India	8K	2K	2K	EnTa
Mixed	English	Kannada	Microsoft Research India	8K	2K	2K	EnKa
Mixed	English	Bangla	Microsoft Research India	10K	2K	2K	EnBa
Western	English	Thai	NECTEC	26K	2K	2K	EnTh
Western	Thai	English	NECTEC	24K	2K	2K	ThEn

Table 1: Source and target languages for the shared task on transliteration.

i. If they are cleaned up manually, we appeal that such data be provided back to the organisers for redistribution to all the participating groups in that language pair; such sharing benefits all participants, and further ensures that the evaluation provides normalisation with respect to data quality.

ii. If automatic cleanup were used, such cleanup would be considered a part of the system fielded, and hence not required to be shared with all participants.

4. *Standard Runs* We expect that the participants to use only the data (parallel names) provided by the Shared Task for transliteration task for a "standard" run to ensure a fair evaluation. One such run (using only the data provided by the shared task) is mandatory for all participants for a given language pair that they participate in.

5. *Non-standard Runs* If more data (either parallel names data or monolingual data) were used, then all such runs using extra data must be marked as "non-standard". For such "non-standard" runs, it is required to disclose the size and characteristics of the data used in the system paper.

6. A participant may submit a maximum of 8 runs for a given language pair (including the mandatory 1 "standard" run marked as "primary submission").

6 Paper Format

Paper submissions to NEWS 2010 should follow the ACL 2010 paper submission policy, including paper format, blind review policy and title and author format convention. Full papers (research paper) are in two-column format without exceeding eight (8) pages of content plus one extra page for references and short papers (task paper) are also in two-column format without exceeding four (4) pages, including references. Submission must conform to the official ACL 2010 style guidelines. For details, please refer to the ACL 2010 website[2].

7 Evaluation Metrics

We plan to measure the quality of the transliteration task using the following 4 metrics. We accept up to 10 output candidates in a ranked list for each input entry.

Since a given source name may have multiple correct target transliterations, all these alternatives are treated equally in the evaluation. That is, any of these alternatives are considered as a correct transliteration, and the first correct transliteration in the ranked list is accepted as a correct hit.

The following notation is further assumed:

[2]http://acl2010.org/authors.html

N	:	Total number of names (source words) in the test set
n_i	:	Number of reference transliterations for i-th name in the test set ($n_i \geq 1$)
$r_{i,j}$	:	j-th reference transliteration for i-th name in the test set
$c_{i,k}$	:	k-th candidate transliteration (system output) for i-th name in the test set ($1 \leq k \leq 10$)
K_i	:	Number of candidate transliterations produced by a transliteration system

1. Word Accuracy in Top-1 (ACC) Also known as Word Error Rate, it measures correctness of the first transliteration candidate in the candidate list produced by a transliteration system. $ACC = 1$ means that all top candidates are correct transliterations i.e. they match one of the references, and $ACC = 0$ means that none of the top candidates are correct.

$$ACC = \frac{1}{N}\sum_{i=1}^{N}\left\{\begin{array}{l} 1 \text{ if } \exists\, r_{i,j} : r_{i,j} = c_{i,1}; \\ 0 \text{ otherwise} \end{array}\right\} \qquad (1)$$

2. Fuzziness in Top-1 (Mean F-score) The mean F-score measures how different, on average, the top transliteration candidate is from its closest reference. F-score for each source word is a function of Precision and Recall and equals 1 when the top candidate matches one of the references, and 0 when there are no common characters between the candidate and any of the references.

Precision and Recall are calculated based on the length of the Longest Common Subsequence between a candidate and a reference:

$$LCS(c, r) = \frac{1}{2}\left(|c| + |r| - ED(c, r)\right) \qquad (2)$$

where ED is the edit distance and $|x|$ is the length of x. For example, the longest common subsequence between "abcd" and "afcde" is "acd" and its length is 3. The best matching reference, that is, the reference for which the edit distance has the minimum, is taken for calculation. If the best matching reference is given by

$$r_{i,m} = \arg\min_j \left(ED(c_{i,1}, r_{i,j})\right) \qquad (3)$$

then Recall, Precision and F-score for i-th word are calculated as

$$R_i = \frac{LCS(c_{i,1}, r_{i,m})}{|r_{i,m}|} \qquad (4)$$

$$P_i = \frac{LCS(c_{i,1}, r_{i,m})}{|c_{i,1}|} \qquad (5)$$

$$F_i = 2\frac{R_i \times P_i}{R_i + P_i} \qquad (6)$$

- The length is computed in distinct Unicode characters.

- No distinction is made on different character types of a language (e.g., vowel vs. consonants vs. combining diereses' etc.)

3. Mean Reciprocal Rank (MRR) Measures traditional MRR *for any right answer* produced by the system, from among the candidates. $1/MRR$ tells approximately the average rank of the correct transliteration. MRR closer to 1 implies that the correct answer is mostly produced close to the top of the n-best lists.

$$RR_i = \left\{\begin{array}{l} \min_j \frac{1}{j} \text{ if } \exists r_{i,j}, c_{i,k} : r_{i,j} = c_{i,k}; \\ 0 \text{ otherwise} \end{array}\right\} \qquad (7)$$

$$MRR = \frac{1}{N}\sum_{i=1}^{N} RR_i \qquad (8)$$

4. MAP$_{ref}$ Measures tightly the precision in the n-best candidates for i-th source name, for which reference transliterations are available. If all of the references are produced, then the MAP is 1. Let's denote the number of correct candidates for the i-th source word in k-best list as $num(i, k)$. MAP$_{ref}$ is then given by

$$MAP_{ref} = \frac{1}{N}\sum_{i}^{N}\frac{1}{n_i}\left(\sum_{k=1}^{n_i} num(i, k)\right) \qquad (9)$$

8 Contact Us

If you have any questions about this share task and the database, please email to

Dr. Haizhou Li
Institute for Infocomm Research (I[2]R), A*STAR
1 Fusionopolis Way
#08-05 South Tower, Connexis
Singapore 138632
hli@i2r.a-star.edu.sg

Dr. A. Kumaran
Microsoft Research India
Scientia, 196/36, Sadashivnagar 2nd Main Road
Bangalore 560080 INDIA
a.kumaran@microsoft.com

Mr. Jack Halpern
CEO, The CJK Dictionary Institute, Inc.
Komine Building (3rd & 4th floors)
34-14, 2-chome, Tohoku, Niiza-shi
Saitama 352-0001 JAPAN
jack@cjki.org

References

[CJKI2010] CJKI. 2010. CJK Institute. http://www.cjk.org/.

[Li et al.2004] Haizhou Li, Min Zhang, and Jian Su. 2004. A joint source-channel model for machine transliteration. In *Proc. 42nd ACL Annual Meeting*, pages 159–166, Barcelona, Spain.

[MSRI2010] MSRI. 2010. Microsoft Research India. http://research.microsoft.com/india.

A Training/Development Data

- File Naming Conventions:
  `NEWS10_train_XXYY_nnnn.xml`
  `NEWS10_dev_XXYY_nnnn.xml`
  `NEWS10_test_XXYY_nnnn.xml`
  - `XX`: Source Language
  - `YY`: Target Language
  - `nnnn`: size of parallel/monolingual names ("25K", "10000", etc)
- File formats:
  All data will be made available in XML formats (Figure 1).
- Data Encoding Formats:
  The data will be in Unicode UTF-8 encoding files without byte-order mark, and in the XML format specified.

B Submission of Results

- File Naming Conventions:
  You can give your files any name you like. During submission online you will need to indicate whether this submission belongs to a "standard" or "non-standard" run, and if it is a "standard" run, whether it is the primary submission.
- File formats:
  All data will be made available in XML formats (Figure 2).
- Data Encoding Formats:
  The results are expected to be submitted in UTF-8 encoded files without byte-order mark only, and in the XML format specified.

```
<?xml version="1.0" encoding="UTF-8"?>

<TransliterationCorpus
    CorpusID = "NEWS2010-Train-EnHi-25K"
    SourceLang = "English"
    TargetLang = "Hindi"
    CorpusType = "Train|Dev"
    CorpusSize = "25000"
    CorpusFormat = "UTF8">

    <Name ID=" 1" >
        <SourceName>eeeeee1</SourceName>
        <TargetName ID="1">hhhhhh1_1</TargetName>
            <TargetName ID="2">hhhhhh1_2</TargetName>
        ...
        <TargetName ID="n">hhhhhh1_n</TargetName>
    </Name>
    <Name ID=" 2" >
        <SourceName>eeeeee2</SourceName>
        <TargetName ID="1">hhhhhh2_1</TargetName>
        <TargetName ID="2">hhhhhh2_2</TargetName>
        ...
        <TargetName ID="m">hhhhhh2_m</TargetName>
    </Name>
    ...
    <!-- rest of the names to follow -->
    ...
</TransliterationCorpus>
```

Figure 1: File: NEWS2010_Train_EnHi_25K.xml

```
<?xml version="1.0" encoding="UTF-8"?>

<TransliterationTaskResults
    SourceLang = "English"
    TargetLang = "Hindi"
    GroupID = "Trans University"
    RunID = "1"
    RunType = "Standard"
    Comments = "HMM Run with params: alpha=0.8 beta=1.25">

    <Name ID="1">
        <SourceName>eeeeee1</SourceName>
        <TargetName ID="1">hhhhhh11</TargetName>
        <TargetName ID="2">hhhhhh12</TargetName>
        <TargetName ID="3">hhhhhh13</TargetName>
        ...
        <TargetName ID="10">hhhhhh110</TargetName>

        <!-- Participants to provide their
        top 10 candidate transliterations -->
    </Name>
    <Name ID="2">
        <SourceName>eeeeee2</SourceName>
        <TargetName ID="1">hhhhhh21</TargetName>
        <TargetName ID="2">hhhhhh22</TargetName>
        <TargetName ID="3">hhhhhh23</TargetName>
        ...
        <TargetName ID="10">hhhhhh110</TargetName>
        <!-- Participants to provide their
        top 10 candidate transliterations -->
    </Name>
    ...
    <!-- All names in test corpus to follow -->
    ...
</TransliterationTaskResults>
```

Figure 2: Example file: NEWS2010_EnHi_TUniv_01_StdRunHMMBased.xml

Report of NEWS 2010 Transliteration Mining Shared Task

A Kumaran
Microsoft Research India
Bangalore, India

Mitesh M. Khapra
Indian Institute of Technology Bombay
Mumbai, India

Haizhou Li
Institute for Infocomm
Research, Singapore

Abstract

This report documents the details of the Transliteration Mining Shared Task that was run as a part of the Named Entities Workshop (NEWS 2010), an ACL 2010 workshop. The shared task featured mining of name transliterations from the paired Wikipedia titles in 5 different language pairs, specifically, between English and one of Arabic, Chinese, Hindi Russian and Tamil. Totally 5 groups took part in this shared task, participating in multiple mining tasks in different languages pairs. The methodology and the data sets used in this shared task are published in the Shared Task White Paper [Kumaran et al, 2010]. We measure and report 3 metrics on the submitted results to calibrate the performance of individual systems on a commonly available Wikipedia dataset. We believe that the significant contribution of this shared task is in (*i*) assembling a diverse set of participants working in the area of transliteration mining, (*ii*) creating a baseline performance of transliteration mining systems in a set of diverse languages using commonly available Wikipedia data, and (*iii*) providing a basis for meaningful comparison and analysis of trade-offs between various algorithmic approaches used in mining. We believe that this shared task would complement the NEWS 2010 transliteration generation shared task, in enabling development of practical systems with a small amount of seed data in a given pair of languages.

1 Introduction

Proper names play a significant role in Machine Translation (MT) and Information Retrieval (IR) systems. When the systems involve multiple languages, The MT and IR system rely on Machine Transliteration systems, as the proper names are not usually available in standard translation lexicons. The quality of the Machine Transliteration systems plays a significant part in determining the overall quality of the system, and hence, they are critical for most multilingual application systems. The importance of Machine Transliteration systems has been well understood by the community, as evidenced by significant publication in this important area.

While research over the last two decades has shown that reasonably good quality Machine Transliteration systems may be developed easily, they critically rely on parallel names corpora for their development. The Machine Transliteration Shared Task of the NEWS 2009 workshop (NEWS 2009) has shown that many interesting approaches exist for Machine Transliteration, and about 10-25K parallel names is sufficient for most state of the art systems to provide a practical solution for the critical need. The traditional source for crosslingual parallel data – the bilingual dictionaries – offer only limited support as they do not include proper names (other than ones of historical importance). The statistical dictionaries, though they contain parallel names, do not have sufficient coverage, as they depend on some threshold statistical evidence [1]. New names and many variations of them are introduced to the vocabulary of a language every day that need to be captured for any good quality end-to-end system such as MT or CLIR. So there is a perennial need for harvesting parallel names data, to support end-user applications and systems well and accurately.

This is the specific focus of the Transliteration Mining Shared Task in NEWS 2010 workshop (an ACL 2010 Workshop): To mine accurately parallel names from a popular, ubiquitous source, the Wikipedia. Wikipedia exists in more than 250 languages, and every Wikipedia article has a link to an equivalent article in other languages[2]. We focused on this specific resource – the Wikipedia titles in multiple languages and the interlinking between them – as the source of parallel names. Any successful mining of parallel names from title would signal copious availability of parallel names data, enabling transliteration generation systems in many languages of the world.

[1] In our experiments with Indian Express news corpora over 2 years shows that 80% of the names occur less than 5 times in the *entire* corpora.

[2] Note that the titles contain concepts, events, dates, etc., in addition to names. Even when the titles are names, parts of them may not be transliterations.

Proceedings of the 2010 Named Entities Workshop, ACL 2010, pages 21–28,
Uppsala, Sweden, 16 July 2010.

2 Transliteration Mining Shared Task

In this section, we provide details of the shared task, and the datasets used for the task and results evaluation.

2.1 Shared Task: Task Details

The task featured in this shared task was to develop a mining system for identifying single word transliteration pairs from the standard interlinked Wikipedia topics (aka, Wikipedia Inter-Language Links, or WIL[3]) in one or more of the specified language pairs. The WIL's link articles on the same topic in multiple languages, and are traditionally used as a parallel language resource for many natural language processing applications, such as Machine Translation, Crosslingual Search, *etc.* Specific WIL's of interest for our task were those that contained proper names – either wholly or partly – which can yield rich transliteration data.

The task involved transliteration mining in the language pairs summarized in Table 1.

Source Language	Target Language	Track ID
English	Chinese	WM-EnCn
English	Hindi	WM-EnHi
English	Tamil	WM-EnTa
English	Russian	WM-EnRu
English	Arabic	WM-EnAr

Table 1: Language Pairs in the shared task

Each WIL consisted of a topic in the source and target language pair, and the task was to identify parts of the topic (in the respective language titles) that are transliterations of each other. A seed data set (of about 1K transliteration pairs) was provided for each language pair, and was the only resource to be used for developing a mining system. The participants were expected to produce a paired list of source-target single word named entities, for every WIL provided. At the evaluation time, a random subset of WIL's (about 1K WIL's) in each language pair were hand labeled, and used to test the results produced by the participants.

Participants were allowed to use only the 1K seed data provided by the organizers to produce "standard" results; this restriction is imposed to provide a meaningful way of comparing the effective methods and approaches. However, "non-standard" runs were permitted where participants were allowed to use more seed data or any language-specific resource available to them.

[3] Wikipedia's Interlanguage Links: http://en.wikipedia.org/wiki/Help:Interlanguage_links

2.2 Data Sets for the Task

The following datasets were used for each language pair, for this task.

Training Data	Size	Remarks
Seed Data (Parallel names)	~1K	Paired names between source and target languages.
To-be-mined Wikipedia Inter-Wiki-Link Data (Noisy)	Variable	Paired named entities between source and target languages obtained directly from Wikipedia
Test Data	~1K	This was a subset of Wikipedia Inter-Wiki-Link data, which was hand labeled for evaluation.

Table 2: Datasets created for the shared task

The first two sets were provided by the organizers to the participants, and the third was used for evaluation.

Seed transliteration data: In addition we provided approximately 1K parallel names in each language pair as seed data to develop any methodology to identify transliterations. For standard run results, only this seed data was to be used, though for non-standard runs, more data or other linguistics resources were allowed.

English Names	Hindi Names
village	विलेज
linden	लिन्डन
market	मार्केट
mysore	मैसूर

Table 3: Sample English-Hindi seed data

English Names	Russian Names
gregory	Григорий
hudson	Гудзон
victor	Виктор
baranowski	барановский

Table 4: Sample English-Russian seed data

To-Mine-Data WIL data: All WIL's were extracted from the Wikipedia around January 2010, and provided to the participants. The extracted names were provided *as-is*, with no hand verification about their correctness, completeness or consistency. As sample of the WIL data for English-Hindi and English-Russian is shown in Tables 5 and 6 respectively. Note that there are 0, 1 or more single-word transliterations from each WIL.

#	English Wikipedia Title	Hindi Wikipedia Title
1	Indian National Congress	भारतीय राष्ट्रीय कांग्रेस
2	University of Oxford	ऑक्सफ़र्ड विश्वविद्यालय
3	Indian Institute of Science	भारतीय विज्ञान संस्थान
4	Jawaharlal Nehru University	जवाहरलाल नेहरू विश्वविद्यालय

Table 5: English-Hindi Wikipedia title pairs

#	English Wikipedia Title	Russian Wikipedia Title
1	Mikhail Gorbachev	Горбачёв, Михаил Сергеевич
2	George Washington	Вашингтон, Джордж
3	Treaty of Versailles	Версальский договор
4	French Republic	Франция

Table 6: English-Russian Wikipedia title pairs

Test set: We randomly selected ~1000 wikipedia links (from the large noisy Inter-wiki-links) as test-set, and manually extracted the single word transliteration pairs associated with each of these WILs. Please note that a given WIL can provide 0, 1 or more single-word transliteration pairs. To keep the task simple, it was specified that only those transliterations would be considered correct that were clear transliterations word-per-word (morphological variations one or both sides are not considered transliterations) These 1K test set was be a subset of Wikipedia data provided to the user. The gold dataset is as shown in Tables 7 and 8.

WIL#	English Names	Hindi Names
1	Congress	कांग्रेस
2	Oxford	ऑक्सफ़र्ड
3	<Null>	<Null>
4	Jawaharlal	जवाहरलाल
4	Nehru	नेहरू

Table 7: Sample English-Hindi transliteration pairs mined from Wikipedia title pairs

WIL#	English Names	Russian Names
1	Mikhail	Михаил
1	Gorbachev	Горбачёв
2	George	Джордж
2	Washington	Вашингтон
3	Versailles	Версальский
4	<Null>	<Null>

Table 8: Sample English-Russian transliteration pairs mined from Wikipedia title pairs

2.3 Evaluation:

The participants were expected to mine such single-word transliteration data for every specific WIL, though the evaluation was done only against the randomly selected, hand-labeled test set. A participant may submit a maximum of 10 runs for a given language pair (including a minimum of one mandatory "standard" run). There could be more standard runs, without exceeding 10 (including the non-standard runs).

At evaluation time, the task organizers checked every WIL in test set from among the user-provided results, to evaluate the quality of the submission on the 3 metrics described later.

3 Evaluation Metrics

We measured the quality of the mining task using the following measures:

1. $Precision_{CorrectTransliterations}(P_{Trans})$
2. $Recall_{CorrectTransliteration}$ (R_{Trans})
3. $F\text{-}Score_{CorrectTransliteration}$ (F_{Trans}).

Please refer to the following figures for the explanations:

A = True Positives (TP) = Pairs that were identified as "Correct Transliterations" by the participant and were indeed "Correct Transliterations" as per the gold standard
B = False Positives (FP) = Pairs that were identified as "Correct Transliterations" by the participant but they were "Incorrect Transliterations" as per the gold standard.
C = False Negatives (FN) = Pairs that were identified as "Incorrect Transliterations" by the participant but were actually "Correct Transliterations" as per the gold standard.
D = True Negatives (TN) = Pairs that were identified as "Incorrect Transliterations" by the participant and were indeed "Incorrect Transliterations" as per the gold standard.

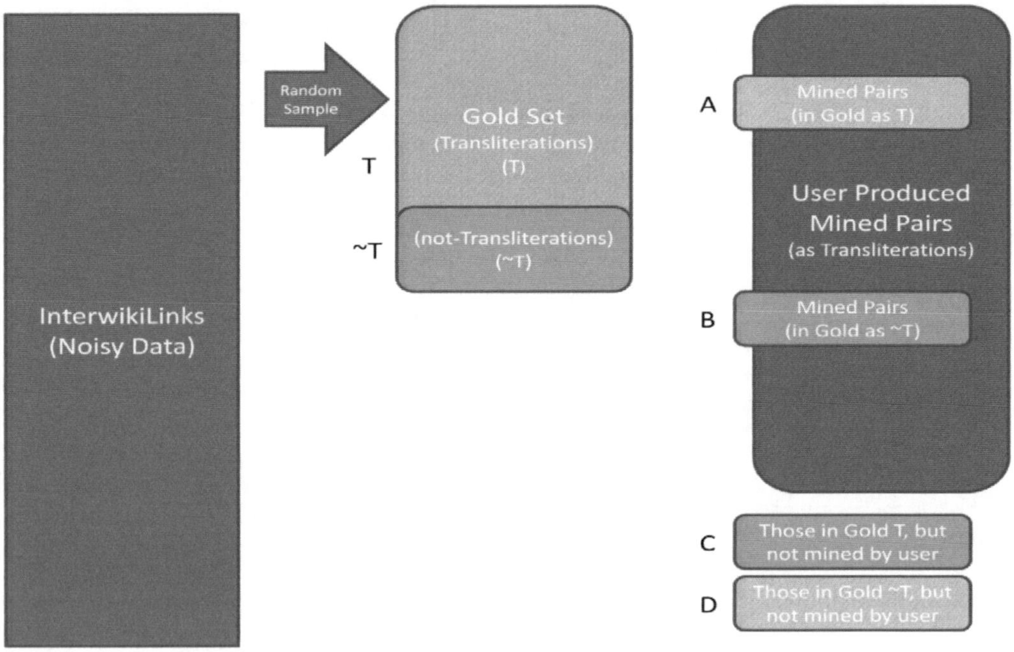

Figure 1: Overview of the mining task and evaluation

1. **Recall$_{\mathbf{CorrectTransliteration}}$ ($\mathbf{R_{Trans}}$)**

The recall was computed using the sample as follows:

$$R_{Trans} = \frac{TP}{TP + FN} = \frac{A}{A + C} = \frac{A}{T}$$

2. **Precision$_{\mathbf{CorrectTransliteration}}$ ($\mathbf{P_{Trans}}$)**

The precision was computed using the sample as follows:

$$P_{Trans} = \frac{TP}{TP + FP} = \frac{A}{A + B}$$

3. **F-Score (F)**

$$F = \frac{2 * P_{Trans} * R_{Trans}}{P_{Trans} + R_{Trans}}$$

4 Participants & Approaches

The following 5 teams participated in the Transliteration Mining Task♣:

#	Team	Organization
1	Alberta	University of Alberta, Canada
2	CMIC	Cairo Microsoft Innovation Centre, Egypt
3	Groningen	University of Groningen, Netherlands
4	IBM Egypt	IBM Egypt, Cairo, Egypt
5	MINT♣	Microsoft Research India, India

Table 9: Participants in the Shared Task

The approaches used by the 4 participating groups can be broadly classified as discriminative and generation based approaches. Discriminative approaches treat the mining task as a binary classification problem where the goal is to build a classifier that identifies whether a given pair is a valid transliteration pair or not. Generation based approaches on the other hand generate transliterations for each word in the source title and measure their similarity with the candidate words in the target title. Below, we give a summary of the various participating systems.

The CMIC team (Darwish et. al., 2010) used a generative transliteration model (***HMM***) to transliterate each word in the source title and compared the transliterations with the words appearing in the target title. For example, for a given word E_i in the source title if the model generates a transliteration F_j which appears in the target title then (E_i, F_j) are considered as transliteration pairs. The results are further improved by using phonetic conflation (***PC***) and iteratively training (***IterT***) the generative model using the mined transliteration pairs. For phonetic conflation a modified SOUNDEX scheme is used wherein vowels are discarded and phonetically similar characters are conflated. Both, phonetic conflation and iterative training, led to an increase in

♣ Non-participating system, included for reference.

recall which was better than the corresponding decline in precision.

The Alberta team (Jiampojamarn et. al., 2010) fielded 5 different systems in the shared task. The first system uses a simple edit distance based method where a pair of strings is classified as a transliteration pair if the Normalized Edit Distance (***NED***) between them is above a certain threshold. To calculate the NED, the target language string is first Romanized by replacing each target grapheme by the source grapheme having the highest conditional probability. These conditional probabilities are obtained by aligning the seed set of transliteration pairs using an M2M-aligner approach (Jiampojamarn et. al., 2007). The second system uses a SVM based discriminative classifier trained using an improved feature representation (***BK 2007***) (Bergsma and Kondrak, 2007). These features include all substring pairs up to a maximum length of three as extracted from the aligned word pairs. The transliteration pairs in the seed data provided for the shared task were used as positive examples. The negative examples were obtained by generating all possible source-target pairs in the seed data and taking those pairs which are not transliterations but have a longest common subsequence ratio above a certain threshold. One drawback of this system is that longer substrings cannot be used due to the combinatorial explosion in the number of unique features as the substring length increases. To overcome this problem they propose a third system which uses a standard n-gram string kernel (***StringKernel***) that implicitly embeds a string in a feature space that has one co-ordinate for each unique n-gram (Shawe-Taylor and Cristianini, 2004). The above 3 systems are essentially discriminative systems. In addition, they propose a generation based approach (***DIRECTL+***) which determines whether the generated transliteration pairs of a source word and target word are similar to a given candidate pair. They use a state-of-the-art online discriminative sequence prediction model based on many-to-many alignments, further augmented by the incorporation of joint n-gram features (Jiampojamarn et. al., 2010). Apart from the four systems described above, they propose an additional system for English Chinese, wherein they formulate the mining task as a matching problem (***Matching***) and greedily extract the pairs with highest similarity. The similarity is calculated using the alignments obtained by training a generation model (Jiampojamarn *et. al.*, 2007) using the seed data.

The IBM Cairo team (Noemans et. al., 2010) proposed a generation based approach which takes inspiration from Phrase Based Statistical Machine Translation (PBSMT) and learns a character-to-character alignment model between the source and target language using GIZA++. This alignment table is then represented using a finite state automaton (***FSA***) where the input is the source character and the output is the target character. For a given word in the source title, candidate transliterations are generated using this FST and are compared with the words in the target title. In addition they also submitted a baseline run which used phonetic edit distance.

The Groningen (Nabende et. al., 2010) team used a generation based approach that uses pair HMMs ***(P-HMM)*** to find the similarity between a given pair of source and target strings. The proposed variant of pair HMM uses transition parameters that are distinct between each of the edit states and emission parameters that are also distinct. The three edits states are substitution state, deletion state and insertion state. The parameters of the pair HMM are estimated using the Baum-Welch Expectation Maximization algorithm (Baum et. al. 1970).

Finally, as a reference, results of a previously published system – MINT (Udupa et. al., 2009) – were also included in this report as a reference. MINT is a large scalable mining system for mining transliterations from comparable corpora, essentially multilingual news articles in the same timeline. While MINT takes a two step approach – first aligning documents based on content similarity, and subsequently mining transliterations based on a name similarity model – for this task, only the transliteration mining step is employed. For mining transliterations a logistic function based similarity model ***(LFS)*** trained discriminatively with the seed parallel names data was employed. It should be noted here that the MINT algorithm was used *as-is* for mining transliterations from Wikipedia paired titles, with no fine-tuning. While the standard runs used only the data provided by the organizers, the non-standard runs used about 15K ***(Seed^{+})*** parallel names between the languages.

5 Results & Analysis

The results for EnAr, EnCh, EnHi, EnRu and EnTa are summarized in Tables 10, 11, 12, 13 and 14 respectively. The results clearly indicate that there is no single approach which performs well across all languages. In fact, there is even no single genre (discriminative v/s generation based) which performs well across all languages. We, therefore, do a case by case analysis of the results and highlight some important observations.

- The discriminative classifier using string kernels proposed by Jiampojamarn *et. al.* (2010) consistently performed well in all the 4 languages that it was tested on. Specifically, it gave the best performance for EnHi and EnTa.
- The simple discriminative approach based on Normalized Edit Distance (NED) gave the best result for EnRu. Further, the authors report that the results of StringKernel and BK-2007 were not significantly better than NED.
- The use of phonetic conflation consistently performed better than the case when phonetic conflation was not used.
- The results for EnCh are significantly lower when compared to the results for other lanaguge pairs. This shows that mining transliteration pairs between alphabetic languages (EnRu, EnAr, EnHi, EnTa) is relatively easier as compared to the case when one of the languages is non-alphabetic (EnCh)

6 Plans for the Future Editions

This shared task was designed as a complementary shared task to the popular NEWS Shared Tasks on Transliteration Generation; successful mining of transliteration pairs demonstrated in this shared task would be a viable source for generating data for developing a state of the art transliteration generation system.

We intend to extend the scope of the mining in 3 different ways: (*i*) extend mining to more language pairs, (*ii*) allow identification of near transliterations where there may be changes do to the morphology of the target (or the source) languages, and, (*iii*) demonstrate an end-to-end transliteration system that may be developed starting with a small seed corpora of, say, 1000 paired names.

References

Baum, L., Petrie, T., Soules, G. and Weiss, N. 1970. *A Maximization Technique Occurring in the Statistical Analysis of Probabilistic Functions of Markov Chains.* In The Annals of Mathematical Statistics, 41 (1): 164-171.

Bergsma, S. and Kondrak, G. 2007. *Alignment Based Discriminative String Similarity.* In Proceedings of the 45th Annual Meeting of the ACL, 2007.

Darwish, K. 2010. *Transliteration Mining with Phonetic Conflation and Iterative Training*. Proceedings of the 2010 Named Entities Workshop: Shared Task on Transliteration Mining, 2010.

Jiampojamarn, S., Dwyer, K., Bergsma, S., Bhargava, A., Dou, Q., Kim, M. Y. and Kondrak, G. 2010. *Transliteration generation and mining with limited training resources.* Proceedings of the 2010 Named Entities Workshop: Shared Task on Transliteration Mining, 2010.

Shawe-Taylor, J and Cristianini, N. 2004. *Kernel Methods for Pattern Analysis.* Cambridge University Press.

Klementiev, A. and Roth, D. 2006. *Weakly supervised named entity transliteration and discovery from multilingual comparable corpora.* Proceedings of the 44th Annual Meeting of the ACL, 2006.

Knight, K. and Graehl, J. 1998. *Machine Transliteration.* Computational Linguistics.

Kumaran, A., Khapra, M. and Li, Haizhou. 2010. *Whitepaper on NEWS 2010 Shared Task on Transliteration Mining.* Proceedings of the 2010 Named Entities Workshop: Shared Task on Transliteration Mining, 2010.

Nabende, P. 2010. *Mining Transliterations from Wikipedia using Pair HMMs.* Proceedings of the 2010 Named Entities Workshop: Shared Task on Transliteration Mining, 2010.

Noeman, S. and Madkour, A. 2010. *Language independent Transliteration mining system using Finite State Automata framework.* Proceedings of the 2010 Named Entities Workshop: Shared Task on Transliteration Mining, 2010.

Udupa, R., Saravanan, K., Kumaran, A. and Jagarlamudi, J. 2009. *MINT: A Method for Effective and Scalable Mining of Named Entity Transliterations from Large Comparable Corpora*. Proceedings of the 12th Conference of the European Chapter of Association for Computational Linguistics, 2009.

Participant	Run Type	Description	Precision	Recall	F-Score
IBM Egypt	Standard	FST, edit distance 2 with normalized characters	0.887	0.945	0.915
IBM Egypt	Standard	FST, edit distance 1 with normalized characters	0.859	0.952	0.903
IBM Egypt	Standard	Phonetic distance, with normalized characters	0.923	0.830	0.874
CMIC	Standard	HMM + IterT	0.886	0.817	0.850
CMIC	Standard	HMM + PC	0.900	0.796	0.845
CMIC	Standard	(HMM + ItertT) + PC	0.818	0.827	0.822
Alberta	Non- Standard		0.850	0.780	0.820
Alberta	Standard	BK-2007	0.834	0.798	0.816
Alberta	Standard	NED+	0.818	0.783	0.800
CMIC	Standard	(HMM + PC + ItertT) + PC	0.895	0.678	0.771
Alberta	Standard	DirecTL+	0.861	0.652	0.742
CMIC	Standard	HMM	0.966	0.587	0.730
CMIC	Standard	HMM + PC + IterT	0.952	0.588	0.727
IBM Egypt	Standard	FST, edit distance 2 without normalized characters	0.701	0.747	0.723
IBM Egypt	Standard	FST, edit distance 1 without normalized characters	0.681	0.755	0.716
IBM Egypt	Standard	Phonetic distance, without normalized characters	0.741	0.666	0.702

Table 10: Results of the English Arabic task

Participant	Run Type	Description	Precision	Recall	F-Score
Alberta	Standard	Matching	0.698	0.427	0.530
Alberta	Non-Standard		0.700	0.430	0.530
CMIC	Standard	(HMM + IterT) + PC	1	0.030	0.059
CMIC	Standard	HMM + IterT	1	0.026	0.05
CMIC	Standard	HMM + PC	1	0.024	0.047
CMIC	Standard	(HMM + PC + IterT) + PC	1	0.022	0.044
CMIC	Standard	HMM	1	0.016	0.032
CMIC	Standard	HMM + PC + IterT	1	0.016	0.032
Alberta	Standard	DirecTL+	0.045	0.005	0.009

Table 11: Results of the English Chinese task

Participant	Run Type	Description	Precision	Recall	F-Score
MINT♣	Non-Standard	LFS + Seed+	0.967	0.923	0.944
Alberta	Standard	StringKernel	0.954	0.895	0.924
Alberta	Standard	NED+	0.875	0.941	0.907
Alberta	Standard	DirecTL+	0.945	0.866	0.904
CMIC	Standard	(HMM + PC + IterT) + PC	0.953	0.855	0.902
Alberta	Standard	BK-2007	0.883	0.880	0.882
CMIC	Standard	(HMM + IterT) + PC	0.951	0.812	0.876
CMIC	Standard	HMM + PC	0.959	0.786	0.864
Alberta	Non-Standard		0.890	0.820	0.860
MINT♣	Standard	LFS	0.943	0.780	0.854
MINT♣	Standard	LFS	0.946	0.773	0.851

♣ Non-participating system

CMIC	Standard	HMM + PC + IterT	0.981	0.687	0.808
CMIC	Standard	HMM + IterT	0.984	0.569	0.721
CMIC	Standard	HMM	0.987	0.559	0.714

Table 10: Results of the English Hindi task

Participant	Run Type	Description	Precision	Recall	F-Score
Alberta	Standard	NED+	0.880	0.869	0.875
CMIC	Standard	HMM + PC	0.813	0.839	0.826
MINT♣	Non-Standard	LFS + Seed$^+$	0.797	0.853	0.824
Groningen♠	Standard	P-HMM	0.780	0.834	0.806
Alberta	Standard	StringKernel	0.746	0.889	0.811
CMIC	Standard	HMM	0.868	0.748	0.804
CMIC	Standard	HMM + PC + IterT	0.843	0.747	0.792
Alberta	Non-Standard		0.730	0.870	0.790
Alberta	Standard	DirecTL+	0.778	0.795	0.786
CMIC	Standard	HMM + IterT	0.716	0.868	0.785
MINT♣	Standard	LFS	0.822	0.752	0.785
CMIC	Standard	(HMM + PC + IterT) + PC	0.771	0.794	0.782
Alberta	Standard	BK-2007	0.684	0.902	0.778
CMIC	Standard	(HMM + IterT) + PC	0.673	0.881	0.763
Groningen	Standard	P-HMM	0.658	0.334	0.444

Table 11: Results of the English Russian task

Participant	Run Type	Description	Precision	Recall	F-Score
Alberta	Standard	StringKernel	0.923	0.906	0.914
MINT♣	Non-Standard	LFS + Seed$^+$	0.910	0.897	0.904
MINT♣	Standard	LFS	0.899	0.814	0.855
MINT♣	Standard	LFS	0.913	0.790	0.847
Alberta	Standard	BK-2007	0.808	0.852	0.829
CMIC	Standard	(HMM + IterT) + PC	0.939	0.741	0.828
Alberta	Non-Standard		0.820	0.820	0.820
Alberta	Standard	DirectL+	0.919	0.710	0.801
Alberta	Standard	NED+	0.916	0.696	0.791
CMIC	Standard	HMM + IterT	0.952	0.668	0.785
CMIC	Standard	HMM + PC	0.963	0.604	0.743
CMIC	Standard	(HMM + PC + IterT) + PC	0.968	0.567	0.715
CMIC	Standard	HMM + PC + IterT	0.975	0.446	0.612
CMIC	Standard	HMM	0.976	0.407	0.575

Table 12: Results of the English Tamil task

♣ Non-participating system

♠ Post-deadline submission of the participating system

Whitepaper of NEWS 2010 Shared Task on Transliteration Mining

A Kumaran
Microsoft Research India
Bangalore, India

Mitesh M. Khapra
Indian Institute of Technology-Bombay
Mumbai, India

Haizhou Li
Institute for Infocomm
Research, Singapore

Abstract

Transliteration is generally defined as phonetic translation of names across languages. Machine Transliteration is a critical technology in many domains, such as machine translation, cross-language information retrieval/extraction, etc. Recent research has shown that high quality machine transliteration systems may be developed in a language-neutral manner, using a reasonably sized good quality corpus (~15-25K parallel names) between a given pair of languages. In this shared task, we focus on acquisition of such good quality names corpora in many languages, thus complementing the machine transliteration shared task that is concurrently conducted in the same NEWS 2010 workshop. Specifically, this task focuses on mining the Wikipedia paired entities data (aka, inter-wiki-links) to produce high-quality transliteration data that may be used for transliteration tasks.

1 Task Description

The task is to develop a system for mining single word transliteration pairs from the standard Wikipedia paired topics (aka, Wikipedia Inter-Language Links, or WIL[1]) in one or more of the specified language pairs. The WIL's link articles on the same topic in multiple languages, and are traditionally used as a parallel language resource for many NLP applications, such as Machine Translation, Crosslingual Search, etc. Specific WIL's of interest for our task are those that contain proper names – either wholly or partly – which can yield rich transliteration data.

Each WIL consists of a topic in the source and the language pair, and the task is to identify parts of the topic (in the respective language titles) that are transliterations of each other. A seed data set (of about 1K transliteration pairs) would be provided for each language pair, and are the only resource to be used for developing a mining system. The participants are expected to produce a paired list of source-target single word named entities, for every WIL provided. At the evaluation time, a random subset of WIL's (about 1K WIL's) in each language pair that are hand labeled would be used to test the results produced by the participants.

Participants may use only the 1K seed data provided by the organizers to produce "standard" results; this restriction is imposed to provide a meaningful way of comparing the effective methods and approaches. However, "non-standard" runs would be permitted where participants may use more seed data or any language-specific resource available to them.

2 Important Dates

SHARED TASK SCHEDULES	
Registration Opens	1-Feb-2010
Registration Closes	13-Mar-2010
Training Data Release	26 -Feb-2010
Test Data Release	13-Mar-2010
Results Submission Due	20-Mar-2010
Evaluation Results Announcement	27-Mar-2010
Short Papers Due	5-Apr-2010
Workshop Paper Submission Closes	5-Apr-2010
Workshop & Task Papers Acceptance	6-May-2010
CRC Due	15-May-2010
Workshop Date	16-Jul-2010

3 Participation

1. Registration (1 Feb 2010)
   a. Prospective participants are to register to the NEWS-2010 Workshop homepage, for this specific task.
2. Training Data Release (26 Feb 2010)
   a. Registered participants are to obtain seed and Wikipedia data from the Shared Task organizers.

[1] Wikipedia's Interlanguage Links: *http://en.wikipedia.org/wiki/Help:Interlanguage_links*.

Proceedings of the 2010 Named Entities Workshop, ACL 2010, pages 29–38,
Uppsala, Sweden, 16 July 2010. ©2010 Association for Computational Linguistics

3. Evaluation Script (1 March 2010)
   a. A sample submission and an evaluation script will be released in due course.
   b. The participants must make sure that their output is produced in a way that the evaluation script may run and produce the expected output.
   c. The same script (with held out test data and the user outputs) would be used for final evaluation.

4. Testing data (13 March 2010)
   a. The test data would be a held out data of approximately 1K "gold-standard" mined data.
   b. The submissions (up to 10) would be tested against the test data, and the results published.

5. Results (27 March 2010)
   a. On the results announcement date, the evaluation results would be published on the Workshop website.
   b. Note that only the scores (in respective metrics) of the participating systems on each language pairs would be published, but no explicit ranking of the participating systems.
   c. Note that this is a shared evaluation task and not a competition; the results are meant to be used to evaluate systems on common data set with common metrics, and not to rank the participating systems. While the participants can cite the performance of their systems (scores on metrics) from the workshop report, they should not use any ranking information in their publications.
   d. Further, all participants should agree not to reveal identities of other participants in any of their publications unless you get permission from the other respective participants. If the participants want to remain anonymous in published results, they should inform the organizers at the time of registration. Note that the results of their systems would still be published, but with the participant identities masked. As a result, in this case, your organization name will still appear in the web site as one of participants, but it is not linked explicitly with your results.

6. Short Papers on Task (5 April 2010)
   a. Each submitting site is required to submit a 4-page system paper (short paper) for its submissions, including their approach, data used and the results.
   b. All system short papers will be included in the proceedings. Selected short papers will be presented in the NEWS 2010 workshop. Acceptance of the system short-papers would be announced together with that of other papers.

4 Languages Involved

The task involves transliteration mining in the language pairs summarized in the following table.

Source Language	Target Language	Track ID
English	Chinese	WM-EnCn
English	Hindi	WM-EnHi
English	Tamil	WM-EnTa
English	Russian	WM-EnRu
English	Arabic	WM-EnAr

Table 1: Language Pairs in the shared task

5 Data Sets for the Task

The following datasets are used for each language pair, for this task.

Training Data	Size	Remarks
Seed Data (Parallel)	~1K	Paired names between source and target languages.
To-be-mined Wikipedia Inter-Wiki-Link Data (Noisy)	Variable	Paired named entities between source and target languages obtained directly from Wikipedia
Test Data	~1K	This is a subset of Wikipedia Inter-Wiki-Link data, which will be hand labeled.

Table 2: Datasets for the shared task

The first two sets would be provided by the organizers to the participants, and the third will be used for evaluation.

To-Mine-Data WIL data: All WIL's from an appropriate download from Wikipedia would be provided. The WIL data might look like the samples shown in Tables 3 and 4, with the single-word transliterations highlighted. Note that there could be 0, 1 or more single-word transliterations from each WIL.

#	English Wikipedia Title	Hindi Wikipedia Title
1	Indian National Congress	भारतीय राष्ट्रीय कांग्रेस
2	University of Oxford	ऑक्सफ़र्ड विश्वविद्यालय
3	Indian Institute of Science	भारतीय विज्ञान संस्थान
4	Jawaharlal Nehru University	जवाहरलाल नेहरू विश्वविद्यालय

Table 3: Sample English-Hindi Wikipedia title pairs

#	English Wikipedia Title	Russian Wikipedia Title
1	Mikhail Gorbachev	Горбачёв, Михаил Сергеевич
2	George Washington	Вашингтон, Джордж
3	Treaty of Versailles	Версальский договор
4	French Republic	Франция

Table 4: Sample English-Russian Wikipedia title pairs

Seed transliteration data: In addition we provide approximately 1K parallel names in each language pair as seed data to develop any methodology to identify transliterations. For standard run results, only this seed data could be used, though for non-standard runs, more data or other linguistics resources may be used.

English Names	Hindi Names
Village	विलेज
Linden	लिन्डन
Market	मार्केट
Mysore	मैसूर

Table 5: Sample English-Hindi seed data

English Names	Russian Names
Gregory	Григорий
Hudson	Гудзон
Victor	Виктор
baranowski	барановский

Table 6: Sample English-Russian seed data

Test set: We plan to randomly select ~1000 wikipedia links (from the large noisy Inter-wiki-links) as test-set, and manually extract the single word transliteration pairs associated with each of these WILs. Please note that a given WIL can provide 0, 1 or more single-word transliteration pairs. To keep the task simple, we consider as correct transliterations only those that are clear transliterations word-per-word (morphological variations one or both sides are not considered transliterations) These 1K test set will be a subset of Wikipedia data provided to the user. The gold dataset might look like the following (assuming the items 1, 2, 3 and 4 in Tables 3 and 4 were among the randomly selected WIL's from To-Mine-Data).

WIL#	English Names	Hindi Names
1	Congress	कांग्रेस
2	Oxford	ऑक्सफ़र्ड
3	<Null>	<Null>
4	Jawaharlal	जवाहरलाल
4	Nehru	नेहरू

Table 7: Sample English-Hindi transliteration pairs mined from Wikipedia title pairs

WIL#	English Names	Russian Names
1	Mikhail	Михаил
1	Gorbachev	Горбачёв
2	George	Джордж
2	Washington	Вашингтон
3	Versailles	Версальский
4	<Null>	<Null>

Table 8: Sample English-Russian transliteration pairs mined from Wikipedia title pairs

Evaluation: The participants are expected to mine such single-word transliteration data for every specific WIL, though the evaluation would be done only against the randomly selected, hand-labeled test set. At evaluation time, the task organizers check every WIL in test set from among the user-provided results, to evaluate the quality of the submission on the 3 metrics described later.

Additional information on data use:

1. Seed data may have ownership and appropriate licenses may need to be procured for use.
2. To-be-mined Wikipedia data is extracted from Wikipedia (in Jan/Feb 2010), and distributed as-is. No assurances that they are correct, complete or consistent.

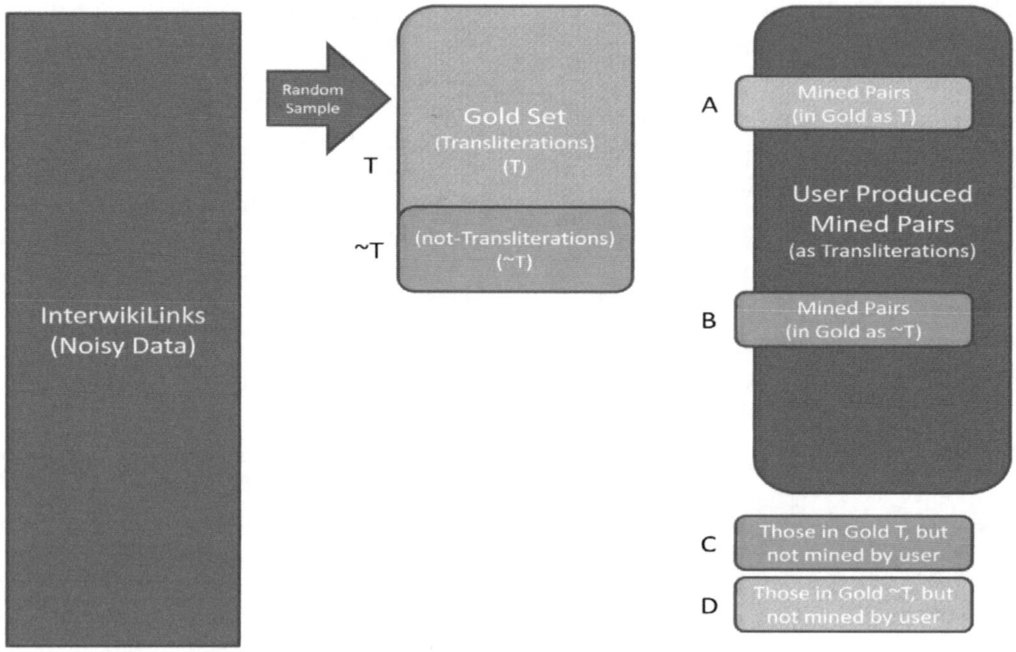

Figure 1: Overview of the mining task and evaluation

3. The hand-labeled test set is created by NEWS shared task organizers, and will be used for computing the metrics for a given submission.
4. We expect that the participants to use only the seed data (parallel names) provided by the Shared Task for a standard run to ensure a fair evaluation and a meaningful comparison between the effectiveness of approaches taken by various systems. At least one such run (using only the data provided by the shared task) is mandatory for all participants for a given task that they participate in.
5. If more data (either parallel names data or monolingual data), or any language-specific modules were used, then all such runs using extra data or resources must be marked as "Non-standard". For such non-standard runs, it is required to disclose the size and characteristics of the data or the nature of languages resources used, in their paper.
6. A participant may submit a maximum of 10 runs for a given language pair (including one or more "standard" run). There could be more standard runs, without exceeding 10 (including the non-standard runs).

6 Paper Format

All paper submissions to NEWS 2010 should follow the ACL 2010 paper submission policy (http://acl2010.org/papers.html), including paper format, blind review policy and title and author format convention. Shared task system short papers are also in two-column format without exceeding four (4) pages plus any extra page for references. However, there is no need for double-blind requirements, as the users may refer to their runs and metrics in the published results.

7 Evaluation Metrics

We plan to measure the quality of the mining task using the following measures:

1. $\text{Precision}_{\text{CorrectTransliterations}}$ (P_{Trans})
2. $\text{Recall}_{\text{CorrectTransliteration}}$ (R_{Trans})
3. $\text{F-Score}_{\text{CorrectTransliteration}}$ (F_{Trans}).

Please refer to the following figures for the explanations:

A = True Positives (TP) = Pairs that were identified as "Correct Transliterations" by the participant and were indeed "Correct Transliterations" as per the gold standard
B = False Positives (FP) = Pairs that were identified as "Correct Transliterations" by the participant but they were "Incorrect Transliterations" as per the gold standard.
C = False Negatives (FN) = Pairs that were identified as "Incorrect Transliterations" by the participant but were actually "Correct Transliterations" as per the gold standard.

D = True Negatives (TN) = Pairs that were identified as "Incorrect Transliterations" by the participant and were indeed "Incorrect Transliterations" as per the gold standard.

1. **$\text{Recall}_{\text{CorrectTransliteration}}$ (R_{Trans})**
The recall is going to be computed using the sample as follows:

$$R_{Trans} = \frac{TP}{TP + FN} = \frac{A}{A + C} = \frac{A}{T}$$

2. **$\text{Precision}_{\text{CorrectTransliteration}}$ (P_{Trans})**
The precision is going to be computed using the sample as follows:

$$P_{Trans} = \frac{TP}{TP + FP} = \frac{A}{A + B}$$

3. **F-Score (F)**

$$F = \frac{2 * P_{Trans} * R_{Trans}}{P_{Trans} + R_{Trans}}$$

8 Contact Us

If you have any questions about this share task and the database, please contact one of the organizers below:

Dr. A. Kumaran
Microsoft Research India
Bangalore 560080 INDIA
a.kumaran@microsoft.com

Mitesh Khapra
Indian Institute of Technology-Bombay
Mumbai, INDIA
MKhapra@cse.iitb.ac.in.

Dr Haizhou Li
Institute for Infocomm Research
Singapore, SINGAPORE 138632
hli@i2r.a-star.edu.sg.

Appendix A: Seed Parallel Names Data

- File Naming Conventions:
  - NEWS09_Seed_XXYY_1K.xml,
    - XX: Source Language
    - YY: Target Language
    - 1K: number of parallel names

- File Formats:
  - All data would be made available in XML formats (Appendix A).

- Data Encoding Formats:
  - The data would be in Unicode, in UTF-8 encoding. The results are expected to be submitted in UTF-8 format only, and in the XML format specified.

File: NEWS2009_Seed_EnHi_1000.xml

```
<?xml version="1.0" encoding="UTF-8"?>
      <SeedCorpus
          CorpusID = "NEWS2009-Seed-EnHi-1K"
          SourceLang = "English"
          TargetLang = "Hindi"
          CorpusType = "Seed"
          CorpusSize = "1000"
          CorpusFormat = "UTF8">
            <Name ID="1">
                  <SourceName>eeeeee1</SourceName>
                  <TargetName ID="1">hhhhhh1_1</TargetName>
                  <TargetName ID="2">hhhhhh1_2</TargetName>
                  ...
                  <TargetName ID="n">hhhhhh1_n</TargetName>
            </Name>
            <Name ID="2">
                  <SourceName>eeeeee2</SourceName>
                  <TargetName ID="1">hhhhhh2_1</TargetName>
                  <TargetName ID="2">hhhhhh2_2</TargetName>
                  ...
                  <TargetName ID="m">hhhhhh2_m</TargetName>
            </Name>
            ...
            <!-- rest of the names to follow -->
            ...
      </SeedCorpus>
```

Appendix B: Wikipedia InterwikiLinks Data

- File Naming Conventions:
  - NEWS09_Wiki_XXYY_nnnn.xml,
    - XX: Source Language
    - YY: Target Language
    - nnnn: size of paired entities culled from Wikipedia ("25K", "10000", etc.)
- File Formats:
  - All data would be made available in XML formats (Appendix A).
- Data Encoding Formats:
  - The data would be in Unicode, in UTF-8 encoding. The results are expected to be submitted in UTF-8 format only, and in the XML format specified.

File: NEWS2009_Wiki_EnHi_10K.xml

```
<?xml version="1.0" encoding="UTF-8"?>
      <WikipediaCorpus
          CorpusID = "NEWS2009-Wiki-EnHi-10K"
          SourceLang = "English"
          TargetLang = "Hindi"
          CorpusType = "Wiki"
          CorpusSize = "10000"
          CorpusFormat = "UTF8">
             <Title ID="1">
                   <SourceEntity>e1 e2 … en</SourceEntity>
                   <TargetEntity>h1 h2 … hm</TargetEntity>
             </Title>
             <Title ID="2">
                   <SourceEntity>e1 e2 … ei</SourceEntity>
                   <TargetEntity>h1 h2 … hj</TargetEntity>
             </Title>
             ...
             <!-- rest of the titles to follow -->
             ...
      </ WikipediaCorpus>
```

Appendix C: Results Submission - Format

- File Naming Conventions:
    - NEWS09_Result_XXYY_gggg_nn_description.xml
        - XX: Source
        - YY: Target
        - gggg: Group ID
        - nn: run ID.
        - description: Description of the run
- File Formats:
    - All results would be submitted in XML formats (Appendix B).
- Data Encoding Formats:
    - The data would be in Unicode, in UTF-8 encoding. The results are expected to be submitted in UTF-8 format only.

Example: NEWS2009_EnHi_TUniv_01_HMMBased.xml

```
<?xml version="1.0" encoding="UTF-8"?>
      <WikipediaMiningTaskResults
          SourceLang = "English"
          TargetLang = "Hindi"
          GroupID = "Trans University"
          RunID = "1"
          RunType = "Standard"
          Comments = "SVD Run with params: alpha=xxx beta=yyy">
             <Title ID="1">
                   <MinedPair ID="1">
                         <SourceName>e1</SourceName>
                         <TargetName>h1</TargetName>
                   </MinedPair>
                   <MinedPair ID="2">
                         <SourceName>e2</SourceName>
                         <TargetName>h2</TargetName>
                   </MinedPair>
             <!—followed by other pairs mined from this title-->
             </Title>
             <Title ID="2">
                   <MinedPair ID="1">
                         <SourceName>e1</SourceName>
                         <TargetName>h1</TargetName>
                   </MinedPair>
```

```
                <MinedPair ID="2">
                        <SourceName>e2</SourceName>
                        <TargetName>h2</TargetName>
                </MinedPair>
        <!—followed by other pairs mined from this title-->
        </Title>
        ...
        <!-- All titles in the culled data to follow -->
        ...
</WikipediaMiningTaskResults>
```

Appendix D: Sample Eng-Hindi Interwikilink Data

```
<?xml version="1.0" encoding="UTF-8"?>
<WikipediaCorpus CorpusID = "NEWS2009-Wiki-EnHi-Sample"
        SourceLang = "English"
        TargetLang = "Hindi"
        CorpusType = "Wiki" CorpusSize = "3"
        CorpusFormat = "UTF8">
                <Title ID="1">
                <SourceEntity>Indian National Congress</SourceEntity>
                <TargetEntity>भारतीय राष्ट्रीय कांग्रेस</TargetEntity>
        </Title>
        <!-- {Congress, कांग्रेस} should be identified by the paricipants-->
        <Title ID="2">
                <SourceEntity>University of Oxford</SourceEntity>
                <TargetEntity>ऑक्सफ़र्ड विश्वविद्यालय</TargetEntity>
        </Title>
        <!-- {Oxford, ऑक्सफ़र्ड} should be identified by the paricipants-->
        <Title ID="3">
                <SourceEntity>Jawaharlal Nehru University</SourceEntity>
                <TargetEntity>जवाहरलाल नेहरू विश्वविद्यालय</TargetEntity>
        </Title>
        <!-- {Jawaharlal, जवाहरलाल} and {Nehru, नेहरू} should be
                                identified by the paricipants-->
        <Title ID="4">
                <SourceEntity>Indian Institute Of Science</SourceEntity>
                <TargetEntity>भारतीय विज्ञान संस्थान</TargetEntity>
        </Title>
        <!--There are no transliteration pairs here -->
</WikipediaCorpus>
```

Appendix E: Eng-Hindi Gold Mined Data (wrt the above WIL Data)

```
<?xml version="1.0" encoding="UTF-8"?>
<WikipediaMiningTaskResults
        SourceLang = "English"
        TargetLang = "Hindi"
        GroupID = "Gold-Standard"
        RunID = ""
        RunType = ""
        Comments = "">
        <Title ID="1">
                <MinedPair ID="1">
                        <SourceName>Congress</SourceName>
                        <TargetName> कांग्रेस</TargetName>
                </MinedPair>
        </Title>
        <Title ID="2">
                <MinedPair ID="1">
```

```
                    <SourceName>Oxford</SourceName>
                    <TargetName> ऑक्सफ़र्ड</TargetName>
            </MinedPair>
      </Title>
      <Title ID="3">
            <MinedPair ID="1">
                    <SourceName>Jawaharlal</SourceName>
                    <TargetName> जवाहरलाल</TargetName>
            </MinedPair>
            <MinedPair ID="2">
                    <SourceName>Nehru</SourceName>
                    <TargetName> नेहरू</TargetName>
            </MinedPair>
      </Title>
      <Title ID="4">
      </Title>
</WikipediaMiningTaskResults>
```

Appendix F: English-Hindi Sample Submission and Evaluation

```
<?xml version="1.0" encoding="UTF-8"?>
<WikipediaMiningTaskResults
      SourceLang = "English"
      TargetLang = "Hindi"
      GroupID = "Gold-Standard"
      RunID = ""
      RunType = ""
      <Title ID="1">
            <MinedPair ID="1">
                    <SourceName>Congress</SourceName>
                    <TargetName> कांग्रेस</TargetName>
            </MinedPair>
The participant mined all correct transliteration pairs
      </Title>
      <Title ID="2">
            <MinedPair ID="1">
                    <SourceName>Oxford</SourceName>
                    <TargetName> ऑक्सफ़र्ड</TargetName>
            </MinedPair>
            <MinedPair ID="1">
                    <SourceName>University</SourceName>
                    <TargetName>विश्वविद्यालय</TargetName>
            </MinedPair>
The participant mined an incorrect transliteration pair {University,विश्वविद्यालय}
      </Title>
      <Title ID="3">
            <MinedPair ID="1">
                    <SourceName>Jawaharlal</SourceName>
                    <TargetName> जवाहरलाल</TargetName>
            </MinedPair>
The participant missed the correct transliteration pair {Nehru, नेहरू}
      </Title>
      <Title ID="4">
            <MinedPair ID="1">
                    <SourceName>Indian</SourceName>
                    <TargetName>भारतीय</TargetName>
            </MinedPair>
The participant mined an incorrect transliteration pair {Indian, भारतीय}
      </Title>
</WikipediaMiningTaskResults>
```

Sample Evaluation

T = |{(Congress, कांग्रेस), (Oxford, ऑक्सफ़र्ड), (Jawaharlal, जवाहरलाल),(Nehru, नेहरू)} | **= 4**
A = TP = | {(Congress, कांग्रेस), (Oxford, ऑक्सफ़र्ड), (Jawaharlal, जवाहरलाल)}| = **3**
B = FP = |{(Indian, भारतीय), (University, विश्वविद्यालय) }| **= 2**
C = FN = |{(Nehru, नेहरू)}| = **1**

$$R_{Trans} = \frac{TP}{TP + FN} = \frac{A}{A + C} = \frac{A}{T} = \frac{3}{4} = 0.75$$

$$P_{Trans} = \frac{TP}{TP+FP} = \frac{A}{A+B} = \frac{3}{5} = 0.60$$

$$F = \frac{2 * P_{Trans} * R_{Trans}}{P_{Trans} + R_{Trans}} = \frac{2 * 0.6 * 0.75}{0.6 + 0.75} = 0.67$$

Transliteration Generation and Mining with Limited Training Resources

Sittichai Jiampojamarn, Kenneth Dwyer, Shane Bergsma, Aditya Bhargava, Qing Dou, Mi-Young Kim, Grzegorz Kondrak
Department of Computing Science
University of Alberta
Edmonton, AB, T6G 2E8, Canada
{sj,dwyer,bergsma,abhargava,qdou,miyoung2,kondrak}@cs.ualberta.ca

Abstract

We present DIRECTL+: an online discriminative sequence prediction model based on many-to-many alignments, which is further augmented by the incorporation of joint n-gram features. Experimental results show improvement over the results achieved by DIRECTL in 2009. We also explore a number of diverse resource-free and language-independent approaches to transliteration mining, which range from simple to sophisticated.

1 Introduction

Many out-of-vocabulary words in statistical machine translation and cross-language information retrieval are named entities. If the languages in question use different writing scripts, such names must be transliterated. Transliteration can be defined as the conversion of a word from one writing script to another, which is usually based on the phonetics of the original word.

DIRECTL+ is our current approach to name transliteration which is an extension of the DIRECTL system (Jiampojamarn et al., 2009). We augmented the feature set with joint n-gram features which allow the discriminative model to utilize long dependencies of joint information of source and target substrings (Jiampojamarn et al., 2010). Experimental results suggest an improvement over the results achieved by DIRECTL in 2009.

Transliteration mining aims at automatically obtaining bilingual lists of names written in different scripts. We explore a number of different approaches to transliteration mining in the context of the NEWS 2010 Shared Task.[1] The sole resource that is provided for each language pair is a "seed" dataset that contains 1K transliteration word pairs. The objective is then to mine transliteration pairs from a collection of Wikipedia titles/topics that are given in both languages.

We explore a number of diverse resource-free and language-independent approaches to transliteration mining. One approach is to bootstrap the seed data by generating pseudo-negative examples, which are combined with the positives to form a dataset that can be used to train a classifier. We are particularly interested in achieving good performance without utilizing language-specific resources, so that the same approach can be applied with minimal or no modifications to an array of diverse language pairs.

This paper is divided in two main parts that correspond to the two tasks of transliteration generation and transliteration mining.

2 Transliteration generation

The structure of this section is as follows. In Section 2.1, we describe the pre-processing steps that were applied to all datasets. Section 2.2 reviews two methods for aligning the source and target symbols in the training data. We provide details on the DIRECTL+ systems in Section 2.3. In Section 2.4, we discuss extensions of DIRECTL+ that incorporate language-specific information. Section 2.5 summarizes our results.

2.1 Pre-processing

For all generation tasks, we pre-process the provided data as follows. First, we convert all characters in the source word to lower case. Then, we remove non-alphabetic characters unless they appear in both the source and target words. We normalize whitespace that surrounds a comma, so that there are no spaces before the comma and exactly one space following the comma. Finally, we separate multi-word titles into single words, using whitespace as the separator. We assume a mono-

[1] http://translit.i2r.a-star.edu.sg/news2010

Proceedings of the 2010 Named Entities Workshop, ACL 2010, pages 39–47,
Uppsala, Sweden, 16 July 2010. ©2010 Association for Computational Linguistics

tonic matching and ignore the titles that have a different number of words on both sides.

We observed that in the ArAe task there are cases where an extra space is added to the target when transliterating from Arabic names to their English equivalents; e.g., “Al Riyad”, “El Sayed”, etc. In order to prevent the pre-processing from removing too many title pairs, we allow non-equal matching if the source title is a single word.

For the English-Chinese (EnCh) task, we convert the English letter “x” to “ks” to facilitate better matching with its Chinese targets.

During testing, we pre-process test data in the same manner, except that we do not remove non-alphabetic characters. After the pre-processing steps, our system proposes 10-best lists for single word titles in the test data. For multi-word titles, we construct 10-best lists by ranking the combination scores of single words that make up the test titles.

2.2 Alignment

In the transliteration tasks, training data consist of pairs of names written in source and target scripts without explicit character-level alignment. In our experiments, we applied two different algorithms to automatically generate alignments in the training data. The generated alignments provide hypotheses of substring mappings in the training data. Given aligned training data, a transliteration model is trained to generate names in the target language given names in the source language.

The M2M-aligner (Jiampojamarn et al., 2007) is based on the expectation maximization (EM) algorithm. It allows us to create alignments between substrings of various lengths. We optimized the maximum substring sizes for the source and target based on the performance of the end task on the development sets. We allowed empty strings (*nulls*) only on the target side. We used the M2M-aligner for all alignment tasks, except for English-Pinyin alignment. The source code of the M2M-aligner is publicly available.[2]

An alternative alignment algorithm is based on the phonetic similarity of graphemes. The key idea of this approach is to represent each grapheme by a phoneme or a sequence of phonemes that is likely to be represented by the grapheme. The sequences of phonemes on the source side and the target side can then be aligned on the basis of phonetic similarity between phonemes. The main advantage of the phonetic alignment is that it requires no training data. We use the ALINE phonetic aligner (Kondrak, 2000), which aligns two strings of phonemes. The example in Figure 1 shows the alignment of the word *Barclay* to its Katakana transliteration *ba-ku-ri*. The one-to-one alignment can then be converted to a many-to-many alignment by grouping the Japanese phonemes that correspond to individual Katakana symbols.

b	a	r	c	-	l	a	y
|	|	|	|	|	|	|	|
b	a	-	k	u	r	-	i

Figure 1: An alignment example.

2.3 DirecTL+

We refer to our present approach to transliteration as DirecTL+. It is an extension of our DirecTL system (Jiampojamarn et al., 2009). It includes additional “joint n-gram” features that allow the discriminative model to correlate longer source and target substrings. The additional features allow our discriminative model to train on information that is present in generative joint n-gram models, and additionally train on rich source-side context, transition, and linear-chain features that have been demonstrated to be important in the transliteration task (Jiampojamarn et al., 2010).

Our model is based on an online discriminative framework. At each training iteration, the model generates an m-best list for each given source name based on the current feature weights. The feature weights are updated according to the gold-standard answers and the generated m-best answer lists using the Margin Infused Relaxed Algorithm (MIRA) (Crammer and Singer, 2003). This training process iterates over the training examples until the model converges. For m-best and n-gram parameters, we set $m = 10$ and $n = 6$ for all language pairs. These parameters as well as others were optimized on the development sets.

We trained our models directly on the data that were provided by the organizers, with three exceptions. In order to improve performance, we gave special treatment to English-Korean (EnKo), English-Chinese (EnCh), and English-Hindi (EnHi). These special cases are described in the next section.

[2] `http://code.google.com/p/m2m-aligner/`

2.4 Beyond DIRECTL+

2.4.1 Korean Jaso

A Korean syllable can be decomposed into two or three components called *Jaso*: an initial consonant, a middle vowel, and optionally a final consonant. The Korean generation for EnKo involves the following three steps: (1) English-to-Jaso generation, (2) correction of illegal Jaso sequences, and (3) Jaso-to-Korean conversion.

In order to correct illegal Jaso sequences that cannot be combined into Korean syllables in step 2, we consider both vowel and consonant rules. A Korean vowel can be either a simple vowel or a complex vowel that combines two simple vowels. We can use this information in order to replace double vowels with one complex vowel. We also use the silent consonant *o* (i-eung) when we need to insert a consonant between double vowels. A Korean vowel - (eu) is most commonly inserted between two English consonants in transliteration. In order to resolve three consecutive consonants, it can be placed into the most probable position according to the probability distribution of the training data.

2.4.2 Japanese Katakana

In the Japanese Katakana generation task, we replace each Katakana symbol with one or two letters using standard romanization tables. This has the effect of expressing the target side in Latin letters, which facilitates the alignment. DIRECTL+ is trained on the converted data to generate the target from the source. A post-processing program then attempts to convert the generated letters back into Katakana symbols. Sequences of letters that cannot be converted into Katakana are removed from the output m-best lists and replaced by lower scoring sequences that pass the back-conversion filter. Otherwise, there is usually a single valid mapping because most Katakana symbols are represented by single vowels or a consonant-vowel pair. The only apparent ambiguity involves the letter n, which can either stand by itself or cluster with the following vowel letter. We resolve the ambiguity by always assuming the latter case unless the letter n occurs at the end of the word.

2.4.3 Chinese Pinyin

Following (Jiampojamarn et al., 2009), we experimented with converting the original Chinese characters to Pinyin as an intermediate representation. Pinyin is the most commonly known romanization system for Standard Mandarin and many free tools are available for converting Chinese characters to Pinyin. Its alphabet contains the same 26 letters as English. Each Chinese character can be transcribed phonetically into Pinyin. A small percentage of Chinese characters have multiple pronunciations, and are thus represented by different Pinyin sequences. For those characters, we manually selected the pronunciations that are normally used for names. This pre-processing step significantly reduces the size of the target symbols: from 370 distinct Chinese characters to 26 Pinyin symbols. This allows our system to produce better alignments.

We developed three models: (1) trained on the original Chinese characters, (2) trained on Pinyin, and (3) the model that incorporates the phonetic alignment described in Section 2.2. The combination of the predictions of the different systems was performed using the following simple algorithm (Jiampojamarn et al., 2009). First, we rank the individual systems according to their top-1 accuracy on the development set. To obtain the top-1 prediction for each input word, we use simple voting, with ties broken according to the ranking of the systems. We generalize this approach to handle n-best lists by first ordering the candidate transliterations according to the rank assigned by each individual system, and then similarly breaking ties by voting and using the ranking of the systems.

2.4.4 Language identification for Hindi

Bhargava and Kondrak (2010) apply support vector machines (SVMs) to the task of identifying the language of names. The intuition here is that language information can inform transliteration. Bhargava and Kondrak (2010) test this hypothesis on the NEWS 2009 English-Hindi transliteration data by training language identification on data manually tagged as being of either Indian or non-Indian origin. It was found that splitting the data disjointly into two sets and training separate transliteration models yields no performance increase due to the decreased size of the data for the models.

We adopt this approach for the NEWS 2010 task, but here we do not use disjoint splits. Instead, we use the SVMs to generate probabilities, and then we apply a threshold to these probabilities to generate two datasets. For example, if we set the threshold to be 0.05, then we determine the probabilities of a given name being of Indian origin (p_{hi}) and of being of non-Indian origin (p_{en}). If $p_{hi} < 0.05$ then the name is excluded from the Indian set, and if $p_{en} < 0.05$ then the name is excluded from the non-Indian set. Using the two obtained non-disjoint sets, we then train a transliteration model for each set using DIRECTL+.

Since the two sets are not disjoint, we must decide how to combine the two results. Given that a name occurs in both sets, and both models provide a ranked list of possible targets for that name, we obtain a combined ranking using a linear combination over the mean reciprocal ranks (MRRs) of the two lists. The weights used are p_{hi} and p_{en} so that the more likely a name is considered to be of Indian origin, the more strongly the result from the Indian set is considered relative to the result from the non-Indian set.

2.5 Evaluation

In the context of the NEWS 2010 Machine Transliteration Shared Task we tested our system on all twelve datasets: from English to Chinese (EnCh), Thai (EnTh), Hindi (EnHi), Tamil (EnTa), Bangla (EnBa), Kannada (EnKa), Korean Hangul (EnKo), Japanese Katakana (EnJa), Japanese Kanji (JnJk); and, in the opposite direction, to English from Arabic (ArAe), Chinese (ChEn), and Thai (ThEn). For all datasets, we trained transliteration models on the provided training and development sets without additional resources.

Table 1 shows our best results obtained on the datasets in terms of top-1 accuracy and mean F-score. We also include the rank in standard runs ordered by top-1 word accuracy. The EnCh result presented in the table refers to the output of the three-system combination, using the combination algorithm described in Section 2.4.3. The respective results for the three component EnCh systems were: 0.357, 0.360, and 0.363. The EnJa result in the table refers the system described in Section 2.4.2 that applied specific treatment to Japanese Katakana. Based on our development results, this specific treatment improves as much as 2% top-1 accuracy over the language-independent model. The EnHi system that incorporates language identification obtained exactly the same top-1 accuracy as the language-independent model. However, the EnKo system with Jaso correction produced the top-1 accuracy of 0.554, which is a significant improvement over 0.387 achieved by the language-independent model.

Task	top-1	F-score	Rank
EnCh	0.363	0.707	2
ChEn	0.137	0.740	1
EnTh	0.378	0.866	2
ThEn	0.352	0.861	2
EnHi	0.456	0.884	1
EnTa	0.390	0.891	2
EnKa	0.341	0.867	2
EnJa	0.398	0.791	1
EnKo	0.554	0.770	1
JnJk	0.126	0.426	1
ArAe	0.464	0.924	1
EnBa	0.395	0.877	2

Table 1: Transliteration generation results

3 Transliteration mining

This section is structured as follows. In Section 3.1, we describe the method of extracting transliteration candidates that serves as the input to the subsequently presented mining approaches. Two techniques for generating negative examples are discussed in Section 3.2. Our language-independent approaches to transliteration mining are described in Section 3.3, and a technique for mining English-Chinese pairs is proposed in Section 3.4. In Section 3.5, we address the issue of overlapping predictions. Finally, Section 3.6 and Section 3.7 summarize our results.

3.1 Extracting transliteration candidates

We cast the transliteration mining task as a binary classification problem. That is, given a word in the source language and a word in the target language, a classifier predicts whether or not the pair constitutes a valid transliteration. As a preprocessing step, we extract candidate transliterations from the pairs of Wikipedia titles. Word segmentation is performed based on sequences of one or more spaces and/or punctuation symbols, which include hyphens, underscores, brackets, and several other non-alphanumeric characters. Apostrophes and single quotes are not used for segmentation (and therefore remain in a given word); however, all single quote-like characters are converted into a generic apostrophe. Once an English title and its target language counterpart have been segmented into words, we form the candidate set for this title as the cross product of the two sets of words after discarding any words that contain fewer than two characters.

After the candidates have been extracted, individual words are flagged for certain attributes that may be used by our supervised learner as additional features. Alternatively, the flags may serve as criteria for filtering the list of candidate pairs prior to classification. We identify words that are capitalized, consist of all lowercase (or all capital) letters, and/or contain one or more digits. We also attempt to encode each word in the target language as an ASCII string, and flag that word if the operation succeeds. This can be used to filter out words that are written in English on both the source and target side, which are not transliterations by definition.

3.2 Generating negative training examples

The main issue with applying a supervised learning approach to the NEWS 2010 Shared Task is that annotated task-specific data is not available to train the system. However, the seed pairs do provide example transliterations, and these can be used as positive training examples. The remaining issue is how to select the negative examples.

We adopt two approaches for selecting negatives. First, we generate all possible source-target pairs in the seed data, and take as negatives those pairs which are not transliterations but have a longest common subsequence ratio (LCSR) above 0.58; this mirrors the approach used by Bergsma and Kondrak (2007). The method assumes that the source and target words are written in the same script (e.g., the foreign word has been romanized).

A second possibility is to generate all seed pairings as above, but then randomly select negative examples, thus mirroring the approach in Klementiev and Roth (2006). In this case, the source and target scripts do not need to be the same. Compared with the LCSR technique, random sampling in this manner has the potential to produce negative examples that are very "easy" (i.e., clearly not transliterations), and which may be of limited utility when training a classifier. On the other hand, at test time, the set of candidates extracted from the Wikipedia data will include pairs that have very low LCSR scores; hence, it can be argued that dissimilar pairs should also appear as negative examples in the training set.

3.3 Language-independent approaches

In this section, we describe methods for transliteration mining that can, in principle, be applied to a wide variety of language pairs without additional modification. For the purposes of the Shared Task, however, we convert all source (English) words to ASCII by removing diacritics and making appropriate substitutions for foreign letters. This is done to mitigate sparsity in the relatively small seed sets when training our classifiers.

3.3.1 Alignment-derived romanization

We developed a simple method of performing romanization of foreign scripts. Initially, the seed set of transliterations is aligned using the one-to-one option of the M2M-aligner approach (Jiampojamarn et al., 2007). We allow nulls on both the source and target sides. The resulting alignment model contains pairs of Latin letters and foreign script symbols (graphemes) sorted by their conditional probability. Then, for each grapheme, we select a letter (or a null symbol) that has the highest conditional probability. The process produces an approximate romanization table that can be obtained without any knowledge of the target script. This method of romanization was used by all methods described in the remainder of Section 3.3.

3.3.2 Normalized edit distance

Normalized edit distance (NED) is a measure of the similarity of two strings. We define a uniform edit cost for each of the three operations: substitution, insertion, and deletion. NED is computed by dividing the minimum edit distance by the length of the longer string, and subtracting the resulting fraction from 1. Thus, the extreme values of NED are 1 for identical strings, and 0 for strings that have no characters in common.

Our baseline method, NED+ is simply the NED measure augmented with filtering of the candidate pairs described in Section 3.1. In order to address the issue of morphological variants, we also filter out the pairs in which the English word ends in a consonant and the foreign word ends with a vowel. With no development set provided, we set the similarity thresholds for individual languages on the basis of the average word length in the seed sets. The values were 0.38, 0.48, 0.52, and 0.58 for Hindi, Arabic, Tamil, and Russian, respectively, with the last number taken from Bergsma and Kondrak (2007).

3.3.3 Alignment-based string similarity

NED selects transliteration candidates when the romanized foreign strings have high character overlap with their English counterparts. The measure is independent of the language pair. This is suboptimal for several reasons. First of all, phonetically unrelated words can share many incidental character matches. For example, the French word 'recettes' and the English word 'proceeds' share the letters *r,c,e,e,s* as a common subsequence, but the words are phonetically unrelated. Secondly, many reliable, recurrent, language-specific substring matches are prevalent in true transliterations. These pairings may or may not involve matching characters. NED can not learn or adapt to these language-specific patterns.

In light of these drawbacks, researchers have proposed string similarity measures that can learn from provided example pairs and adapt the similarity function to a specific task (Ristad and Yianilos, 1998; Bilenko and Mooney, 2003; McCallum et al., 2005; Klementiev and Roth, 2006).

One particularly successful approach is by Bergsma and Kondrak (2007), who use discriminative learning with an improved feature representation. The features are substring pairs that are consistent with a character-level alignment of the two strings. This approach strongly improved performance on cognate identification, while variations of it have also proven successful in transliteration discovery (Goldwasser and Roth, 2008). We therefore adopted this approach for the transliteration mining task.

We produce negative training examples using the LCSR threshold approach described in Section 3.2. For features, we extract from the aligned word pairs all substring pairs up to a maximum length of three. We also append characters marking the beginning and end of words, as described in Bergsma and Kondrak (2007). For our classifier, we use a Support Vector Machine (SVM) training with the very efficient LIBLINEAR package (Fan et al., 2008). We optimize the SVM's regularization parameter using 10-fold cross validation on the generated training data. At test time, we apply our classifier to all the transliteration candidates extracted from the Wikipedia titles, generating transliteration pairs whenever there is a positive classification.

3.3.4 String kernel classifier

The alignment-based classifier described in the preceding section is limited to using substring features that are up to (roughly) three or four letters in length, due to the combinatorial explosion in the number of unique features as the substring length increases. It is natural to ask whether longer substrings can be utilized to learn a more accurate predictor.

This question inspired the development of a second SVM-based learner that uses a string kernel, and therefore does not have to explicitly represent feature vectors. Our kernel is a standard n-gram (or spectrum) kernel that implicitly embeds a string in a feature space that has one co-ordinate for each unique n-gram (see, e.g., (Shawe-Taylor and Cristianini, 2004)). Let us denote the alphabet over input strings as A. Given two input strings x and x', this kernel function computes:

$$k(x, x') = \sum_{s \in A^n} \#(s, x)\#(s, x')$$

where s is an n-gram and $\#(a, b)$ counts the number of times a appears as a substring of b.

An extension of the n-gram kernel that we employ here is to consider all n-grams of length $1 \leq n \leq k$, and weight each n-gram as a function of its length. In particular, we specify a value λ and weight each n-gram by a factor of λ^n. We implemented this kernel in the LIBSVM software package (Chang and Lin, 2001). Optimal values for k, λ, and the SVM's regularization parameter were estimated for each dataset using 5-fold cross-validation. The values of (k, λ) that we ultimately used were: EnAr $(3, 0.8)$, EnHi $(8, 0.8)$, EnRu $(5, 1.2)$, and EnTa $(5, 1.0)$.

Our input string representation for a candidate pair is formed by first aligning the source and target words using M2M-aligner (Jiampojamarn et al., 2007). Specifically, an alignment model is trained on the seed examples, which are subsequently aligned and used as positive training examples. We then generate 20K negative examples by random sampling (cf. Section 3.2) and apply the alignment model to this set. Not all of these 20K word pairs will necessarily be aligned; we randomly select 10K of the successfully aligned pairs to use as negative examples in the training set.

Each aligned pair is converted into an "alignment string" by placing the letters that appear in

Word pair	zubtsov	зубцов
Aligned pair	z|u|b|t|s|o|v|	з|у|б|ц|_|о|в|
Align't string	zз|uу|bб|tц|s_|oо|vв	

Table 2: An example showing how an alignment string (the input representation for the string kernel) is created from a word pair.

the same position in the source and target next to one another, while retaining the separator characters (see Table 2). We also appended beginning and end of word markers. Note that no romanization of the target words is necessary for this procedure.

At test time, we apply the alignment model to the candidate word pairs that have been extracted from the *train* data, and retain *all* the successfully aligned pairs. Here, M2M-aligner also acts as a filter, since we cannot form alignment strings from unaligned pairs — these yield negative predictions by default. We also filter out pairs that met any of the following conditions: 1) the English word consists of all all capital or lowercase letters, 2) the target word can be converted to ASCII (cf. Section 3.1), or 3) either word contains a digit.

3.3.5 Generation-based approach

In the mining tasks, we are interested in whether a candidate pair (x, y) is a transliteration pair. One approach is to determine if the generated transliterations of a source word $\hat{y} = \alpha(x)$ and a target word $\hat{x} = \beta(y)$ are similar to the given candidate pair. We applied DIRECTL+ to the mining tasks by training transliteration generation models on the provided seed data in forward and backward transliteration directions, creating $\alpha(x)$ and $\beta(y)$ models. We now define a transliteration score function in Eq. 1. $N(\hat{x}, x)$ is the normalized edit distance between string $\hat{x}$ and x, and w_1 and w_2 are combination weights to favor forward and backward transliteration models.

$$S(x,y) = \frac{w_1 \cdot N(\hat{y}, y) + w_2 \cdot N(\hat{x}, x)}{w_1 + w_2} \quad (1)$$

A candidate pair is considered a transliteration pair if its $S(x, y) > \tau$. Ideally, we would like to optimize these parameters, τ, w_1, w_2 based on a development set for each language pair. Unfortunately, no development sets were provided for the Shared Task. Therefore, following Bergsma and Kondrak (2007), we adopt the threshold of $\tau = 0.58$. We experimented with three sets of values for w_1 and w_2: $(1, 0)$, $(0.5, 0.5)$, and $(0, 1)$. Our final predictions were made using $w_0 = 0$ and $w_1 = 1$, which appeared to produce the best results. Thus, only the backward transliteration model was ultimately employed.

3.4 English-Chinese string matching

Due to the fact that names transliterated into Chinese consist of multiple Chinese characters and that the Chinese text provided in this shared task is not segmented, we have to adopt a different approach to the English-Chinese mining task (Unlike many other languages, there are no clear boundaries between Chinese words). We first train a generation model using the seed data and then apply a greedy string matching algorithm to extract transliteration pairs.

The generation model is built using the discriminative training framework described in (Jiampojamarn et al., 2008). Two models are learned: one is trained using English and Chinese characters, while the other is trained on English and Pinyin (a standard phonetic representation of Chinese characters). In order to mine transliteration pairs from Wikipedia titles, we first use the generation model to produce transliterations for each English token on the source side as both Chinese characters and Pinyin. The generated Chinese characters are ultimately converted to Pinyin during string matching. We also convert all the Chinese characters on the target side to their Pinyin representations when performing string matching.

The transliteration pairs are then mined by combining two different strategies. First of all, we observe that most of the titles that contain a separation symbol " · " on the target side are transliterations. In this case, the number of tokens on both sides is often equal. Therefore, the mining task can be formulated as a matching problem. We use a competitive linking approach (Melamed, 2000) to find the best match. First, we select links between all possible pairs if similarity of strings on both sides is above a threshold $(0.6 * length(Pinyin))$. We then greedily extract the pairs with highest similarity until the number of unextracted segments on either side becomes zero.

The problem becomes harder when there is no indication of word segmentation for Chinese. Instead of trying to segment the Chinese characters first, we use an incremental string matching strategy. For each token on the source side, the algorithm calculates its similarity with all possible n-grams ($2 \leq n \leq L$) on the target side, where L is the length of the Chinese title (i.e., the number of characters). If the similarity score of n-gram with the highest similarity surpasses a threshold ($0.5 \times length(Pinyin)$), the n-gram sequence is proposed as a possible transliteration for the current source token.

3.5 Resolving overlapping predictions

Given a set of candidate word pairs that have been extracted from a given Wikipedia title according to the procedure described in Section 3.1, our classifiers predict a class label for each pair independently of the others. Pairs that receive negative predictions are discarded immediately and are never reported as mined pairs. However, it is sometimes necessary to arbitrate between positive predictions, since it is possible for a classifier to mark as transliterations two or more pairs that involve the same English word or the same target word in the title. Clearly, mining multiple overlapping pairs will lower the system's precision, since there is (presumably) at most one correct transliteration in the target language version of the title for each English word.[3]

Our solution is to apply a greedy algorithm that sorts the word pair predictions for a given title in descending order according to the scores that were assigned by the classifier. We make one pass through the sorted list and report a pair of words as a mined pair unless the English word or the target language word has already been reported (for this particular title).[4]

3.6 Results

In the context of the NEWS 2010 Shared Task on Transliteration Generation we tested our system on all five data sets: from English to Russian (EnRu), Hindi (EnHi), Tamil (EnTa), Arabic (EnAr), and Chinese (EnCh). The EnCh set differs from the remaining sets in the lack of transparent word segmentation on the Chinese side. There were no development sets provided for any of the language pairs.

Task	System	F	P	R
EnRu	NED+	**.875**	.880	.869
	BK-2007	.778	.684	.902
	StringKernel*	.811	.746	.889
	DIRECTL+	.786	.778	.795
EnHi	NED+	.907	.875	.941
	BK-2007	.882	.883	.880
	StringKernel	**.924**	.954	.895
	DIRECTL+	.904	.945	.866
EnTa	NED+	.791	.916	.696
	BK-2007	.829	.808	.852
	StringKernel	**.914**	.923	.906
	DIRECTL+	.801	.919	.710
EnAr	NED+	.800	.818	.783
	BK-2007	.816	.834	.798
	StringKernel*	**.827**	.917	.753
	DIRECTL+	.742	.861	.652
EnCh	GreedyMatch	**.530**	.698	.427
	DIRECTL+	.009	.045	.005

Table 3: Transliteration mining results. An asterisk (*) indicates an unofficial result.

Table 3 shows the results obtained by our various systems on the final test sets, measured in terms of F-score (F), precision (P), and recall (R). The systems referred to as NED+, BK-2007, StringKernel, DIRECTL+, and GreedyMatch are described in Section 3.3.2, Section 3.3.3, Section 3.3.4, Section 3.3.5, and Section 3.4 respectively. The runs marked with an asterisk (*) were produced after the Shared Task deadline, and therefore are not included in the official results.

3.7 Discussion

No fixed ranking of the four approaches emerges across the four alphabetic language pairs (all except EnCh). However, StringKernel appears to be the most robust, achieving the highest F-score on three language pairs. This suggests that longer substring features are indeed useful for classifying candidate transliteration pairs. The simple NED+ method is a clear winner on EnRu, and obtains decent scores on the remaining alphabetic language pairs. The generation-based DIRECTL+ approach ranks no higher than third on any language pair, and it fails spectacularly on EnCh because of the word segmentation ambiguity.

Finally, we observe that there are a number of cases where the results for our discriminatively trained classifiers, BK-2007 and StringKernel, are

[3]On the other hand, mining all such pairs *might* improve recall.

[4]A bug was later discovered in our implementation of this algorithm, which had failed to add the words in a title's first mined pair to the "already reported" list. This sometimes caused up to two additional mined pairs per title to be reported in the prediction files that were submitted.

not significantly better than those of the simple NED+ approach. We conjecture that automatically generating training examples is suboptimal for this task. A more effective strategy may be to filter all possible word pairs in the seed data to only those with NED above a fixed threshold. We would then apply the same threshold to the Wikipedia candidates, only passing to the classifier those pairs that surpass the threshold. This would enable a better match between the training and test operation of the system.

4 Conclusion

The results obtained in the context of the NEWS 2010 Machine Transliteration Shared Task confirm the effectiveness of our discriminative approaches to transliteration generation and mining.

Acknowledgments

This research was supported by the Alberta Ingenuity Fund, Informatics Circle of Research Excellence (iCORE), and the Natural Sciences and Engineering Research Council of Canada (NSERC).

References

Shane Bergsma and Grzegorz Kondrak. 2007. Alignment-based discriminative string similarity. In *Proc. ACL*.

Aditya Bhargava and Grzegorz Kondrak. 2010. Language identification of names with SVMs. In *Proc. NAACL-HLT*.

Mikhail Bilenko and Raymond J. Mooney. 2003. Adaptive duplicate detection using learnable string similarity measures. In *Proc. KDD*.

Chih-Chung Chang and Chih-Jen Lin. 2001. LIBSVM: a library for support vector machines. Software available at `http://www.csie.ntu.edu.tw/~cjlin/libsvm`.

Koby Crammer and Yoram Singer. 2003. Ultraconservative online algorithms for multiclass problems. *Journal of Machine Learning Research*, 3:951–991.

Rong-En Fan, Kai-Wei Chang, Cho-Jui Hsieh, Xiang-Rui Wang, and Chih-Jen Lin. 2008. LIBLINEAR: A library for large linear classification. *JMLR*, 9:1871–1874.

Dan Goldwasser and Dan Roth. 2008. Transliteration as constrained optimization. In *Proc. EMNLP*.

Sittichai Jiampojamarn, Grzegorz Kondrak, and Tarek Sherif. 2007. Applying many-to-many alignments and Hidden Markov Models to letter-to-phoneme conversion. In *Proc. HLT-NAACL*.

Sittichai Jiampojamarn, Colin Cherry, and Grzegorz Kondrak. 2008. Joint processing and discriminative training for letter-to-phoneme conversion. In *Proc. ACL*.

Sittichai Jiampojamarn, Aditya Bhargava, Qing Dou, Kenneth Dwyer, and Grzegorz Kondrak. 2009. DirecTL: a language-independent approach to transliteration. In *NEWS '09: Proceedings of the 2009 Named Entities Workshop: Shared Task on Transliteration*, pages 28–31.

Sittichai Jiampojamarn, Colin Cherry, and Grzegorz Kondrak. 2010. Integrating joint n-gram features into a discriminative training framework. In *Proc. NAACL-HLT*.

Alexandre Klementiev and Dan Roth. 2006. Named entity transliteration and discovery from multilingual comparable corpora. In *Proc. HLT-NAACL*.

Grzegorz Kondrak. 2000. A new algorithm for the alignment of phonetic sequences. In *Proc. NAACL*, pages 288–295.

Andrew McCallum, Kedar Bellare, and Fernando Pereira. 2005. A conditional random field for discriminatively-trained finite-state string edit distance. In *Proc. UAI*.

I. Dan Melamed. 2000. Models of translational equivalence among words. *Computational Linguistics*, 26(2):221–249.

Eric Sven Ristad and Peter N. Yianilos. 1998. Learning string-edit distance. *IEEE Trans. Pattern Analysis and Machine Intelligence*, 20(5).

John Shawe-Taylor and Nello Cristianini. 2004. *Kernel Methods for Pattern Analysis*. Cambridge University Press.

Transliteration using a Phrase-based Statistical Machine Translation System to Re-score the Output of a Joint Multigram Model

Andrew Finch
NICT
3-5 Hikaridai
Keihanna Science City
619-0289 JAPAN
andrew.finch@nict.go.jp

Eiichiro Sumita
NICT
3-5 Hikaridai
Keihanna Science City
619-0289 JAPAN
eiichiro.sumita@nict.go.jp

Abstract

The system presented in this paper uses a combination of two techniques to directly transliterate from grapheme to grapheme. The technique makes no language specific assumptions, uses no dictionaries or explicit phonetic information; the process transforms sequences of tokens in the source language directly into to sequences of tokens in the target. All the language pairs in our experiments were transliterated by applying this technique in a single unified manner. The approach we take is that of hypothesis re-scoring to integrate the models of two state-of-the-art techniques: phrase-based statistical machine translation (SMT), and a joint multigram model. The joint multigram model was used to generate an *n*-best list of transliteration hypotheses that were re-scored using the models of the phrase-based SMT system. The both of the models' scores for each hypothesis were linearly interpolated to produce a final hypothesis score that was used to re-rank the hypotheses. In our experiments on development data, the combined system was able to outperform both of its component systems substantially.

1 Introduction

In statistical machine translation the re-scoring of hypotheses produced by a system with additional models that incorporate information not available to the original system has been shown to be an effective technique to improve system performance (Paul et al., 2006). Our approach uses a re-scoring technique to integrate the models of two transliteration systems that are each capable in their own right: a phrase-based statistical machine translation system (Koehn et al., 2003), and a joint multigram model (Deligne and Bimbot, 1995; Bisani and Ney, 2008).

In this work we treat the process of transliteration as a process of direct transduction from sequences of tokens in the source language to sequences of tokens in the target language with no modeling of the phonetics of either source or target language (Knight and Graehl, 1997). Taking this approach allows for a very general transliteration system to be built that does not require any language specific knowledge to be incorporated into the system (for some language pairs this may not be the best strategy since linguistic information can be used to overcome issues of data sparseness on smaller datasets).

2 Component Systems

For this shared task we chose to combine two systems through a process of re-scoring. The systems were selected because of their expected strong level of performance (SMT systems have been used successfully in the field, and joint multigram models have performed well both in grapheme to phoneme conversion and Arabic-English transliteration). Secondly, the joint multigram model relies on key features not present in the SMT system, that is the history of bilingual phrase pairs used to derive the target. For this reason we felt the systems would complement each other well. We now briefly describe the component systems.

2.1 Joint Multigram Model

The joint multigram approach proposed by (Deligne and Bimbot, 1995) has arisen as an extension of the use of variable-length *n*-grams (multigrams) in language modeling. In a joint multigram, the units in the model consist of multiple input and output symbols. (Bisani and Ney, 2008) refined the approach and applied to it grapheme-to-phoneme conversion, where its performance was shown to be comparable to state-of-the-art systems. The approach was later applied to Arabic-English transliteration (Deselaers et al., 2009) again with promising results.

Joint multigram models have the following characteristics:

- The symbols in the source and target are co-segmented

Proceedings of the 2010 Named Entities Workshop, ACL 2010, pages 48–52,
Uppsala, Sweden, 16 July 2010.

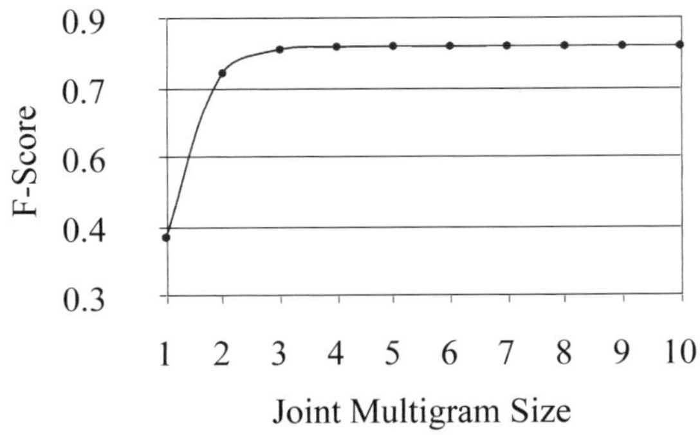

Figure 1: The effect on F-score by tuning with respect to joint multigram size

  - Maximum likelihood training using an EM algorithm (Deligne and Bimbot, 1995)

- The probability of sequences of joint multigrams is modeled using an *n*-gram model

In these respects the model can be viewed as a close relative of the joint source channel model proposed by (Li et al., 2004) for transliteration.

2.2 Phrase-based SMT

It is possible to view the process of transliteration as a process of translation at the character level, without re-ordering. From this perspective it is possible to directly employ a phrase-based SMT system in the task of transliteration (Finch and Sumita, 2008; Rama and Gali, 2009). A phrase-based SMT system has the following characteristics:

- The symbols in the source and target are aligned one to many in both directions. Joint sequences of source and target symbols are heuristically extracted given these alignments
- Transliteration is performed using a log-linear model with weights tuned on development data
- The models include: a translation model (with 5 sub-models), and a target language model

The bilingual phrase-pairs are analogous to the joint multigrams, however the translation model of the SMT system doesn't use the context of previously translated phrase-pairs, instead relying on a target language model.

3 Experimental Conditions

3.1 SMT Decoder

In our experiments we used an in-house phrase-based statistical machine translation decoder called CleopATRa. This decoder operates on exactly the same principles as the publicly available MOSES decoder (Koehn et al., 2003). Our decoder was modified to be able to decode source sequences with reference to a target sequence; the decoding process being forced to generate the target. The decoder was also configured to combine scores of multiple derivations yielding the same target sequence. In this way the models in the decoder were used to derive scores used to re-score the *n*-best (we used n=20 for our experiments) hypotheses generated by the joint multigram model. The phrase-extraction process was symmetrized with respect to token order using the technique proposed in (Finch and Sumita, 2010). In order to adapt the SMT system to the task of transliteration, the decoder was constrained decode in a monotone manner, and furthermore during training, the phrase extraction process was constrained such that only phrases with monotone order were extracted in order to minimize the effects of errors in the word alignment process.

In a final step the scores from both systems were linearly interpolated to produce a single integrated hypothesis score. The hypotheses were then re-ranked according to this integrated score for the final submission.

3.2 Joint Multigram model

For the joint multigram system we used the publicly available Sequitur G2P grapheme-to-phoneme converter (Bisani and Ney, 2008). The system was used with its default settings, and pilot experiments were run on development data to determine appropriate settings for the maximum size of the multigrams. The results for the English-to-Japanese task are shown in Figure 1. As can be seen in the figure, the system rapidly improves to a near-optimal value with a maximum multigram size of 4. No improvement at all was observed for sizes over 7. We therefore chose a maximum multigram size of 8 for the experiments presented in this paper, and for the systems entered in the shared task.

3.3 Pre-processing

In order to reduce data sparseness we took the decision to work with data in only its lowercase form.

We chose not to perform any tokenization or phonetic mapping for any of the language pairs

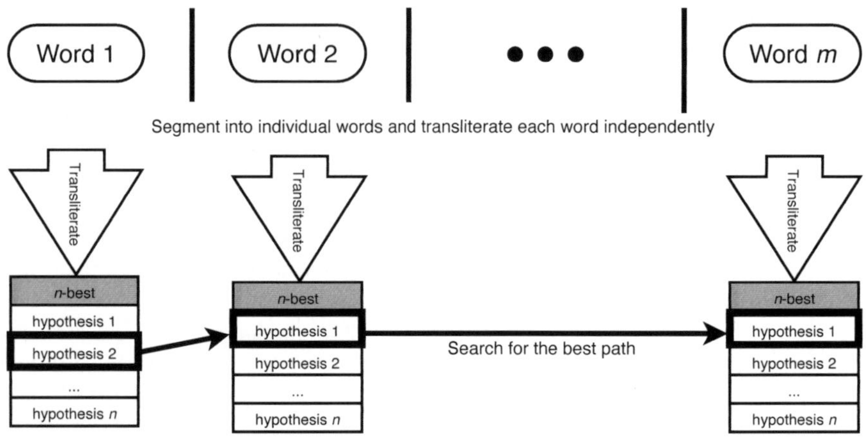

Figure 2: The transliteration process for multi-word sequences

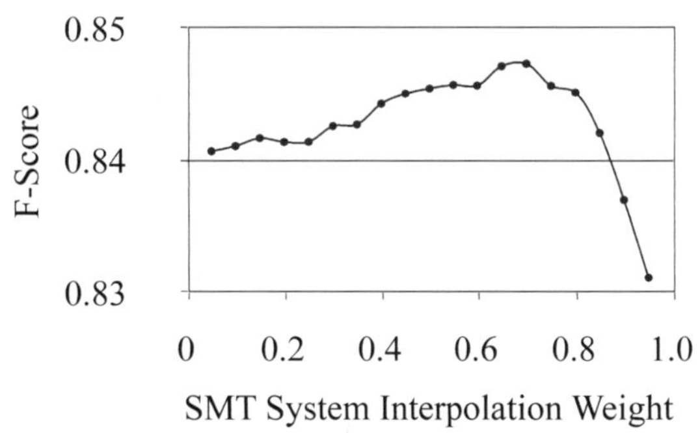

Figure 3: The effect on the F-score of the integrated system by tuning with respect to the SMT system's interpolation weight

in the shared task. We adopted this approach because:

- It allowed us to have a single unified approach for all language pairs
- It was in the spirit of the shared task, as it did not require extra knowledge outside of the supplied corpora

3.4 Handling Multi-Word Sequences

The data for some languages contained some multi-word sequences. To handle these we had to consider the following strategies:

- Introduce a <space> token into the sequence, and treat it as one long character sequence to transliterate; or
- Segment the word sequences into individual words and transliterate these independently, combining the *n*-best hypothesis lists for all the individual words in the sequence into a single output sequence.

We adopted both approaches: for those multi-word sequences where the number of words in the source and target matched, the latter approach was taken; for those where the numbers of source and target words differed, the former approach was taken. The decoding process for multi-word sequences is shown in Figure 2. During recombination, the score for the target word sequence was calculated as the product of the scores of each hypothesis for each word. Therefore a search over all combinations of hypotheses is required. In almost all cases we were able to perform a full search. For the rare long word sequences in the data, a beam search strategy was adopted.

3.5 Building the Models

For the final submissions, all systems were trained on the union of the training data and development data. It was felt that the training set was sufficiently small that the inclusion of the development data into the training set would yield a reasonable boost in performance by increasing the coverage of the systems. All tunable parameters were tuned on development data using systems built using only the training data. Under the assumption that these parameters would perform well in the systems trained on the combined development/training corpora, these tuned parameters were transferred directly to the systems trained on all available data.

3.6 Parameter Tuning

The SMT systems were tuned using the minimum error rate training procedure introduced in (Och, 2003). For convenience, we used BLEU as a proxy for the various metrics used in the shared task evaluation. The BLEU score is commonly used to evaluate the performance of

Language Pair	Accuracy in top-1	Mean F-score	MRR	MAP_{ref}
English → Thai	0.412	0.883	0.550	0.412
Thai → English	0.397	0.873	0.525	0.397
English → Hindi	0.445	0.884	0.574	0.445
English → Tamil	0.390	0.887	0.522	0.390
English → Kannada	0.371	0.871	0.506	0.371
English → Japanese	0.378	0.783	0.510	0.378
Arabic → English	0.403	0.891	0.512	0.327
English → Bangla	0.412	0.883	0.550	0.412

Table 1: The results of our system in the official evaluation on the test data on all performance metrics.

machine translation systems and is a function of the geometric mean of *n*-gram precision. The use of BLEU score as a proxy has been shown to be a reasonable strategy for the metrics used in these experiments (Finch and Sumita, 2009). Nonetheless, it is reasonable to assume that one would be able to improve the performance in a particular evaluation metric by doing minimum error rate training specifically for that metric. The interpolation weight was tuned by a grid search to find the value that gave the maximal f-score (according to the official f-score evaluation metric for the shared task) on the development data, the process for English-Japanese is shown in Figure 3.

4 Results

The results of our experiments are shown in Table 1. These results are the official shared task evaluation results on the test data, and the scores for all of the evaluation metrics are shown in the table. The reader is referred to the workshop white paper (Li et al., 2010) for details of the evaluation metrics. The system achieved a high level of performance on most of the language pairs. Comparing the individual systems to each other, and to the integrated system, the joint multigram system outperformed the phrase-based SMT system. In experiments run on the English-to-Japanese katakana task, the joint multigram system in isolation achieved an F-score of 0.837 on development data, whereas the SMT system in isolation achieved an F-score of 0.824. When integrated the models of the systems complemented each other well, and on the same English-Japanese task the integrated system achieved an F-score of 0.843.

We feel that for some language pairs, most notably Arabic-English where a large difference existed between our system and the top-ranked system, there is much room for improvement. One of the strengths in terms of the utility of our approach is that it is free from dependence on the linguistic characteristics of the languages being processed. This property makes it generally applicable, but due to the limited amounts of data available for the shared task, we believe that in order to progress, a language-dependent approach will be required.

5 Conclusion

We applied a system that integrated two state-of-the-art systems through a process of re-scoring, to the NEWS 2010 Workshop shared task on transliteration generation. Our systems gave a strong performance on the shared task test set, and our experiments show the integrated system was able to outperform both of its component systems. In future work we would like to depart from the direct grapheme-to-grapheme approach taken here and address the problem of how best to represent the source and target sequences by either analyzing their symbols further, or agglomerating them. We would also like to investigate the use of co-segmentation schemes that do not rely on maximum likelihood training to overcome the issues inherent in this technique.

Acknowledgements

The results presented in this paper draw on the following data sets. For English-Japanese and Arabic-English, the reader is referred to the CJK website: http://www.cjk.org. For English-Hindi, English-Tamil, and English-Kannada, and English-Bangla the data sets originated from the work of Kumaran and Kellner, 2007.

References

Peter Brown, Stephen Della Pietra, Vincent Della Pietra, and Robert Mercer, 1991. The mathematics of statistical machine translation: parameter estimation. *Computational Linguistics*, 19(2), 263-311.

Sabine Deligne, and Frédéric Bimbot, 1995. Language modeling by variable length sequences: theoretical formulation and evaluation of multigrams. *In: Proc. IEEE Internat. Conf. on Acoustics, Speech and Signal Processing*, Vol. 1, Detroit, MI, USA, pp. 169–172.

Maximilian Bisani and Hermann Ney, 2008. Joint-Sequence Models for Grapheme-to-Phoneme Conversion. Speech Communication, Volume 50, Issue 5, Pages 434-451.

Thomas Deselaers, Sasa Hasan, Oliver Bender, and Hermann Ney, 2009. A Deep Learning Approach to Machine Transliteration. *In Proceedings of the EACL 2009 Workshop on Statistical Machine Translation (WMT09)*, Athens, Greece.

Andrew Finch and Eiichiro Sumita, 2008. Phrase-based machine transliteration. *In Proceedings of WTCAST'08*, pages 13-18.

Andrew Finch and Eiichiro Sumita, 2009. Transliteration by Bidirectional Statistical Machine Translation, *Proceedings of the 2009 Named Entities Workshop: Shared Task on Transliteration*, Singapore.

Andrew Finch and Eiichiro Sumita, 2010. Exploiting Directional Asymmetry in Phrase-table Generation for Statistical Machine Translation, *In Proceedings of NLP2010*, Tokyo, Japan.

Kevin Knight and Jonathan Graehl, 1997. Machine Transliteration. *Proceedings of the Thirty-Fifth Annual Meeting of the Association for Computational Linguistics and Eighth Conference of the European Chapter of the Association for Computational Linguistics*, pp. 128-135, Somerset, New Jersey.

Philipp Koehn, Franz Josef Och, and Daniel Marcu, 2003. Statistical Phrase-Based Translation. *In Proceedings of the Human Language Technology Conference 2003 (HLT-NAACL 2003)*, Edmonton, Canada.

Franz Josef Och, 2003. Minimum error rate training for statistical machine translation, *Proceedings of the ACL.*

A Kumaran and Tobias Kellner, 2007. A generic framework for machine transliteration, *Proc. of the 30th SIGIR.*

Haizhou Li, Min Zhang, Jian Su, 2004. A joint source channel model for machine transliteration, *Proc. of the 42nd ACL.*

Haizhou Li, A Kumaran, Min Zhang and Vladimir Pervouchine, 2010. Whitepaper of NEWS 2010 Shared Task on Transliteration Generation. In *Proc. of ACL2010 Named Entities Workshop.*

Michael Paul, Eiichiro Sumita and Seiichi Yamamoto, 2006, Multiple Translation-Engine-based Hypotheses and Edit-Distance-based Rescoring for a Greedy Decoder for Statistical Machine Translation, *Information and Media Technologies*, Vol. 1, No. 1, pp.446-460 .

Taraka Rama and Karthik Gali, 2009. Modeling machine transliteration as a phrase based statistical machine translation problem, *Proceedings of the 2009 Named Entities Workshop: Shared Task on Transliteration*, Singapore.

Transliteration Mining with Phonetic Conflation and Iterative Training

Kareem Darwish
Cairo Microsoft Innovation Center
Cairo, Egypt
kareemd@microsoft.com

Abstract

This paper presents transliteration mining on the ACL 2010 NEWS workshop shared transliteration mining task data. Transliteration mining was done using a generative transliteration model applied on the source language and whose output was constrained on the words in the target language. A total of 30 runs were performed on 5 language pairs, with 6 runs for each language pair. In the presence of limited resources, the runs explored the use of phonetic conflation and iterative training of the transliteration model to improve recall. Using letter conflation improved recall by as much as 48%, with improvements in recall dwarfing drops in precision. Using iterative training improved recall, but often at the cost of significant drops in precision. The best runs typically used both letter conflation and iterative learning.

1 Introduction

Transliteration Mining (TM) is the process of finding transliterated word pairs in parallel or comparable corpora. TM has many potential applications such as building training data for training transliterators and improving lexical coverage for machine translation and cross language search via translation resource expansion. TM has been gaining some attention of late with a shared task in the ACL 2010 NEWS workshop[1]. In this paper, TM was performed using a transliterator that was used to generate possible transliterations of a word while constraining the output to tokens that exist in a target language word sequence. The paper presents the use of phonetic letter conflation and iterative transliterator training to improve TM when only limited transliteration training data is available. For phonetic letter conflation, a variant of SOUNDEX (Russell, 1918) was used to improve the coverage of existing training data. As for iterative transliterator training, an initial transliterator, which was trained on initial set of transliteration pairs, was used to mine transliterations in parallel text. Then, the automatically found transliterations pairs were considered correct and were used to re-train the transliterator.

The proposed improvements in TM were tested using the ACL 2010 NEWS workshop data for Arabic, English-Chinese, English-Hindi, English-Russian, and English-Tamil. For language pair, a base set of 1,000 transliteration pairs were available for training.

The rest of the paper is organized as follows: Section 2 surveys prior work on transliteration mining; Section 3 describes the TM approach and the proposed improvements; Section 4 describes the experimental setup including the evaluation sets; Section 5 reports on experimental results; and Section 6 concludes the paper.

2 Background

Much work has been done on TM for different language pairs such as English-Chinese (Kuo et al., 2006; Kuo et al., 2007; Kuo et al., 2008; Jin et al. 2008;), English-Tamil (Saravanan and Kumaran, 2008; Udupa and Khapra, 2010), English-Korean (Oh and Isahara, 2006; Oh and Choi, 2006), English-Japanese (Brill et al., 2001; Oh and Isahara, 2006), English-Hindi (Fei et al., 2003; Mahesh and Sinha, 2009), and English-Russian (Klementiev and Roth, 2006). The most common approach for determining letter sequence mapping between two languages is using automatic letter alignment of a training set of transliteration pairs. Automatic alignment can be performed using different algorithms such as the EM algorithm (Kuo et al., 2008; Lee and Chang, 2003) or using an HMM aligner (Udupa et al., 2009a; Udupa et al., 2009b). Another method is to use automatic speech recognition confusion tables to extract phonetically equivalent character sequences to discover monolingual and cross lingual pronunciation variations (Kuo and Yang, 2005). Alternatively, letters can be mapped into a common character set. One example of that is to use a predefined transliteration scheme to transliterate a word in one character set into another character set (Oh and Choi, 2006). Different methods were proposed to ascertain if two words can be transliterations of each other. One such way is to use a generative model that attempts to generate possible transliterations given the character mappings between two character sets (Fei et al., 2003; Lee and Chang, 2003, Udupa et al., 2009a). A similar alternative is to use back-transliteration to de-

[1] http://translit.i2r.a-star.edu.sg/news2010/

Proceedings of the 2010 Named Entities Workshop, ACL 2010, pages 53–56,
Uppsala, Sweden, 16 July 2010.

termine if one sequence could have been generated by successively mapping character sequences from one language into another (Brill et al., 2001; Bilac and Tanaka, 2005; Oh and Isahara, 2006). Another mapping method is to map candidate transliterations into a common representation space (Udupa et al., 2010). When using a predefined transliteration scheme, edit distance was used to determine if candidate transliterations were indeed transliterations (Oh and Choi, 2006). Also letter conflation was used to find transliterations (Mahesh and Sinha, 2009). Different methods were proposed to improve the recall of mining. For example, Oh and Choi (2006) used a SOUNDEX like scheme to minimize the effect of vowels and different schemes of phonetically coding names. SOUNDEX is used to convert English words into a simplified phonetic representation, in which vowels are removed and phonetically similar characters are conflated. Another method involved expanding character sequence maps by automatically mining transliteration pairs and then aligning these pairs to generate an expanded set of character sequence maps (Fei et al., 2003).

3 Transliteration Mining

TM proposed in this paper uses a generative transliteration model, which is trained on a set of transliteration pairs. The training involved automatically aligning character sequences. SOUNDEX like letter conflation and iterative transliterator training was used to improve recall. Akin to phrasal alignment in machine translation, character sequence alignment was treated as a word alignment problem between parallel sentences, where transliterations were treated as if they were sentences and the characters from which they were composed were treated as if they were words. The alignment was performed using a Bayesian learner that trained on word dependent transition models for HMM based word alignment (He, 2007). Alignment produced a mapping of source character sequence to a target character sequence along with the probability of source given target.

For all the work reported herein, given an English-foreign language transliteration candidate pair, English was treated as the target language and the foreign language as the source. Given a foreign source language word sequence F_1^n and an English target word sequence E_1^m, $F_i \in F_1^n$ is a potential transliteration of $E_j \in E_1^m$. Given F_i, composed of the character sequence $f_1 \dots f_o$, and E_j, composed of the character sequence $e_1 \dots e_p$, $P(F_i|E_j)$ is calculated using the trained model, as follows:

$$P(E_i|F_j) = \prod_{alt\, f_x \cdots f_y} P(f_x \dots f_y | e'_k \dots e'_l)$$

The non-overlapping segments $f_x \dots f_y$ are generated by finding all possible 2^{n-1} segmentations of the word F_i. For example, given "man" then all possible segmentations are (m,a,n), (ma,n), (m,an), and (man). The segmentation producing the highest probability is chosen. All segment sequences $e'_k \dots e'_l$ known to produce $f_x \dots f_y$ for each of the possible segmentations are produced. If a set of non-overlapping sequences of $e'_k \dots e'_l$ generates the sequence $e_1 \dots e_p$ (word $E_j \in E_1^m$), then E_j is considered a transliteration of F_i. If multiple target words have $P(F_i|E_j) > 0$, then E_j that maximizes $P(F_i|E_j)$ is taken as the proper transliteration. A suffix tree containing E_1^m was used to constrain generation, improving efficiency. No smoothing was used.

To improve recall, a variant of SOUNDEX was used on the English targets. The original SOUNDEX scheme applies the following rules:

1. Retain the first letter in a word
2. Remove all vowels, H, and W
3. Perform the following mappings:

B, F, P, V → 1	C, G, J, K, Q, S, X, Z → 2
D,T → 3	L → 4
M,N → 5	R → 6

4. Trim all result sequences to 4 characters
5. Pad short sequences with zeros to have exactly 4 characters.

SOUNDEX was modified as follows:

1. The first letter in a word was not retained and was changed according the mapping in step 3 of SOUNDEX.
2. Resultant sequences longer than 4 characters were not trimmed.
3. Short resultant strings were not padded with zeros.

SOUNDEX after the aforementioned modifications is referred at S-mod. Alignment was performed between transliteration pairs where English words were replaced with their S-mod representation. Case folding was always applied to English.

Iterative transliterator training involved training a transliterator using an initial seed of transliteration pairs, which was used to automatically mine transliterations from a large set of parallel words sequences. Automatically mined transliteration pairs were assumed to be correct and were used to retrain the transliterator. S-mod and iterative training were used in isolation or in combination as is shown in the next section.

Russian and Arabic were preprocessed as follows:

- Russian: characters were case-folded
- Arabic: the different forms of *alef* (*alef, alef maad, alef with hamza on top*, and *alef with hamza below it*) were normalized to *alef*, *ya* and *alef maqsoura* were normalized to *ya*, and *ta marbouta* was mapped to *ha*.

No preprocessing was performed for the other languages. Since Wikipedia English entries often had non-English characters, the following letter conflations were performed:

ž, ż ➔ z	á, â, ä, à, ã, ā, ą, æ ➔ a
é, ę, è ➔ e	ć, č, ç ➔ c
ł ➔ l	ï, í, ì, î ➔ i
ó, ō, ö, õ ➔ o	ń, ñ, ṅ ➔ n
ş, ś, ß, š ➔ s	ř ➔ r
ý ➔ y	ū, ü, ú, û ➔ u

Language Pair	# of Parallel Sequences
English-Arabic	90,926
English-Chinese	196,047
English-Hindi	16,963
English-Russian	345,969
English-Tamil	13,883

Table 1: Language pairs and no. of parallel sequences

Run	Precision	Recall	F-score
1	0.900	0.796	0.845
2	**0.966**	0.587	0.730
3	0.952	0.588	0.727
4	0.886	0.817	**0.850**
5	0.895	0.678	0.771
6	0.818	**0.827**	0.822

Table 2: English-Arabic mining results

Run	Precision	Recall	F-score
1	1.000	0.024	0.047
2	1.000	0.016	0.032
3	1.000	0.016	0.032
4	1.000	0.026	0.050
5	1.000	0.022	0.044
6	1.000	0.030	0.059

Table 3: English-Chinese mining results

Run	Precision	Recall	F-score
1	0.959	0.786	0.864
2	**0.987**	0.559	0.714
3	0.984	0.569	0.721
4	0.951	0.812	**0.876**
5	0.981	0.687	0.808
6	0.953	**0.855**	0.902

Table 4: English-Hindi mining results

Run	Precision	Recall	F-score
1	0.813	0.839	**0.826**
2	**0.868**	0.748	0.804
3	0.843	0.747	0.792
4	0.716	0.868	0.785
5	0.771	0.794	0.782
6	0.673	**0.881**	0.763

Table 5: English-Russian mining results

Run	Precision	Recall	F-score
1	0.963	0.604	0.743
2	**0.976**	0.407	0.575
3	0.975	0.446	0.612
4	0.952	0.668	0.785
5	0.968	0.567	0.715
6	0.939	**0.741**	**0.828**

Table 6: English-Tamil mining results

For each foreign language (F) and English (E) pair, a set of 6 runs were performed. The first two runs involved training a transliterator using the 1,000 transliteration pairs and using it for TM as in section 3. The runs were:

Run 1: align F with S-mod(E)
Run 2: align F with E

The four other runs involved iterative training in which all automatically mined transliterations from Runs 1 and 2 were considered correct, and were used to retrain the transliterator. The runs were:

Run 3: Use Run 2 output, align F with E
Run 4: Use Run 2 output, align F with S-mod(E)
Run 5: Use Run 1 output, align F with E
Run 6: Use Run 1 output, align F with S-mod(E)

For evaluation, the system would mine transliterations and a set of 1,000 parallel sequences were chosen randomly for evaluation. The figures of merit are precision, recall, F1 measure.

4 Experimental Setup

The experiments were done on the ACL-2010 NEWS Workshop TM shared task datasets. The datasets cover 5 language pairs. For each pair, a dataset includes a list of 1,000 transliterated words to train a transliterator, and list of parallel word sequences between both languages. The parallel sequences were extracted parallel Wikipedia article titles for which cross language links exist between both languages. Table 1 lists the language pairs and the number of the parallel word sequences.

5 Experimental Results

Tables 2, 3, 4, 5, and 6 report results for Arabic, Chinese, Hindi, Russian and Tamil respectively. As shown in Table 3, the recall for English-Chinese TM was dismal and suggests problems in experimental setup. This would require further investigation. For the other 4 languages, the results show that not using S-mod and not using iterative training, as in Run 2, led to the highest precision. Using both S-mod and iterative training, as in Run 6, led to the highest recall.

In comparing Runs 1 and 2, where 1 uses S-mod and 2 does not, using S-mod led to 35.6%, 40.6%, 12.2%, and 48.4% improvement in recall and to 6.8%, 2.8%, 6.3%, and 1.3% decline in precision for Arabic, Chinese, Russian, and Tamil respectively. Except for Russian, the improvements in recall dwarf decline in precision, leading to overall improvements in F-measure for all 4 languages.

In comparing runs 2 and 3 where iterative training is used, iterative training had marginal impact on precision and recall. When using S-mod, comparing run 6 where iterative training was performed over the output from run 1, recall increased by

3.9%, 8.8%, 5.0%, and 22.7% for Arabic, Chinese, Russian, and Tamil respectively. The drop in precision was 9.1% and 17.2% for Arabic and Russian respectively and marginal for Hindi and Tamil. Except for Russian, the best runs for all languages included the use of S-mod and iterative training. The best runs were 4 for Arabic and Hindi and 6 for Tamil. For Russian, the best runs involved using S-mod only without iterative training. The drop in Russian could be attributed to the relatively large size of training data compared to the other languages (345,969 parallel word sequences).

6 Conclusion

This paper presented two methods for improving transliteration mining, namely phonetic conflation of letters and iterative training of a transliteration model. The methods were tested using on the ACL 2010 NEWS workshop shared transliteration mining task data. Phonetic conflation of letters involved using a SOUNDEX like conflation scheme for English. This led to much improved recall and general improvements in F-measure. The iterative training of the transliteration model led to improved recall, but recall improvements were often offset by decreases in precision. However, the best experimental setups typically involved the use of both improvements.

The success of phonetic conflation for English may indicate that similar success may be attained if phonetic conflation is applied to other languages. Further, the use of smoothing of the transliteration model may help improve recall. The recall for transliteration mining between English and Chinese were dismal and require further investigation.

References

Slaven Bilac, Hozumi Tanaka. Extracting transliteration pairs from comparable corpora. NLP-2005, 2005.

Eric Brill, Gary Kacmarcik, Chris Brockett. Automatically harvesting Katakana-English term pairs from search engine query logs. NLPRS 2001, pages 393–399, 2001.

Huang Fei, Stephan Vogel, and Alex Waibel. 2003. Extracting Named Entity Translingual Equivalence with Limited Resources. TALIP, 2(2):124–129.

Xiaodong He, 2007. Using Word-Dependent Transition Models in HMM based Word Alignment for Statistical Machine Translation. ACL-07 2nd SMT workshop.

Chengguo Jin, Dong-Il Kim, Seung-Hoon Na, Jong-Hyeok Lee. 2008. Automatic Extraction of English-Chinese Transliteration Pairs using Dynamic Window and Tokenizer. Sixth SIGHAN Workshop on Chinese Language Processing, 2008.

Alexandre Klementiev and Dan Roth. 2006. Named Entity Transliteration and Discovery from Multilingual Comparable Corpora. HLT Conf. of the North American Chapter of the ACL, pages 82–88.

Jin-Shea Kuo, Haizhou Li, Ying-Kuei Yang. 2006. Learning Transliteration Lexicons from the Web. COLING-ACL2006, Sydney, Australia, 1129 – 1136.

Jin-shea Kuo, Haizhou Li, Ying-kuei Yang. A phonetic similarity model for automatic extraction of transliteration pairs. TALIP, 2007

Jin-Shea Kuo, Haizhou Li, Chih-Lung Lin. 2008. Mining Transliterations from Web Query Results: An Incremental Approach. Sixth SIGHAN Workshop on Chinese Language Processing, 2008.

Jin-shea Kuo, Ying-kuei Yang. 2005. Incorporating Pronunciation Variation into Extraction of Transliterated-term Pairs from Web Corpora. Journal of Chinese Language and Computing, 15 (1): (33-44).

Chun-Jen Lee, Jason S. Chang. Acquisition of English-Chinese transliterated word pairs from parallel-aligned texts using a statistical machine transliteration model. Workshop on Building and Using Parallel Texts, HLT-NAACL-2003, 2003.

R. Mahesh, K. Sinha. 2009. Automated Mining Of Names Using Parallel Hindi-English Corpus. 7th Workshop on Asian Language Resources, ACL-IJCNLP 2009, pages 48–54, Suntec, Singapore, 2009.

Jong-Hoon Oh, Key-Sun Choi. 2006. Recognizing transliteration equivalents for enriching domain-specific thesauri. 3rd Intl. WordNet Conf. (GWC-06), pages 231–237, 2006.

Jong-Hoon Oh, Hitoshi Isahara. 2006. Mining the Web for Transliteration Lexicons: Joint-Validation Approach. pp.254-261, 2006 IEEE/WIC/ACM Intl. Conf. on Web Intelligence (WI'06), 2006.

Raghavendra Udupa, K. Saravanan, Anton Bakalov, and Abhijit Bhole. 2009a. "They Are Out There, If You Know Where to Look": Mining Transliterations of OOV Query Terms for Cross-Language Information Retrieval. ECIR-2009, Toulouse, France, 2009.

Raghavendra Udupa, K. Saravanan, A. Kumaran, and Jagadeesh Jagarlamudi. 2009b. MINT: A Method for Effective and Scalable Mining of Named Entity Transliterations from Large Comparable Corpora. EACL 2009.

Raghavendra Udupa and Mitesh Khapra. 2010. Transliteration Equivalence using Canonical Correlation Analysis. ECIR-2010, 2010.

Robert Russell. 1918. Specifications of Letters. US patent number 1,261,167.

K Saravanan, A Kumaran. 2008. Some Experiments in Mining Named Entity Transliteration Pairs from Comparable Corpora. The 2nd Intl. Workshop on Cross Lingual Information Access addressing the need of multilingual societies, 2008.

Language Independent Transliteration Mining System Using Finite State Automata Framework

Sara Noeman and Amgad Madkour
Human Language Technologies Group
IBM Cairo Technology Development Center
P.O.Box 166 El-Haram, Giza, Egypt
{noemans,amadkour}@eg.ibm.com

Abstract

We propose a Named Entities transliteration mining system using Finite State Automata (FSA). We compare the proposed approach with a baseline system that utilizes the Editex technique to measure the length-normalized phonetic based edit distance between the two words. We submitted three standard runs in NEWS2010 shared task and ranked first for English to Arabic (WM-EnAr) and obtained an F-measure of 0.915, 0.903, and 0.874 respectively.

1 Introduction

Named entities transliteration is a crucial task in many domains such as cross lingual information retrieval, machine translation, and other natural language processing applications. In the previous NEWS 2009 transliteration task, we introduced a statistical approach for transliteration generation only using the bilingual resources (about 15k parallel names) provided for the shared task. For NEWS2010, the shared task focuses on acquisition of a reasonably sized, good quality names corpus to complement the machine transliteration task. Specifically, the task focuses on mining the Wikipedia paired entities data (inter-wiki-links) to produce high-quality transliteration data that may be used for transliteration generation tasks.

2 Related Work

Finite state Automata is used to tackle many Natural Language Processing challenges. Hassan (2008) et al. proposed the use of finite state automata for language-independent text correction. It consists of three phases : detecting misspelled words, generating candidate corrections for them and ranking corrections. In detecting the misspelled words, they compose the finite state automaton representation of the dictionary with the input string. Onaizan (2002) et al. proposed the use of probabilistic finite state machines for machine transliteration of names in Arabic text. They used a hybrid approach between phonetic-based and spelling-based models. Malik (2008) et al. proposed a Hindi Urdu machine transliteration system using finite state machines. They introduced UIT (universal intermediate transcription) on the same pair according to thier phonetic properties as a means of representing the language and created finite state transducers to represent them. Sherif (2007) proposed the use of memoryless stochastic transducer for extracting transliteration through word similarity metrics.

Other approaches for transliteration include translation of names through mining or through using machine translation systems resources. Hassan (2007) et al. proposed a framework for extraction of named entity translation pairs. This is done through searching for candidate documents pairs through an information retrieval system and then using a named entity matching system which relies on the length-normalized phonetic based edit distance between the two words. They also use a phrase-based translation tables to measure similarity of extracted named entities. Noeman (2009) also used a phrase based statistical machine translation (PBSMT) approach to create a substring based transliteration system through the generated phrase table, thus creating a language independent approach to transliteration. Other resources have been used to perform transliteration. Chang (2009) et. al proposed the use of a romanization table in conjunction with an unsupervised constraint driven learning algorithm in order to identify transliteration pairs without any labelled data.

3 System architecture

The approach consists of three main phases which are (1) Transliteration model learning, (2) Fi-

Proceedings of the 2010 Named Entities Workshop, ACL 2010, pages 57–61,
Uppsala, Sweden, 16 July 2010. ©2010 Association for Computational Linguistics

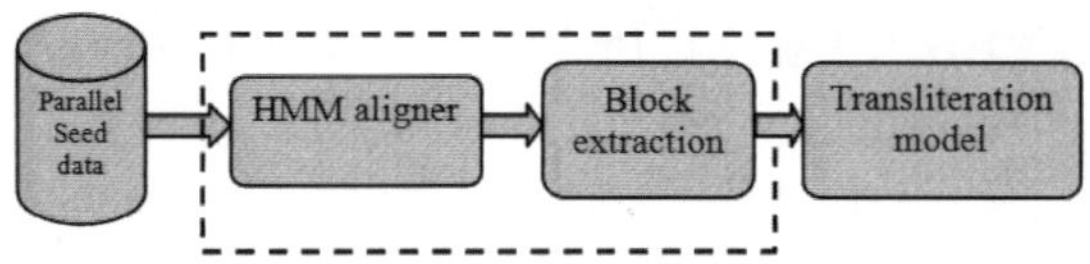

Figure 1: Transliteration table learning in PBSMT

nite State machine formalization of the generated transliteration model and (3) Generating Candidate transliterations. Figure (1) illustrates Transliteration table learning in PBSMT framework. A detailed description of each phase is given in the following sections.

3.1 Transliteration model learning

The objective of NEWS2010 shared task is to develop a system for mining single word transliteration pairs from the standard Wikipedia paired topics (Wikipedia Inter-Language Links, or WIL1), using a seed data of only 1000 parallel names. The aim is to learn one-to-many character sequence mappings on both directions.

We propose the use of MOSES framework[1] for PBSMT training which was applied on the 1k parallel seed data. The proposed approach depends on the formulation of the transliteration problem using the PBSMT approach used in Machine translation. Giza++ Hidden Markov Model (HMM) aligner[2] proposed by Och (1999) was also used over the parallel character sequences. Heuristics were used to extend substring to substring mappings based on character-to-character alignment. This generated a substring to substring translation model such as in Koehn (2003). The phrase "substring" table was filtered out to obtain all possible substrings alignment of each single character in the language alphabet in both directions. This means that for each character in the source language (English) alphabet, substrings mapped to it are filtered with a threshold. Also for each character in the target language (Arabic) alphabet, all English substrings mapped to it are filtered with a threshold. These two one-to-many alignments were intersected in one "Transliteration Arabic-to-English mapping". We obtained a character alignment table which we refer to as "Ar2En list". Figure(2) illustrates a sample one-to-many alignment mapping.

[1]MOSES Framework: http://www.statmt.org/moses/
[2]GIZA++ Aligner: http://fjoch.com/GIZA++.html

ص | s 0.833334 | z 0.166667 |
خ | k h 0.65 | c h 0.3 | j 0.05 |
د | d 0.899543 |
ض | d 1 |
م | m 0.863924 |
ب | b 0.571984 | p 0.272374 |
ر | r 0.909449 |
ت | t 0.901408 |
ن | n 0.856618 |
ش | s h 0.506173 | c h 0.148148 | s c h 0.148148 |
ك | k 0.465278 | c 0.326389 | c k 0.0590278 |

Figure 2: One to Many Alignment Mapping

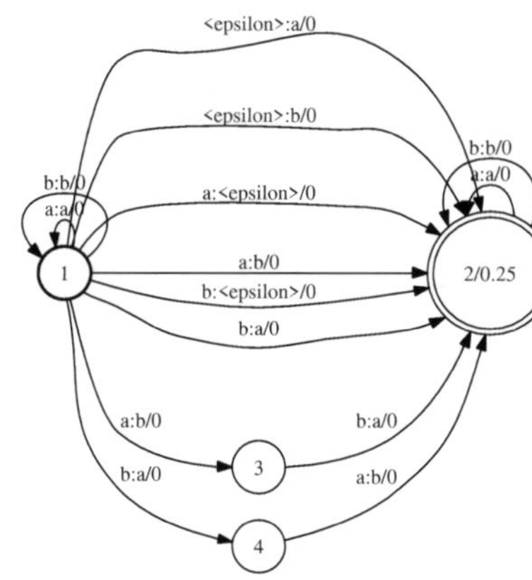

Figure 3: Edit distance 1 FSM

3.2 FSM formalization of Transliteration Model

The proposed method makes use of the finite state automaton representation for the Ar2En character alignment list, where the input is the source character and the output is the target character. We refer to this finite state transducer (FST) as "Ar2En FST". For each source word, we build a Finite State Acceptor (FSA), such that each candidate source word FSA is composed with the "Ar2En FST". For the target words list, we build a finite state acceptor (FSA) that contains a path for each word in the target Wiki-Link.

3.3 Generating Candidate transliterations

The task of generating candidate transliterations at edit distance k from initial source candidate transliterations using Levenshtein transducer can be divided into two sub tasks: Generating a list of words that have edit distance less than or equal k to the input word, and selecting the words inter-

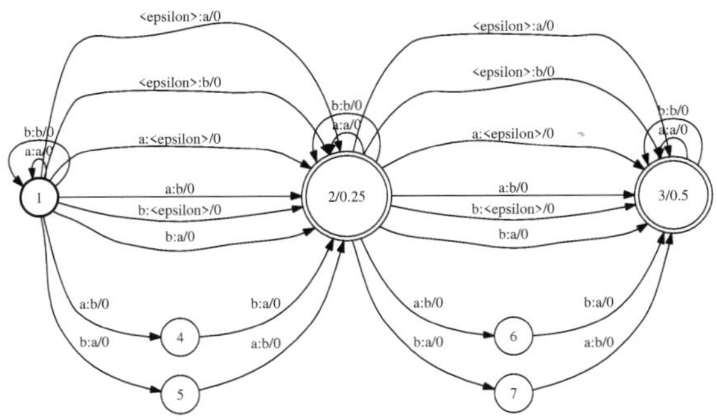

Figure 4: Edit distance 2 FSM

```
For each Wiki-Link-Title
{
   @EnWords = English word list;
   @ArWords_a = Arabic word list;
   Create FSA for English word list "@EnWords" =
FSA[@EnWords];
   Create FSA for Arabic word list "@ArWords" =
FSA[@ArWords];
   Out1_FST = Compose FSA[@ArWords] with FST[Ar2En];
   Out2_FST = Compose Out1_FST with FST[Edit-1];
   Out3_FST = Compose Out2_FST with FSA[@EnWords];
   If(Out3_FST is empty)
   {
          Arabic word @ArWords has no transliteration;
   }
   Else
   {
          Get Mined pair @ArMatched with @EnMatched
   }
}
```

Figure 5: Using Levenshtein edit-1 FST

secting with the target inter-wiki-link words. This is similar to the spelling correction technique that used FSM which was introduced by Hassan (2008) et. al. In the spelling correction task , after generating the list of words within edit distance *k* to the input word, the system selects a subset of those words that exist in a large dictionary. In order to accomplish this same scenario, we created a single transducer (Levenshtein transducer) that when composed with an FSM representing a word generates all words within an edit distance *k* from the input word. We then compose the resulting FSM with an FSA (finite state acceptor) of all words in the target inter-wiki-link. The Levenshtein transducer is language independent and is built only using the alphabet of the target language. Figure (3) and Figure (4) illustrate the Levenshtein transducer for edit distance 1 and 2 over a limited set of vocabulary (a, b).

4 Data and Resources Processing

After revising the training data (inter-wiki-links) released, we discovered that English and Arabic words contained many stress marks and non normalized characters. We therefore applied normalization on Arabic and English characters to increase source target matching probability, thus increasing the recall of data mining. We also normalized Arabic names, removing all diacritics and kashida. Kashida is a type of justification used in some cursive scripts such as Arabic. Also we normalized Alef () with hamza and madda to go to "bare Alef".

5 Standard runs

We submitted 6 runs derived from 3 experiments. For each experiment, we submitted 2 runs, one with normalized Arabic and English characters, and the other with the stress marks and special characters. It is important to note that we run the mining in the Arabic to English direction, thus the Arabic side is the source and the English side is the target.

5.1 Using Levenshtein edit distance 1 FST

Figure (5) illustrates the algorithm used to conduct the first experiment. We subjected all source words to be composed with Levenshtein edit distance 1. For each Wiki-Link, we build a finite state acceptor (FSA) that contains a path for each word in the Arabic Wiki-Link. We refer to it as FSA[@ArWords]. Similarly, for the English name candidates we build a finite state acceptor (FSA) that contains a path for each word in the English Wiki-Link. We refer to it as FSA[@EnWords]. The generated @ArWords and @EnWords are the lists of words in the Arabic and English wiki-links respectively. The result of this experiment was reported as Standard-3 "normalized characters" and Standard-4 "without normalized characters".

5.2 Using Levenshtein up to edit distance 2 FST

Figure (6) illustrates the algorithm used to conduct the second experiment. We use a threshold on the number of characters in a word to decide whether it will be subjected for "composed with" edit dis-

```
For each Wiki-Link-Title
{
  @EnWords = English word list;
  @ArWords = Arabic word list;
  Create FSA for English word list "@EnWords" =
FSA[@EnWords];
  For each Arabic word "wa" (@ArWords)
  {
        Create FSA [wa];
        Out1_FST = Compose FSA[wa] with FST[Ar2En];
        Where |wa| = length of "wa"
        If( |wa| <= 3 letters)
        {
          Out2_FST = Out1_FST;
        }
        Else if( 3 letters < |wa| <= 7 letters )
        {
          Out2_FST = Compose Out1_FST with FST[Edit-1];
        }
        Else
        {
          Out2_FST = Compose Out1_FST with FST[Edit-2];
        }
        Out3_FST = Compose Out2_FST with FSA[@EnWords];
        If(Out3_FST is empty)
        {
          Arabic word "wa" has no transliteration.
        }
        Else
        {
          Get best path: mined pair "wa" with best path output
        }
  }
}
```

Figure 6: Using Levenshtein edit-2 FST

tance 0 or 1 or 2. We use a threshold of 3 for edit distance 1 and a threshold of 7 for edit distance 2. The threshold values are set based on our previous experience from dealing with Arabic text and could be derived from the data we obtained. If word length is less than or equal 3 letters, then it is not composed with Levenshtein FSTs, and if word length is between 4 to 7 letters, we compose it with edit distance 1 FST. Longer words are composed with edit distance 2 FST. The result of the experiment was reported in two submitted runs: Standard-5 "normalized characters" and Standard-6 "without normalized characters".

5.3 Baseline

We use a length-normalized phonetic edit distance to measure the phonetic similarity between the source and target Named Entities in the inter-wiki-links. We use the Editex technique Zobel (1996) that makes use of the phonetic characteristics of individual characters to estimate their similarity. Editex measures the phonetic distance between pairs of words by combining the properties of edit distances with a letter grouping strategy that groups letters with similar pronunciations. The result of this experiment was reported in two submitted runs: Standard-1 "normalized characters" and Standard-2 "without normalized characters".

Submission	F-Score	Precision	Recall
Standard-6	***0.915***	0.887	0.945
Standard-4	0.903	0.859	***0.952***
Standard-2	0.874	***0.923***	0.830
Standard-5	0.723	0.701	0.747
Standard-3	0.716	0.681	0.755
Standard-1	0.702	0.741	0.666

Table 1: Shared Task Results

6 Results

Table (1) illustrates the results of the shared task given on the runs we submitted.

Our baseline run (Standard-2) reports highest precision of 0.923 and lowest recall of 0.830 (lowest F-score = 0.874). The reason is that Editex technique measures the edit distance based on letter grouping strategy which groups letters with similar pronunciations. It operates on character to character level. Letters that are mapped to multi-characters will suffer a large edit distance and may exceed the matching threshold used.

The two runs Standard-4 and Standard-6 are implemented using edit-distance FSM matching between source and target. They cover one-to-many character mapping. We notice that Standard-6 run reports higher precision of 0.887 compared to 0.859 for Standard-4 run. This reflects the effect of using variable edit-distance according to the source word length. The Standard-6 reports a Recall of 0.945 producing our best F-Score of 0.915. Standard-6 recall degrades only 0.7% from Standard-4 Recall (0.952).

7 Conclusion

We proposed a language independent transliteration mining system that utilizes finite state automaton. We demonstrated how statistical techniques could be used to build a language independent machine transliteration system through utilizing PBMT techniques. We performed 3 standard experiments each containing two submissions. FSM edit distance matching outperformed Editex in F-Score and Recall. The proposed approach obtained the highest F-Score of 0.915 and a recall of 0.945 in the shared task.

References

Ahmed Hassan, Haytham Fahmy, Hany Hassan 2007. *Improving Named Entity Translation by Exploiting Comparable and Parallel Corpora*. AMML07

Ahmed Hassan, Sara Noeman, Hany Hassan 2008. *Language Independent Text Correction using Finite State Automata*. IJCNLP08.

Franz Josef Och, Christoph Tillmann, and Hermann Ney 1999. *Improved Alignment Models for Statistical Machine Translation*. EMNLP.

Justin Zobel and Philip Dart 1996. *Phonetic string matching: Lessons from information retrieval*. In Proceedings of the Annual ACM References Conference on Research and Development in Information Retrieval (SIGIR).

M. G. Abbas Malik, Christian Boitet, Pushpak Bhattacharyya 2008. *Hindi Urdu Machine Transliteration using Finite-state Transducers*. Proceedings of the 22nd International Conference on Computational Linguistics (Coling 2008), pages 537544

Ming-Wei Chang, Dan Goldwasser, Dan Roth, Yuancheng Tu 2009. *Unsupervised Constraint Driven Learning For Transliteration Discovery*. Proceedings of Human Language Technologies: The 2009 Annual Conference of the North American Chapter of the Association for Computational Linguistics.

Philipp Koehn, Franz Josef Och, Daniel Marc 2003. *Statistical Phrase-Based Translation*. Proc. Of the Human Language Technology Conference, HLT-NAACL2003, May.

Sara Noeman 2009. *Language Independent Transliteration system using PBSMT approach on substrings*. Proceedings of the 2009 Named Entities Workshop: Shared Task on Transliteration.

Tarek Sherif, Grzegorz Kondrak 2007. *Bootstrapping a Stochastic Transducer for Arabic-English Transliteration Extraction*. Proceedings of the 45th Annual Meeting of the Association of Computational Linguistics, pages 864871

Yasser Al-Onaizan, Kevin Knight 2002. *Machine Transliteration of Names in Arabic Text*. ACL Workshop on Comp. Approaches to Semitic Languages.

Reranking with Multiple Features for Better Transliteration

Yan Song[†] **Chunyu Kit**[†] **Hai Zhao**[‡†]
[†]Department of Chinese, Translation and Linguistics
City University of Hong Kong, 83 Tat Chee Ave., Kowloon, Hong Kong
[‡]Department of Computer Science and Engineering
Shanghai Jiao Tong University, #800, Dongchuan Rd, Shanghai, China
{yansong,ctckit}@cityu.edu.hk, zhaohai@cs.sjtu.edu.cn

Abstract

Effective transliteration of proper names via grapheme conversion needs to find transliteration patterns in training data, and then generate optimized candidates for testing samples accordingly. However, the top-1 accuracy for the generated candidates cannot be good if the right one is not ranked at the top. To tackle this issue, we propose to rerank the output candidates for a better order using the averaged perceptron with multiple features. This paper describes our recent work in this direction for our participation in NEWS2010 transliteration evaluation. The official results confirm its effectiveness in English-Chinese bidirectional transliteration.

1 Introduction

Since transliteration can be considered a direct orthographic mapping process, one may adopt general statistical machine translation (SMT) procedures for its implementation. Aimed at finding phonetic equivalence in another language for a given named entity, however, different transliteration options with different syllabification may generate multiple choices with the symphonic form for the same source text. Consequently, even the overall results by SMT output are acceptable, it is still unreliable to rank the candidates simply by their statistical translation scores for the purpose of selecting the best one. In order to make a proper choice, the direct orthographic mapping requires a precise alignment and a better transliteration option selection. Thus, powerful algorithms for effective use of the parallel data is indispensable, especially when the available data is limited in volume.

Interestingly, although an SMT based approach could not achieve a precise top-1 transliteration result, it is found in (Song et al., 2009) that, in contrast to the ordinary top-1 accuracy (ACC) score, its recall rate, which is defined in terms of whether the correct answer is generated in the n-best output list, is rather high. This observation suggests that if we could rearrange those outputs into a better order, especially, push the correct one to the top, the overall performance could be enhanced significantly, without any further refinement of the original generation process. This reranking strategy is proved to be efficient in transliteration generation with a multi-engine approach (Oh et al., 2009).

In this paper, we present our recent work on reranking the transliteration candidates via an online discriminative learning framework, namely, the averaged perceptron. Multiple features are incorporated into it for performance enhancement. The following sections will give the technical details of our method and present its results for NEWS2010 shared task for named entity transliteration.

2 Generation

For the generation of transliteration candidates, we follow the work (Song et al., 2009), using a phrase-based SMT procedure with the log-linear model

$$P(t|s) = \frac{exp[\sum_{i=1}^{n} \lambda_i h_i(s,t)]}{\sum_t exp[\sum_{i=1}^{n} \lambda_i h_i(s,t)]} \quad (1)$$

for decoding. Originally we use two directional phrase[1] tables, which are learned for both directions of source-to-target and target-to-source, containing different entries of transliteration options. In order to facilitate the decoding by exploiting all possible choices in a better way, we combine the forward and backward directed phrase tables together, and recalculate the probability for each en-

[1]It herein refers to a character sequence as described in (Song et al., 2009).

Proceedings of the 2010 Named Entities Workshop, ACL 2010, pages 62–65,
Uppsala, Sweden, 16 July 2010.

try in it. After that, we use a phoneme resource[2] to refine the phrase table by filtering out the wrongly extracted phrases and cleaning up the noise in it. In the decoding process, a dynamic pruning is performed when generating the hypothesis in each step, in which the threshold is variable according to the current searching space, for we need to obtain a good candidate list as precise as possible for the next stage. The parameter for each feature function in log-linear model is optimized by MERT training (Och, 2003). Finally, a maximum number of 50 candidates are generated for each source name.

3 Reranking

3.1 Learning Framework

For reranking training and prediction, we adopt the averaged perceptron (Collins, 2002) as our learning framework, which has a more stable performance than the non-averaged version. It is presented in Algorithm 1. Where $\vec{\omega}$ is the vector of parameters we want to optimize, x, y are the corresponding source (with different syllabification) and target graphemes in the candidate list, and Φ represents the feature vector in the pair of x and y. In this algorithm, reference y_i^* is the most appropriate output in the candidate list according to the true target named entity in the training data. We use the Mean-F score to identify which candidate can be the reference, by locating the one with the maximum Mean-F score value. This process updates the parameters of the feature vector and also relocate all of the candidates according to the ranking scores, which are calculated in terms of the resulted parameters in each round of training as well as in the testing process. The number of iteration for the final model is determined by the development data.

Algorithm 1 Averaged perceptron training

Input: Candidate list with reference $\{LIST(x_j, y_j)_{j=1}^n, y_i^*\}_{i=1}^N$

Output: Averaged parameters

$\vec{\omega} \leftarrow 0$, $\vec{\omega}_a \leftarrow 0$, $c \leftarrow 1$
for $t = 1$ **to** T **do**
  for $i = 1$ **to** N **do**
    $\hat{y}_i \leftarrow argmax_{y \in LIST(x_j, y_j)} \vec{\omega} \cdot \Phi(x_i, y_i)$
    if $\hat{y}_i \neq y_i^*$ **then**
      $\vec{\omega} \leftarrow \vec{\omega} + \Phi(x_i^*, y_i^*) - \Phi(\hat{x}_i, \hat{y}_i)$
      $\vec{\omega}_a \leftarrow \vec{\omega}_a + c \cdot \{\Phi(x_i^*, y_i^*) - \Phi(\hat{x}_i, \hat{y}_i)\}$
    end if
    $c \leftarrow c + 1$
  end for
end for
return $\vec{\omega} - \vec{\omega}_a / c$

3.2 Multiple Features

The following features are used in our reranking process:

Transliteration correspondence feature, $f(s_i, t_i)$;

This feature describes the mapping between source and target graphemes, similar to the transliteration options in the phrase table in our previous generation process, where s and t refer to the source and target language respectively, and i to the current position.

Source grapheme chain feature, $f(s_{i-1}^i)$;

It measures the syllabification for a given source text. There are two types of units in different levels. One is on syllable level, e.g., "*aa/bye*", "*aa/gaar/d*", reflecting the segmentation of the source text, and the other on character level, such as "*a/b*", "*a/g*", "*r/d*", showing the combination power of several characters. These features on different source grapheme levels can help the system to achieve a more reliable syllabification result from the candidates. We only consider bi-grams when using this feature.

Target grapheme chain feature, $f(t_{i-2}^i)$;

This feature measures the appropriateness of the generated target graphemes on both character and syllables level. It performs in a similar way as the language model for SMT decoding. We use *tri*-gram syllables in this learning framework.

Paired source-to-target transition feature, $f(<s, t>_{i-1}^i)$;

This type of feature is firstly proposed in (Li et al., 2004), aiming at generating source and target graphemes simultaneously under a suitable constraint. We use this feature to restrict the synchronous transition of both source and target graphemes, measuring how well are those transitions, such as for "*st*",

[2]In this work, we use Pinyin as the phonetic representation for Chinese.

whether "*s*" transliterated by "*斯*" is followed by "*t*" transliterated by "*特*". In order to deal with the data sparseness, only bi-gram transition relations are considered in this feature.

Hidden Markov model (HMM) style features;

There are a group of features with HMM style constraint for evaluating the candidates generated in previous SMT process, including, previous syllable HMM features, $f(s_{i-n+1}^{i}, t_i)$, posterior syllable HMM features, $f(s_i^{i+n-1}, t_i)$, and posterior character HMM features, $f(s_i, l, t_i)$, where l denotes the character following the previous syllable in the source language. For the last feature, it is effective to use both the current syllable and the first letter of the next syllable to bound the current target grapheme. The reason for applying this feature in our learning framework is that, empirically, the letters following many syllables strongly affect the transliteration for them, e.g., *Aves* → *埃维斯*, "*a*" followed by "*v*" is always translated into "*埃*" rather than "*阿*".

Target grapheme position feature, $f(t_i, p)$;

This feature is an improved version of that proposed in (Song et al., 2009), where p refers to the position of t_i. We have a measure for the target graphemes according to their source graphemes and the current position of their correspondent target characters. There are three categories of such position, namely, start (S), mediate (M) and end (E). S refers to the first character in a target name, E to the final, and the others belong to M. This feature is used to exploit the observation that some characters are more likely to appear at certain positions in the target name. Some are always found at the beginning of a named entity while others only at the middle or the end. For example, "*re*" associated to first character in a target name is always transliterated as "*雷*", such as *Redd* → *雷德*. When "*re*" appears at the end of a source name, however, its transliteration will be "*尔*" in most cases, just like *Gore* → *戈尔*.

Target tone feature;

This feature is only applied to the transliteration task with Chinese as the target language. It can be seen as a combination of a target grapheme chain with some position features, using tone instead of the target grapheme itself for evaluation. There are 5 tones (0,1,2,3,4) for Chinese characters. It is easy to conduct a comprehensive analysis for the use of a higher ordered transition chain as a better constraint. Many fixed tone patterns can be identified in the Chinese transliteration training data. The tone information can also be extracted from the Pinyin resource we used in the previous stage.

Besides the above string features, we also have some numeric features, as listed below.

Transliteration score;

This score is the joint probabilities of all transliteration options, included in the output candidates generated by our decoder.

Target language model score;

This score is calculated from the probabilistic tri-gram language model.

Source/target Pinyin feature;

This feature uses Pinyin representation for a source or target name, depending on what side the Chinese language is used. It measures how good the output candidates can be in terms of the comparison between English text and Pinyin representation. The resulted score is updated according to the Levenshtein distance for the two input letter strings of English and Pinyin.

For a task with English as the target language, we add the following two additional features into the learning framework.

Vowel feature;

It is noticed that when English is the target language, vowels can sometimes be missing in the generated candidates. This feature is thus used to punish those outputs unqualified to be a valid English word for carrying no vowel.

Syllable consistent feature;

This feature measures whether an English target name generated in the previous step has the same number of syllables as the source name. In Chinese-to-English transliteration, Chinese characters are single-syllabled, thus

Table 1: Evaluation results for our NEWS2010 task.

Task	Source	Target	ACC	Mean F	MRR	Map_ref	Recall	ACC_{SMT}
EnCh	English	Chinese	0.477	0.740	0.506	0.455	0.561	0.381
ChEn	Chinese	English	0.227	0.749	0.269	0.226	0.371	0.152

we can easily identify their number. For syllabification, we have an independent segmentation process for calculating the syllables.

4 Results

For NEWS2010, we participated in all two Chinese related transliteration tasks, namely, EnCh (English-to-Chinese) and ChEn (Chinese-to-English back transliteration). The official evaluation scores for our submissions are presented in Table 1 with recall rate, and the ACC score (ACC_{SMT}) for original SMT outputs. It is easy to see the performance gain for the reranking, and also from the recall rate that there is still some room for improvement, in spite of the high ratio of ACC/Recall[3] calculated from Table 1. However, it is also worth noting that, some of the source texts cannot be correctly transliterated, due to many multiple-word name entities with semantic components in the test data, e.g., "*MANCHESTER BRIDGE*", "*BRIGHAM CITY*" etc. These semantic parts are beyond our transliteration system's capability to tackle, especially when the training data is limited and the only focus of the system is on the phonetic equivalent correspondence.

Compared to the EnCh transliteration, we get a rather low ACC score for the ChEn back transliteration, suggesting that ChEn task is somewhat harder than the EnCh (in which Chinese characters are always limited). The ChEn task is a one-to-many translation, involving a lot of possible choices and combinations of English syllables. This certainly makes it a more challengeable task than EnCh. However, looking into the details of the outputs, we find that, in the ChEn back transliteration, some characters in the test corpus are unseen in the training and the development data, resulting in incorrect transliterations for many graphemes. This is another factor affecting our final results for the ChEn task.

5 Conclusion

In this paper, we have presented our work on multiple feature based reranking for transliteration generation. It NEWS2010 results show that this approach is effective and promising, in the sense that it ranks the best in EnCh and ChEn tasks. The reranking used in this work can also be considered a regeneration process based on an existing set, as part of our features are always used directly to generate the initial transliteration output in other researches. Though, those features are strongly dependent on the nature of English and Chinese languages, it is thus not an easy task to transplant this model for other language pairs. It is an interesting job to turn it into a language independent model that can be applied to other languages.

[3] Compared to the results from (Song et al., 2009)

Acknowledgments

The research described in this paper was partially supported by City University of Hong Kong through the Strategic Research Grants (SRG) 7002267 and 7008003. Dr. Hai Zhao was supported by the Natural Science Foundation of China (NSFC) through the grant 60903119. We also thank Mr. Wenbin Jiang for his helpful suggestions on averaged perceptron learning.

References

Michael Collins. 2002. Discriminative training methods for hidden markov models: Theory and experiments with perceptron algorithms. In *Proceedings of EMNLP-2002*, pages 1–8, July.

Haizhou Li, Min Zhang, and Jian Su. 2004. A joint source-channel model for machine transliteration. In *Proceedings of ACL-04*, pages 159–166, Barcelona, Spain, July.

Franz Josef Och. 2003. Minimum error rate training in statistical machine translation. In *Proceedings of ACL-03*, pages 160–167, Sapporo, Japan, July.

Jong-Hoon Oh, Kiyotaka Uchimoto, and Kentaro Torisawa. 2009. Machine transliteration using target-language grapheme and phoneme: Multi-engine transliteration approach. In *Proceedings of NEWS 2009*, pages 36–39, Suntec, Singapore, August.

Yan Song, Chunyu Kit, and Xiao Chen. 2009. Transliteration of name entity via improved statistical translation on character sequences. In *Proceedings of NEWS 2009*, pages 57–60, Suntec, Singapore, August.

Syllable-based Thai-English Machine Transliteration

Chai Wutiwiwatchai and Ausdang Thangthai
National Electronics and Computer Technology Center
Pathumthani, Thailand
{chai.wutiwiwatchai,ausdang.thangthai}@nectec.or.th

Abstract

This article describes the first trial on bidirectional Thai-English machine transliteration applied on the NEWS 2010 transliteration corpus. The system relies on segmenting source-language words into syllable-like units, finding unit's pronunciations, consulting a syllable transliteration table to form target-language word hypotheses, and ranking the hypotheses by using syllable n-gram. The approach yields 84.2% and 70.4% mean F-scores on English-to-Thai and Thai-to-English transliteration. Discussion on existing problems and future solutions are addressed.

1 Introduction

Transliteration aims to phonetically transcribe text in source languages with text in target languages. The task is crucial for various natural language processing research and applications such as machine translation, multilingual text-to-speech synthesis and information retrieval. Most of current Thai writings contain both Thai and English scripts. Such English words when written in Thai are mainly their translations. Without official translation forms, transliterations often take place.

Thai-English machine transliteration and related research have been investigated for many years. Works for Thai word romanization or Thai-to-English transliteration are such as Charoenporn et al. (1999), Aroonmanakun and Rivepiboon (2004). Both works proposed statistical romanization models based on the syllable unit. Generating Thai scripts of English words are mainly via automatic transcription of English words. Aroonmanakun (2005) described a chunk-based n-gram model where the chunk is a group of characters useful for mapping to Thai transcriptions. Thangthai et al. (2007) proposed a method for generating Thai phonetic transcriptions of English words for use in Thai/English text-to-speech synthesis. The CART learning machine was adopted to map English characters to Thai phonetics. As our literature review, a general algorithm for bi-directional Thai-to-English and English-to-Thai transliteration has not been investigated.

The NEWS machine transliteration shared task has just included Thai-English words as a part of its corpus in 2010, serving as a good source for algorithm benchmarking. In this article, a Thai-English machine transliteration system is evaluated on the NEWS 2010 corpus. The system was developed under intuitive concepts that transliteration among Thai-English is mostly done on the basis of sound mimicking of syllable units. Therefore, the algorithm firstly segments the input word in a source language into syllable-like units and finding pronunciations of each unit. The pronunciation in the form of phonetic scripts is used to find possible transliteration forms given a syllable translation table. The best result is determined by using syllable n-gram.

The next section describes more details of Thai-English transliteration problems and the Thai-English NEWS 2010 corpus. The detail of proposed system is given in Section 3 and its evaluation is reported in Section 4. Section 5 discusses on existing problems and possible solutions.

2 Thai-English Transliteration

As mentioned in the Introduction, the current Thai writing often contains both Thai and English scripts especially for English words without compact translations. Many times, transliterations take place when only Thai scripts are needed. This is not only restricted to names but also some common words like "computer", "physics", etc.

The Thai Royal Institute (http://www.royin.go.th) is authorized to issue official guidelines for Thai transcriptions of foreign words and also romanization of Thai words, which are respectively equivalent to English-to-Thai and Thai-to-English transliteration. Romanization of Thai words is based on sound transcription. Thai con-

Proceedings of the 2010 Named Entities Workshop, ACL 2010, pages 66–70,
Uppsala, Sweden, 16 July 2010. ©2010 Association for Computational Linguistics

sonant and vowel alphabets are defined to map to roman alphabets. Similarly, English-to-Thai transliteration is defined based on the phonetic transcription of English words. However, in the latter case, an English phoneme could be mapped to multiple Thai alphabets. For example, the sound /k/ could be mapped to either "ก", "ข", "ค", or "ฆ". Moreover, the guideline reserves for transliterations generally used in the current writing and also transliterations appeared in the official Royal Institute dictionaries, even such transliterations do not comply with the guideline.

Since the guidelines are quite flexible and it is also common that lots of Thai people may not strictly follow the guidelines, ones can see many ways of transliteration in daily used text. To solve this ambiguity, both the official guidelines and statistics of usage must be incorporated in the machine transliteration system.

The Thai-English part of NEWS 2010 corpus developed by the National Electronics and Computer Technology Center (NECTEC) composes of word pairs collected mainly from 3 sources; press from the Thai Royal Institute, press from other sources, and the NEWS 2009 corpus. The first two sources, sharing about 40% of the corpus, mostly contain common English words often transliterated into Thai and the transliteration is almost restricted to the Royal Institute guidelines. The rest are English names selected from the NEWS 2009 corpus based on their frequencies found by the Google search. Such English names were transliterated into Thai and rechecked by linguists using the Royal Institute transliteration guideline.

3 Proposed Transliteration System

Our proposed model is similar to what proposed by Jiang et al. (2009), which introduced translation among Chinese and English names based on syllable units and determined the best candidate using the statistical n-gram model. The overall structure of our model is shown in Figure 1.

3.1 Syllabification and letter-to-sound

An input word in the source language is first segmented into syllable-like units. It is noted that there are some cases where segmented units are not really a syllable. For examples, "S" in the word "SPECTOR" might actually be pronounced as a single consonant without vowel. The Thai word "เสนอ"/s-a n-ɛ:/ is unbreakable as the letter expressed for the first syllable /s-a/ is enclosed in the letters of the second syllable /n-ɛ:/. These cases are considered exceptional syllables.

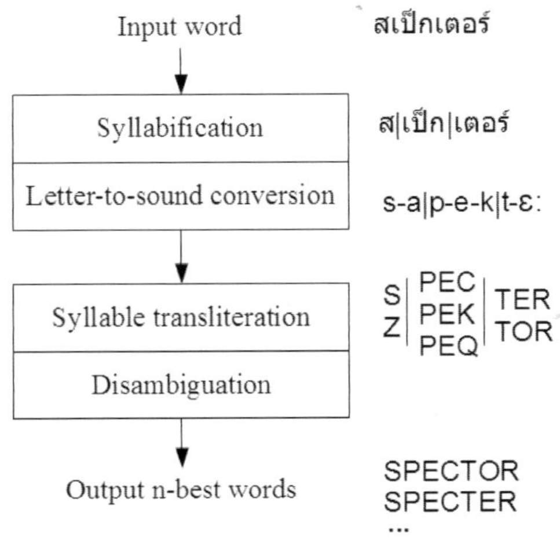

Figure 1. The overall system architecture.

In the Thai-to-English system, syllabification of Thai words is a part of a Thai letter-to-sound conversion tool provided by Thangthai et al. (2006). It is performed using context-free grammar (CFG) rules created by Tarsaku et al. (2001). The CFG rules produce syllable-sequence hypotheses, which are then disambiguated by using syllable n-gram. Simultaneously, the tool provides the phonetic transcription of the best syllable sequence by using a simple syllable-to-phone mapping. Figure 1 shows an example of an input Thai word "สเป็กเตอร์" which is segmented into 3 syllables "ส|เป็ก|เตอร์" and converted to the phonetic transcription defined for Thai "s-a|p-e-k|t-ɛ:".

In the English-to-Thai system, a simple syllabification module of English words is created using the following rules.

1) Marking all vowel letters "a, e, i, o, u", e.g. L[o]m[o]c[a]t[i]v[e], J[a]nsp[o]rt
2) Using some rules, merging consonantal letters surrounding each vowel to form basic syllables, e.g. Lo|mo|ca|ti|ve, Jan|sport
3) Post-processing by merging the syllable with "e" vowel into its preceding syllable e.g. Lo|mo|ca|tive, and re-segmenting for syllables without vowel letters, e.g. mcdo|nald to mc|do|nald, sport to s|port

Letter-to-sound conversion of English words can actually be conducted by several public tools like Festival (http://www.cstr.ed.ac.uk/projects/ festival/). However, the tool does not meet our requirement as it could not output syllable boundaries of the phonetic sequence and finding such boundaries is not trivial. Instead, a tool for converting English words to Thai phonetic transcriptions developed by Thangthai et al. (2007) is adopted. In this tool, the CART learning machine is used to capture the relationship among alphabets and English phone transcriptions of English words and Thai phone transcriptions. Since the Thai phonetic transcription is defined based on the syllable structure, the syllable boundaries of phonetic transcriptions given by this tool can be obtained.

3.2 Syllable transliteration and disambiguation

In the training phase, both Thai and English words in pairs are syllabified and converted to phonetic transcriptions using the methods described in the previous subsection. To reduce the effect of errors caused by automatic syllabification, only word pairs having equal number of syllables are kept for building a syllable transliteration table. The table consists of a list of syllable phonetic transcriptions and its possible textual syllables in both languages. An n-gram model of textual syllables in each language is also prepared from the training set.

In the testing phase, each syllable in the source-language word is mapped to possible syllables in the target language via its phonetic transcription using the syllable transliteration table described above. Since each syllable could be transliterated to multiple hypotheses, the best hypothesis can be determined by considering syllable n-gram probabilities.

4 Experiments

The Thai-English part of NEWS 2010 were deployed in our experiment. The training set composes of 24,501 word pairs and two test sets, 2,000 words for English-to-Thai and 1,994 words for Thai-to-English are used for evaluation. All training words were syllable segmented and converted to phonetic transcriptions using the tools described in the Section 3.1. Since the CFG rules could not completely cover all possible syllables in Thai, some words failed from automatically generating phonetic transcriptions were filtered out. As mentioned also in the Section 3.1, only word pairs with equal number of segmented syllables were kept for training. Finally, 16,705 out of 24,501 word pairs were reserved for building the syllable transliteration table and for training syllable 2-gram models.

Table 1 shows some statistics of syllables collected from the training word pairs. Since the Thai-English word pairs provided in NEWS 2010 were prepared mainly by transliterating English words and names into Thai, it is hence reasonable that the number of distinct syllables in Thai is considerably lower than in English. Similarly, the other statistics like the numbers of homophones per syllable phonetic-transcription are in the same manner.

Total no. of syllables	39,537
Avg. no. of syllables per word	2.4
No. of distinct syllables	4,367 (Thai) 6,307 (English)
No. of distinct syllable phonetic-transcriptions	1,869
Avg. no. of homophones per syllable phonetic-transcription	2.3 (Thai) 3.4 (English)
Max. no. of homophones per syllable phonetic-transcription	16 (Thai) 38 (English)

Table 2. Some statistics of syllables extracted from the training set.

As seen from the Table 1 that there could be up to 38 candidates of textual syllables given a syllable phonetic transcription. To avoid the large search space of syllable combinations, only top-frequency syllables were included in the search space. Table 2 shows transliteration results regarding 4 measures defined in the NEWS 2010 shared task. Both experiments on English-to-Thai and Thai-to-English transliteration are non-standard tests as external letter-to-sound conversion tools are incorporated.

Measure	Eng-to-Thai	Thai-to-Eng
ACC in Top-1	0.247	0.093
Mean F-score	0.842	0.707
MRR	0.367	0.132
MAP_{ref}	0.247	0.093

Table 2. Transliteration results based on the NEWS 2010 measurement.

5 Analysis and Discussion

There are still some problematic issues regarding the transliteration format including hyphenation and case sensitivity in the test data. Ignoring both problems leads to 0.5% and 8.3% improvement on the English-to-Thai and Thai-to-English tests respectively. Figure 2 illustrates the distribution of test words and error words with respect to the word length in the unit of syllables. More than 80% of test words are either 2 or 3 syllables. It can be roughly seen that the ratio of error words over test words increases with respect to the length of words. This is by the fact that the whole word will be considered incorrect even if only a syllable in the word is wrongly transliterated. Out of 3,860 syllable units extracted from all error words, over 57% are correctly transliterated.

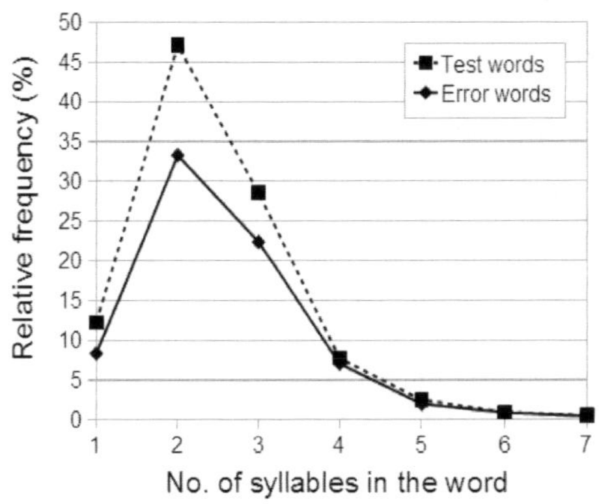

Figure 2. The distribution of test words and error words with respect to the word length.

Another issue largely affecting the system performance is as mentioned in the Section 2 that the Thai Royal Institute's guideline is somewhat flexible for multiple ways of transliteration. However, the corpus used to train and test currently provides only one way of transliteration. Improving the corpus to cope with such transliteration flexibility is needed. In developing the Thai-English NEWS 2010 transliteration corpus, some foreign names are difficult to pronounce even by linguists. Errors in the corpus are then unavoidable and required further improvement.

Many algorithms could be conducted to help improve the system accuracy. First, the current system uses only syllable n-gram probabilities to determine the best result without considering how likely the target syllable is close to the source syllable. For example, the source syllables "BIKE" and "BYTE" are transliterated to Thai as "ไบค์"and "ไบท์" respectively. Both Thai transliterated syllables are pronounced in the same way as /b-ai/. It can be seen that both syllables "BIKE" and "BYTE" can be linked to both "ไบค์"and "ไบท์". Selecting the best syllable takes only the syllable n-gram into account without considering its right transliteration. Direct mapping between source and target syllables could solve this problem but leads to another problem of unseen syllables. A better way is to incorporate in the search space another score representing the closeness of source and target syllables. As the example, the syllable "BIKE" is closer to "ไบค์" than to "ไบท์" as the letter "K" is normally pronounced like "ค" /k/, not "ท" /t^h/. We have tried incorporating such knowledge by introducing a syllable similarity score in the search space. Given a pair of source and target syllables, the syllable similarity score is the number of consonants having the same sound like "K" and "ค" divided by the total number of consonants in the syllable. Unfortunately, this approach could not yield any improvement currently as many syllable pairs happened to have the same similarity score. A better definition of the score will be conducted in the future work.

6 Conclusion

The Thai-English part of NEWS 2010 transliteration corpus was briefly described and its use in building a Thai-English machine transliteration system was reported. The system is based on transliteration of syllable units extracted from the whole input word. Within the space of candidate transliterated syllables, the best output was determined by using the statistical syllable n-gram model. There are many issues left for further improvement. First, possible transliterations of each word should be added to the corpus. Second, the system itself could be improved by e.g. incorporating better syllabification approaches, defining a better syllable similarity score, and comparing with other potential algorithms. Finally, as the Thai-to-English part of the transliteration corpus is actually back-transliteration of English-to-Thai, it is interesting to extend the corpus to cope with real-use Thai-to-English word pairs.

Acknowledgments

The authors would like to thank the Thai Royal Institute and Assoc. Prof. Dr. Wirote Aroonmanakun from the Faculty of Arts, Chulalongkorn University, who help supply parts of the Thai-English NEWS 2010 transliteration corpus.

References

Ausdang Thangthai, Chatchawarn Hansakunbuntheung, Rungkarn Siricharoenchai, and Chai Wutiwiwatchai. 2006. *Automatic syllable-pattern induction in statistical Thai text-to-phone transcription*, In Proc. of INTERSPEECH 2006, pp. 1344-1347.

Ausdang Thangthai, Chai Wutiwiwatchai, Anocha Ragchatjaroen, Sittipong Saychum. 2007. *A learning method for Thai phonetization of English words*, In Proc. of INTERSPEECH 2007, pp. 1777-1780.

Thatsanee Charoenporn, Ananlada Chotimongkol, and Virach Sornlertlamvanich. 1999. *Automatic romanization for Thai*, In Proc. of the Oriental COCOSDA 1999, Taipei, Taiwan.

Wirote Aroonmanakun and Wanchai Rivepiboon. 2004. *A unified model of Thai word segmentation and romanization*, In Proc. of the 18th Pacific Asia Conference on Language, Information and Computation, Tokyo, Japan, pp. 205-214.

Wirote Aroonmanakun. 2005. *A chunk-based n-gram English to Thai transliteration,* In Proc. of the 6th Symposium on Natural Language Processing, Chiang Rai, Thailand, pp. 37-42.

Xue Jiang, Le Sun, Dakun Zhang. 2009. *A syllable-based name transliteration system*, In Proc. of the 2009 Named Entities Workshop, ACL-IJCNLP 2009, pp. 96–99.

English to Indian Languages Machine Transliteration System at NEWS 2010

Amitava Das[1], Tanik Saikh[2], Tapabrata Mondal[3], Asif Ekbal[4], Sivaji Bandyopadhyay[5]
Department of Computer Science and Engineering[1,2,3,5]
Jadavpur University,
Kolkata-700032, India
amitava.santu@gmail.com[1], tanik4u@gmail.com[2], tapabratamondal@gmail.com[3], sivaji_cse_ju@yahoo.com[5]
Department of Computational Linguistics[4]
University of Heidelberg
Im Neuenheimer Feld 325
69120 Heidelberg, Germany
ekbal@cl.uni-heidelberg.de

Abstract

This paper reports about our work in the NEWS 2010 Shared Task on Transliteration Generation held as part of ACL 2010. One standard run and two non-standard runs were submitted for English to Hindi and Bengali transliteration while one standard and one non-standard run were submitted for Kannada and Tamil. The transliteration systems are based on Orthographic rules and Phoneme based technology. The system has been trained on the NEWS 2010 Shared Task on Transliteration Generation datasets. For the standard run, the system demonstrated mean F-Score values of 0.818 for Bengali, 0.714 for Hindi, 0.663 for Kannada and 0.563 for Tamil. The reported mean F-Score values of non-standard runs are 0.845 and 0.875 for Bengali non-standard run-1 and 2, 0.752 and 0.739 for Hindi non-standard run-1 and 2, 0.662 for Kannada non-standard run-1 and 0.760 for Tamil non-standard run-1. Non-Standard Run-2 for Bengali has achieved the highest score among all the submitted runs. Hindi Non-Standard Run-1 and Run-2 runs are ranked as the 5th and 6th among all submitted Runs.

1 Introduction

Transliteration is the method of translating one source language word into another target language by expressing and preserving the original pronunciation in their source language. Thus, the central problem in transliteration is predicting the pronunciation of the original word. Transliteration between two languages that use the same set of alphabets is trivial: the word is left as it is. However, for languages those use different alphabet sets the names must be transliterated or rendered in the target language alphabets. Transliteration of words is necessary in many applications, such as machine translation, corpus alignment, cross-language Information Retrieval, information extraction and automatic lexicon acquisition. In the literature, a number of transliteration algorithms are available involving English (Li et al., 2004; Vigra and Khudanpur, 2003; Goto et al., 2003), European languages (Marino et al., 2005) and some of the Asian languages, namely Chinese (Li et al., 2004; Vigra and Khudanpur, 2003), Japanese (Goto et al., 2003; Knight and Graehl, 1998), Korean (Jung et al., 2000) and Arabic (Al-Onaizan and Knight, 2002a; Al-Onaizan and Knight, 2002c). Recently, some works have been initiated involving Indian languages (Ekbal et al., 2006; Ekbal et al., 2007; Surana and Singh, 2008). The detailed report of our participation in NEWS 2009 could be found in (Das et al., 2009).

One standard run for Bengali (Bengali Standard Run: BSR), Hindi (Hindi Standard Run: HSR), Kannada (Kannada Standard Run: KSR) and Tamil (Tamil Standard Run: TSR) were submitted. Two non-standard runs for English to Hindi (Hindi Non-Standard Run 1 & 2: HNSR1 & HNSR2) and Bengali (Bengali Non-Standard Run 1 & 2: BNSR1 & BNSR1) transliteration were submitted. Only one non-standard run were submitted for Kannada (Kannada Non-Standard Run-1: KNSR1) and Tamil (Tamil Non-Standard Run-1: TNSR1).

Proceedings of the 2010 Named Entities Workshop, ACL 2010, pages 71–75,
Uppsala, Sweden, 16 July 2010.

2 Machine Transliteration Systems

Five different transliteration models have been proposed in the present report that can generate the transliteration in Indian language from an English word. The transliteration models are named as Trigram Model (Tri), Joint Source-Channel Model (JSC), Modified Joint Source-Channel Model (MJSC), Improved Modified Joint Source-Channel Model (IMJSC) and International Phonetic Alphabet Based Model (IPA). Among all the models the first four are categorized as orthographic model and the last one i.e. IPA based model is categorized as phoneme based model.

An English word is divided into Transliteration Units (TUs) with patterns C*V*, where C represents a consonant and V represents a vowel. The targeted words in Indian languages are divided into TUs with patterns C+M?, where C represents a consonant or a vowel or a conjunct and M represents the vowel modifier or matra. The TUs are the basic lexical units for machine transliteration. The system considers the English and Indian languages contextual information in the form of collocated TUs simultaneously to calculate the plausibility of transliteration from each English TU to various Indian languages candidate TUs and chooses the one with maximum probability. The system learns the mappings automatically from the bilingual NEWS 2010 training set being guided by linguistic features/knowledge. The output of the mapping process is a decision-list classifier with collocated TUs in the source language and their equivalent TUs in collocation in the target language along with the probability of each decision obtained from the training set. A Direct example base has been maintained that contains the bilingual training examples that do not result in the equal number of TUs in both the source and target sides during alignment. The Direct example base is checked first during machine transliteration of the input English word. If no match is obtained, the system uses direct orthographic mapping by identifying the equivalent TU in Indian languages for each English TU in the input and then placing the target language TUs in order. The IPA based model has been used for English dictionary words. Words which are not present in the dictionary are handled by other orthographic models as Trigram, JSC, MJSC and IMJSC.

The transliteration models are described below in which S and T denotes the source and the target words respectively:

3 Orthographic Transliteration models

The orthographic models work on the idea of TUs from both source and target languages. The orthographic models used in the present system are described below. For transliteration, P(*T*), i.e., the probability of transliteration in the target language, is calculated from a English-Indian languages bilingual database If, *T* is not found in the dictionary, then a very small value is assigned to P(*T*). These models have been desribed in details in Ekbal et al. (2007).

3.1 Trigram

This is basically the Trigram model where the previous and the next source TUs are considered as the context.

$$P(S \mid T) = \prod_{k=1}^{K} P(<s,t>_k \mid s_{k-1}, s_{k+1})$$

$$S \rightarrow T(S) = \arg\max_T \{P(T) \times P(S \mid T)\}$$

3.2 Joint Source-Channel Model (JSC)

This is essentially the Joint Source-Channel model (Hazhiou et al., 2004) where the previous TUs with reference to the current TUs in both the source (s) and the target sides (t) are considered as the context.

$$P(S \mid T) = \prod_{k=1}^{K} P(<s,t>_k \mid <s,t>_{k-1})$$

$$S \rightarrow T(S) = \arg\max_T \{P(T) \times P(S \mid T)\}$$

3.3 Modified Joint Source-Channel Model (MJSC)

In this model, the previous and the next TUs in the source and the previous target TU are considered as the context. This is the Modified Joint Source-Channel model.

$$P(S \mid T) = \prod_{k=1}^{K} P(<s,t>_k \mid <s,t>_{k-1}, s_{k+1})$$

$$S \rightarrow T(S) = \arg\max_T \{P(T) \times P(S \mid T)\}$$

3.4 Improved Modified Joint Source-Channel Model (IMJSC)

In this model, the previous two and the next TUs in the source and the previous target TU are considered as the context. This is the Improved Modified Joint Source-Channel model.

$$P(S \mid T) = \prod_{k=1}^{K} P(< s,t >_k \mid s_{k+1} < s,t >_{k-1,}\ s_{k+1})$$

$$S \rightarrow T(S) = \arg\max_T \{P(T) \times P(S \mid T)\}$$

4 International Phonetic Alphabet (IPA) Model

The NEWS 2010 Shared Task on Transliteration Generation challenge addresses general domain transliteration problem rather than named entity transliteration. Due to large number of dictionary words as reported in Table 1 in NEWS 2010 data set a phoneme based transliteration algorithm has been devised.

	Train	Dev	Test
Bengali	7.77%	5.14%	6.46%
Hindi	27.82%	15.80%	3.7%
Kannada	27.60%	14.63%	4.4%
Tamil	27.87%	17.31%	3.0%

Table 1: Statistics of Dictionary Words

The International Phonetic Alphabet (IPA) is a system of representing phonetic notations based primarily on the Latin alphabet and devised by the International Phonetic Association as a standardized representation of the sounds of spoken language. The machine-readable Carnegie Mellon Pronouncing Dictionary [1] has been used as an external resource to capture source language IPA structure. The dictionary contains over 125,000 words and their transcriptions with mappings from words to their pronunciations in the given phoneme set. The current phoneme set contains 39 distinct phonemes. As there is no such parallel IPA dictionary available for Indian languages, English IPA structures have been mapped to TUs in Indian languages during training. An example of such mapping between phonemes and TUs are shown in Table 3, for which the vowels may carry lexical stress as reported in Table 2. This phone set is based on the ARPAbet[2] symbol set developed for speech recognition uses.

Representation	Stress level
0	No
1	Primary
2	Secondary

Table 2: Stress Level on Vowel

A pre-processing module checks whether a targeted source English word is a valid dictionary word or not. The dictionary words are then handled by phoneme based transliteration module.

Phoneme	Example	Translation	TUs
AA	odd	AA0-D	অ-ড
AH	hut	HH0-AH-T	হা-ট
D	dee	D-IY1	ড-ী

Table 3: Phoneme Map Patterns of English Words and TUs

In the target side we use our TU segregation logic to get phoneme wise transliteration pattern. We present this problem as a sequence labelling problem, because transliteration pattern changes depending upon the contextual phonemes in source side and TUs in the target side. We use a standard machine learning based sequence labeller Conditional Random Field (CRF)[3] here.

IPA based model increased the performance for Bengali, Hindi and Tamil languages as reported in Section 6. The performance has decreased for Kannada.

5 Ranking

The ranking among the transliterated outputs follow the order reported in Table 4: The ranking decision is based on the experiments as described in (Ekbal et al., 2006) and additionally based on the experiments on NEWS 2010 development dataset.

Word Type	Ranking Order				
	1	2	3	4	5
Dictionary	IPA	IMJSC	MJSC	JSC	Tri
Non-Dictionary	IMJSC	MJSC	JSC	Tri	-

Table 4: Phoneme Patterns of English Words

In BSR, HSR, KSR and TSR the orthographic TU based models such as: IMJSC, MJSC, JSC and Tri have been used only trained by NEWS 2010 dataset. In BNSR1 and HNSR1 all the orthographic models have been trained with additional census dataset as described in Section 6. In case of BNSR2, HNSR2, KNSR1 and TNSR1 the output of the IPA based model has been added with highest priority. As no census data is available for Kannada and Tamil therefore there is only one Non-Standard Run was submitted for these two languages only with the output of IPA based model along with the output of Standard Run.

6 Experimental Results

We have trained our transliteration models using the NEWS 2010 datasets obtained from the NEWS 2010 Machine Transliteration Shared Task (Li et al., 2010). A brief statistics of the

[1] www.speech.cs.cmu.edu/cgi-bin/cmudict

[2] http://en.wikipedia.org/wiki/Arpabet

[3] http://crfpp.sourceforge.net

datasets are presented in Table 5. During training, we have split multi-words into collections of single word transliterations. It was observed that the number of tokens in the source and target sides mismatched in various multi-words and these cases were not considered further. Following are some examples:

Paris Charles de Gaulle पेरिस रॉसे चार्ल्स डे ग्यूले

Suven Life Scie ಸುವೆನ್ ಲೈಫ್ ಸೈನ್ಸ್

Delta Air Lines டெல்டா ஏர்லைன்ஸ்

In the training set, some multi-words were partly translated and not transliterated. Such examples were dropped from the training set. In the following example the English word "National" is being translated in the target as "राष्ट्रीय".

Australian National University ऑस्ट्रेलियन राष्ट्रीय यूनिवर्सिटी

Set	Number of examples			
	Bng	Hnd	Kn	Tm
Training	11938	9975	7990	7974
Development	992	1974	1968	1987
Test	991	1000	1000	1000

Table 5: Statistics of Dataset

There is less number of known examples in the NEWS 2010 test set from training set. The exact figure is reported in the Table 6.

	Matches with training
Bengali	14.73%
Hindi	0.2%
Kannada	0.0%
Tamil	0.0%

Table 6: Statistics of Dataset

If the outputs of any two transliteration models are same for any word then only one output are provided for that particular word. Evaluation results of the final system are shown in Table 7 for Bengali, Table 8 for Hindi, Table 9 for Kannada and Table 10 for Tamil.

Parameters	Accuracy		
	BSR	BNSR1	BNSR2
Accuracy in top-1	0.232	0.369	0.430
Mean F-score	0.818	0.845	0.875
Mean Reciprocal Rank (MRR)	0.325	0.451	0.526
Mean Average Precision $(MAP)_{ref}$	0.232	0.369	0.430

Table 7: Results on Bengali Test Set

Parameters	Accuracy		
	HSR	HNSR1	HNSR2
Accuracy in top-1	0.150	0.254	0.170
Mean F-score	0.714	0.752	0.739
Mean Reciprocal Rank (MRR)	0.308	0.369	0.314
Mean Average Precision $(MAP)_{ref}$	0.150	0.254	0.170

Table 8: Results on Hindi Test Set

Parameters	Accuracy	
	KSR	KNSR1
Accuracy in top-1	0.056	0.055
Mean F-score	0.663	0.662
Mean Reciprocal Rank (MRR)	0.112	0.169
Mean Average Precision $(MAP)_{ref}$	0.056	0.055

Table 9: Results on Kannada Test Set

Parameters	Accuracy	
	TSR	TNSR1
Accuracy in top-1	0.013	0.082
Mean F-score	0.563	0.760
Mean Reciprocal Rank (MRR)	0.121	0.142
Mean Average Precision $(MAP)_{ref}$	0.013	0.082

Table 10: Results on Tamil Test Set

The additional dataset used for the non-standard runs is mainly the census data consisting of only Indian person names that have been collected from the web[4]. In the BNSR1 and HNSR1 we have used an English-Bengali/Hindi bilingual census example dataset. English-Hindi set consist of 961,890 examples and English-Bengali set consist of 582984 examples. This database contains the frequency of the corresponding English-Bengali/Hindi name pair.

7 Conclusion

This paper reports about our works as part of the NEWS 2010 Shared Task on Transliteration Generation. We have used both the orthographic and phoneme based transliteration modules for the present task. As our all previous efforts was for named entity transliteration. The Transliteration Generation challenge addresses general domain transliteration problem rather than named entity transliteration. To handle general transliteration problem we proposed a IPA based methodology.

[4]http://www.eci.gov.in/DevForum/Fullname.asp

References

A. Das, A. Ekbal, Tapabrata Mondal and S. Bandyopadhyay. English to Hindi Machine Transliteration at NEWS 2009. In Proceedings of the NEWS 2009, In Proceeding of ACL-IJCNLP 2009, August 7th, 2009, Singapore.

Al-Onaizan, Y. and Knight, K. 2002a. Named Entity Translation: Extended Abstract. In Proceedings of the Human Language Technology Conference, 122– 124.

Al-Onaizan, Y. and Knight, K. 2002b. Translating Named Entities using Monolingual and Bilingual Resources. In Proceedings of the 40th Annual Meeting of the ACL, 400–408, USA.

Ekbal, A. Naskar, S. and Bandyopadhyay, S. 2007. Named Entity Transliteration. International Journal of Computer Processing of Oriental Languages (IJCPOL), Volume (20:4), 289-310, World Scientific Publishing Company, Singapore.

Ekbal, A., Naskar, S. and Bandyopadhyay, S. 2006. A Modified Joint Source Channel Model for Transliteration. In Proceedings of the COLING-ACL 2006, 191-198, Australia.

Goto, I., Kato, N., Uratani, N. and Ehara, T. 2003. Transliteration Considering Context Information based on the Maximum Entropy Method. In Proceeding of the MT-Summit IX, 125–132, New Orleans, USA.

Jung, Sung Young , Sung Lim Hong and Eunok Paek. 2000. An English to Korean Transliteration Model of Extended Markov Window. In Proceedings of International Conference on Computational Linguistics (COLING 2000), 383-389.

Knight, K. and Graehl, J. 1998. Machine Transliteration, Computational Linguistics, Volume (24:4), 599–612.

Kumaran, A. and Tobias Kellner. 2007. A generic framework for machine transliteration. In Proc. of the 30th SIGIR.

Li, Haizhou, A Kumaran, Min Zhang and Vladimir Pervouchine. 2010. Whitepaper: NEWS 2010 Shared Task on Transliteration Generation. In the ACL 2010 Named Entities Workshop (NEWS-2010), Uppsala, Sweden, Association for Computational Linguistics, July 2010.

Li, Haizhou, Min Zhang and Su Jian. 2004. A Joint Source-Channel Model for Machine Transliteration. In Proceedings of the 42nd Annual Meeting of the ACL, 159-166. Spain.

Marino, J. B., R. Banchs, J. M. Crego, A. de Gispert, P. Lambert, J. A. Fonollosa and M. Ruiz. 2005. Bilingual n-gram Statistical Machine Translation. In Proceedings of the MT-Summit X, 275–282.

Surana, Harshit, and Singh, Anil Kumar. 2008. A More Discerning and Adaptable Multilingual Transliteration Mechanism for Indian Languages. In Proceedings of the 3rd International Joint Conference on Natural Language Processing (IJCNLP-08), 64-71, India.

Vigra, Paola and Khudanpur, S. 2003. Transliteration of Proper Names in Cross-Lingual Information Retrieval. In Proceedings of the ACL 2003 Workshop on Multilingual and Mixed-Language Named Entity Recognition, 57–60.

Mining Transliterations from Wikipedia using Pair HMMs

Peter Nabende
Alfa-Informatica, University of Groningen
The Netherlands
p.nabende@rug.nl

Abstract

This paper describes the use of a pair Hidden Markov Model (pair HMM) system in mining transliteration pairs from noisy Wikipedia data. A pair HMM variant that uses nine transition parameters, and emission parameters associated with single character mappings between source and target language alphabets is identified and used in estimating transliteration similarity. The system resulted in a *precision* of 78% and *recall* of 83% when evaluated on a random selection of English-Russian Wikipedia topics.

1 Introduction

The transliteration mining task as defined in the NEWS 2010 White paper (Kumaran et al., 2010) required identifying single word transliteration pairs from a set of candidate transliteration pairs. In the case of Wikipedia data, we have a collection of corresponding source and target language topics that can be used for extracting candidate transliterations. We apply a pair HMM edit-distance based method to obtain transliteration similarity estimates. The similarity estimates for a given set of source and target language words are then compared with the aim of identifying potential transliteration pairs. Generally, the pair HMM method uses the notion of transforming a source string to a target string through a series of edit operations. The three edit operations that we consider for use in transliteration similarity estimation include: *substitution*, *insertion*, and *deletion*. These edit operations are represented as hidden states of a pair HMM. Depending on the source and target language alphabets, it is possible to design or use a specific pair HMM algorithm for estimating paired character emission parameters in the edit operation states, and transition parameters for a given design of transitions between the pair HMM's states. Before applying the pair HMM method, we use external datasets to identify a pair HMM variant that we consider as suitable for application to transliteration similarity estimation. We then use the shared task datasets to train the selected pair HMM variant, and finally apply an algorithm that is specific to the trained pair HMM for computing transliteration similarity estimates. In section 2, we discuss transliteration similarity estimation with regard to applying the pair HMM method; section 3 describes the experimental setup and results; section 4 concludes the paper with pointers to future work.

2 Transliteration Similarity Estimation using Pair HMMs

To describe the transliteration similarity estimation process, consider examples of corresponding English (as *source* language) and Russian (as *target* language) Wikipedia topics as shown in Table 1. Across languages, Wikipedia topics are written in different ways and all words in a topic could be important for mining transliterations. One main step in the transliteration mining task is to identify a set of words in each topic for consideration as candidate transliterations. As seen in Table 1, it is very likely that some words will not be selected as

id	**English topic**	**Russian topic**
1	Johnston Atoll	Джонстон (атолл)
2	Oleksandr Palyanytya	Паляница, Александр Витальевич
3	Ministers for Foreign Affairs of Luxembourg	Категория:Министры иностранных дел Люксембурга
	...	...

Table 1: Example of corresponding English Russian Wikipedia topics

Proceedings of the 2010 Named Entities Workshop, ACL 2010, pages 76–80,
Uppsala, Sweden, 16 July 2010. ©2010 Association for Computational Linguistics

candidate transliterations depending on the criteria for selection. For example, if a criterion is such that we consider only words starting with uppercase characters for English and Russian datasets, then the Russian word 'атолл' in the topic pair 1 in Table 1 will not be used as a candidate transliteration and that in turn makes the system loose the likely pair of 'Atoll, атолл'. After extracting candidate transliterations, the approach we use in this paper takes each candidate word on the source language side and determines a transliteration estimate with each candidate word on the target language side. Consider the example for topic id 1 in Table 1 where we expect to have 'Johnston' and 'Atoll' as candidate source language transliterations, and 'Джонстон' and 'атолл' as candidate target language transliterations. The method used is expected to compare 'Johnston' against 'Джонстон' and 'атолл', and then compare 'Atoll' to the Russian candidate transliterations. We expect the output to be 'Johston, Джонстон' and 'Atoll, атолл' as the most likely single word transliterations from topic pair 1 after sorting out all the four transliteration similarity estimates in this particular case. We employ the pair HMM approach to estimate transliteration similarity for candidate source-target language words.

A pair HMM has an emission state or states that generate two observation sequences instead of one observation sequence as is the case in standard HMMs. Pair HMMs originate from work in Biological sequence analysis (Durbin et al., 1998; Rivas and Eddy, 2001) from which variants were created and successfully applied in cognate identification (Mackay and Kondrak, 2005), Dutch dialect comparison (Wieling et al., 2007), transliteration identification (Nabende et al., 2010), and transliteration generation (Nabende, 2009). As mentioned earlier, we have first, tested two pair HMM variants on manually verified English-Russian datasets which we obtain from the previous shared task on machine transliteration (NEWS 2009) (Kumaran and Kellner, 2007). This preliminary test is aimed at determining the effect of pair HMM parameter changes on the quality of the transliteration similarity estimates. For the first pair HMM variant, no transitions are modeled between edit states; we only use transtion parameters associated with transiting from a start state to each of the edit operation states, and from each of the edit operation states to an end state. The

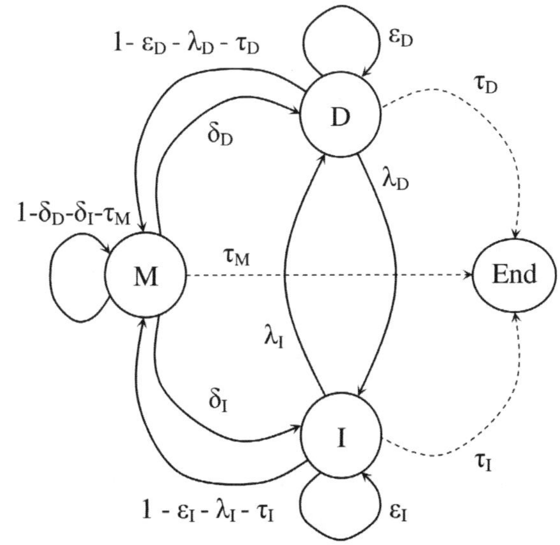

Figure 1: Pair HMM with nine distinct transition parameters. Emission parameters are specified with emitting states and their size is dependent on the characters used in the source and target languages

second pair HMM variant uses nine distinct transition parameters between the pair HMM's states as shown in Figure 1. The node M in Figure 1 represents the substitution state in which emission parameters encode relationships between each of the source and target language characters. D denotes the deletion state where emission parameters specify relationships between source language characters and a target language gap. I denotes the insertion state where emission parameters encode relationships between target language characters and a source language gap. Starting parameters for the pair HMM in Figure 1 are assoicated with transiting from the M state to one of the edit operation states including transiting back to M.

The pair HMM parameters are estimated using the well-known Baum-Welch Expectation Maximization (EM) algorithm (Baum et al., 1970). For each pair HMM variant, the training algorithm starts with a uniform distribution for substitution, deletion, insertion, and transition parameters, and iterates through the data until a local maximum.

A method referred to as *stratified ten fold cross validation* (Olson and Delen, 2008) is used to evaluate the two pair HMM variants. In each fold, 7056 pairs of English-Russian names from the previous shared task on machine transliteration (Ku-

Pair HMM Model		CVA	CVMRR
phmm00edtrans	Viterbi	0.788	0.809
	Forward	0.927	0.954
phmm09edtrans	Viterbi	0.943	0.952
	Forward	**0.987**	**0.991**

Table 2: CVA and CVMRR results two pair HMM variants on a preliminary transliteration identificatio experiment. phmm00edtrans is the pair HMM variant with no transition parameters between the edit states while phmm09edtrans is the pair HMM variant with nine distinct transition parameters.

maran and Kellner, 2007) are used for training and 784 name pairs for testing. The Cross Validation Accuracy (CVA) and Cross Validation Mean Reciprocal Rank (CVMRR) results obtained from applying the Forward and Viterbi algorithms of the two pair HMM variants on this particular dataset are shown in Table 2.

The CVA and CVMRR values in Table 2 suggest that it is necessary to model for transition parameters when using pair HMMs for transliteration similarity estimation. Table 2 also suggests that it is better to use the Forward algorithm for a given pair HMM variant. Based on the results in Table 2, the pair HMM variant illustrated in Figure 1 is chosen for application in estimating transliteration similarity for the mining task.

3 Experimental setup and Results

To simplify the analysis of the source and target strings, the pair HMM system requires unique whole number representations for each character in the source and target language data. This is not suitable for all the different types of writing systems. In this paper, we look at only the English and Russian languages where many characters are associated with a phonemic alphabet and where numbered representations are hardly expected to contribute to errors from loss of information inherent in the original orthography. A preliminary run on Chinese-English[1] datasets from the previous shared task on machine transliteration (NEWS 2009) resulted in an *accuracy* of 0.213 and *MRR* of 0.327 using the pair HMM variant in Figure 1. In the following subsection we discuss some data preprocessing steps on the English-Russian Wikipedia dataset.

3.1 English and Russian candidate transliteration extraction

The English-Russian Wikipedia dataset that was provided for the transliteration mining task is very noisy meaning that it has various types of other entities in addition to words for each language's orthography. A first step in simplifying the transliteration mining process was to remove any unnecessary entities.

We observed the overlap of writing systems in both the English and Russian Wikipedia datasets. We therefore made sure that there is no topic where the same writing system is used in both the English and Russian data. Any strings that contain characters that are not associated with the writing systems for English and Russian were also removed.

We also observed the presence of many temporal and numerical expressions that are not necessary on both the English and Russian Wikipedia datasets. We applied different sets of rules to remove such expressions while leaving any necessary words.

Using knowledge about the initial formatting of strings in both the English and Russian data, a set of rules was applied to split most of the strings based on different characters. For example almost all strings in the English side had the underscore '_' character as a string separator. We also removed characters such as: colons, semi-colons, commas, question marks, exclamation marks, dashes, hyphens, forward and back slashes, mathematical operator symbols, currency symbols, etc. Some strings were also split based on string patterns, for example where different words are joined into one string and it was easy to identify that the uppercase character for each word still remained in the combined string just like when it is alone. We also removed many abbreviations and titles in the datasets that were not necessary for analysis during the transliteration mining process.

After selecting candidate words based on most of the criteria above, we determine all characters in our extracted candidate transliteration data and compare against those in the shared task's seed data (Kumaran et al., 2010) with the aim of finding all characters that are missing in the seed data. Matching transliteration pairs with the the miss-

[1] In this case Chinese is the source language while English is the target language

ing characters are then hand picked from the candidate words dataset and added to the seed data before training the pair HMM variant that is selected from the previous section. The process for identifying missing characters and words that have them is carried out seperately for each language. However, a matching word in the other language is identified to constitute a transliteration pair that can be added to the seed dataset. For the English-Russian dataset, we use 142 transliteration pairs in addition to the 1000 transliteration pairs in the initial seed data. We hence apply the Baum-Welch algorithm for the selected pair HMM specification from section 2 on a total of 1142 transliteration pairs. The algorithm performed 182 iterations before converging for this particular dataset.

3.2 Results

To obtain transliteration similarity measures, we apply the Forward algorithm of the trained pair HMM from section 3.1 to all the remaining Wikipedia topics. For each word in an English topic, the algorithm computes transliteration similarity estimates for all words in the Russian topic. After observing transliteration similarity estimates for a subset of candidate transliteration words, we specify a single threshold value (*th*) and use it for identifying potential transliteration pairs. A threshold value of 1×10^{-13} was chosen after observing that many of the pairs that had a similarity estimate above this threshold were indeed transliteration pairs. Therefore, a pair of words was taken as a potential transliteration pair only when its transliteration estimate (*tr_sim*) was such that $tr\_sim > th$. This resulted in a total of 299389 potential English-Russian transliteration pairs. This collection of potential transliteration pairs has been evaluated using a random set of corresponding English and Russian Wikipedia topics as specified in the NEWS 2010 White paper for the transliteration mining task (Kumaran et al., 2010). Table 3 shows the *precision*, *recall*, and *f-score* results[2] that were obtained after applying the Forward algorithm for the pair HMM of Figure 1.

Despite using the pair HMM method with its basic probabilistic one-to-one mapping for each of the source target character representations, the result in Table 3 suggests a promising application of pair HMMs in mining transliterations from Wikipedia.

[2]The numbers in Table 3 were obtained from a post evaluation after correcting a number of processing errors in the pair HMM transliteration mining system. The errors initially led to relatively lower values associated with the measures in this Table. The values in this Table are therefore not part of the initial shared task results

Model	***precision***	***recall***	***f-score***
phmm09edtrans	0.780	0.834	0.806

Table 3: Evaluation results for the Pair HMM of Figure 1 on a random selection of 1000 corresponding English Russian Wikipedia topics.

4 Conclusions and Future Work

We have described the application of Pair HMMs to mining transliterations from Wikipedia. The transliteration mining evaluation results suggest a valuable application of Pair HMMs to mining transliterations. Currently, the pair HMM system is considered to be best applicable to languages whose writing system mostly uses a phonemic alphabet. Although an experimental test run was done for Chinese-English data, a conclusion about the general applicability of the pair HMM necessitates additional tests using other language pairs such as Hindi and Tamil which were also part of the shared task.

As future work, we would like to investigate the performance of Pair HMMs on additional writing systems. This may require additional modifications to a pair HMM system to minimize on input formatting errors for other types of writing systems. It is also necessary to determine the transliteration mining performance of pair HMMs when more tolerant criteria are used on the noisy Wikipedia data. Currently, the pair HMM is applied in its most basic form, that is, no complex modifications have been implemented for example modeling for context in source and target language words, and other factors that may affect the quality of a transliteration similarity estimate; it should be interesting to investigate perfromance of complex pair HMM variants in transliteration mining.

Acknowledgments

Research in this paper is funded through a second NPT (Uganda) Project.

References

A Kumaran, Mitesh Khapra, and Haizhou Li. 2010. Whitepaper on NEWS 2010 Shared Task on

Transliteration Mining.

A Kumaran and Tobias Kellner. 2007. A Generic Framework for Machine Transliteration. *Proceedings of the* 30th *Annual International ACM SIGIR Conference on Research and Development in Information Retrieval (SIGIR 2007)*, pp 721–722, Amsterdam, The Netherlands.

Leonard E. Baum, Ted Petrie, George Soules, and Norman Weiss. 1970. A Maximization Technique Occurring in the Statistical Analysis of Probabilistic Functions of Markov Chains. *Annals of Mathematical Statistics*, 41(1):164–171.

David L. Olson and Dursun Delen. 2008. *Advanced Data Mining Techniques*. Springer.

Elena Rivas and Sean R. Eddy. 2001. Noncoding RNA Gene Detection using Comparative Sequence Analysis. *BMC Bioinformatics 2001*, 2:8.

Martijn Wieling, Therese Leinonen, and John Nerbonne. 2007. Inducing Sound Segment Differences using Pair Hidden Markov Models. In John Nerbonne, Mark Ellison, and Grzegorz Kondrak (eds.) *Computing Historical Phonology:* 9th *Meeting of the ACL Special Interest Group for Computational Morphology and Phonology Workshop*, pp 48–56, Prague, Czech Republic.

Peter Nabende. 2009. Transliteration System using Pair HMMs with Weighted FSTs. Proceedings of the Named Entities Workshop, NEWS'09, pp 100–103, Suntec, Singapore.

Peter Nabende, Jorg Tiedemann, and John Nerbonne. 2010. Pair Hidden Markov Model for Named Entity Matching. In Tarek Sobh (ed.) *Innovations and Advances in Computer Sciences and Engineering*, pp 497–502, Springer, Heidelberg.

Richard Durbin, Sean R. Eddy, Anders Krogh, Graeme Mitchison. 1998. *Biological Sequence Analysis: Probabilistic Models of Proteins and Nucleic Acids.* Cambridge University Press, Cambridge, UK.

Wesley Mackay and Grzegorz Kondrak. 2005. Computing Word Similarity and Identifying Cognates with Pair Hidden Markov Models. *Proceedings of the ninth Conference on Computational Natural Language Learning (CoNLL 2005)*, pp 40–47, Ann Arbor, Michigan.

Phrase-based Transliteration System with Simple Heuristics

Avinesh PVS and **Ankur Parikh**
IIIT Hyderabad
Language Technologies Research Centre
{avinesh,shaileshkumar.parikh}@students.iiit.ac.in

Abstract

This paper presents modeling of transliteration as a phrase-based machine translation system. We used a popular phrase-based machine translation system for English-Hindi machine transliteration. We have achieved an accuracy of 38.1% on the test set. We used some basic rules to modulate the existing phrased-based transliteration system. Our experiments show that phrase-based machine translation systems can be adopted by modulating the system to fit the transliteration problem.

1 Introduction

Transliteration is the practice of converting a text from one writing system into another in a systematic way. Most significantly it is used in Machine Translation (MT) systems, Information Retrieval systems where a large portion of unknown words (out of vocabulary) are observed. Named entities (NE), technical words, borrowed words and loan words constitute the majority of the unknown words. So, transliteration can also be termed as the process of obtaining the phonetic translation of names across various languages (Shishtla et al., 2009). Transcribing the words from one language to another without the help of bilingual dictionary is a challenging task.

Previous work in transliteration include (Surana and Singh, 2009) who propose a transliteration system using two different approaches of transliterating the named entities based on their origin. (Sherif and Kondrak, 2007) use the Viterbi based monotone search algorithm for searching possible candidate sub-string transliterations. (Malik, 2006) solved some special cases of transliteration for Punjabi using a set of transliteration rules.

In the recent years Statistical Machine Translation (SMT) systems (Brown et al., 1990), (Yamada and Knight, 2001), (Chiang, 2005), (Charniak et al., 2003) have been in focus. It is easy to develop a MT system for a new pair of language using an existing SMT system and a parallel corpora. It isn't a surprise to see SMT being attractive in terms of less human labour as compared to other traditional systems. These SMT systems have also become popular in the transliteration field (Finch and Sumita, 2008), (Finch and Sumita, 2009), (Rama and Gali, 2009). (Finch and Sumita, 2008) use a bi-directional decoder whereas (Finch and Sumita, 2009) use a machine translation system comprising of two phrase-based decoders. The first decoder generated from first token of the target to the last. The second decoder generated the target from last to first. (Rama and Gali, 2009) modeled the phrase-based SMT system using minimum error rate training (MERT) for learning model weights.

In this paper we present a phrase-based machine transliteration technique with simple heuristics for transliterating named entities of English-Hindi pair using small amount of training and development data. The structure of our paper is as follows. Section 2 describes the modeling of translation problem to transliteration. Modeling of the parameters and the heuristics are presented in Section 3. Section 4 and 5 we give a brief description about the data-set and error-analysis. Finally we conclude in Section 6.

2 Modeling Approach

Transliteration can be viewed as a task of character-level machine translation process. Both the problems involve transformation of source tokens in one language to target tokens in another language.
Transliteration differs from machine translation in two ways (Finch and Sumita, 2009):

1. Reordering of the target tokens is generally

Proceedings of the 2010 Named Entities Workshop, ACL 2010, pages 81–84,
Uppsala, Sweden, 16 July 2010.

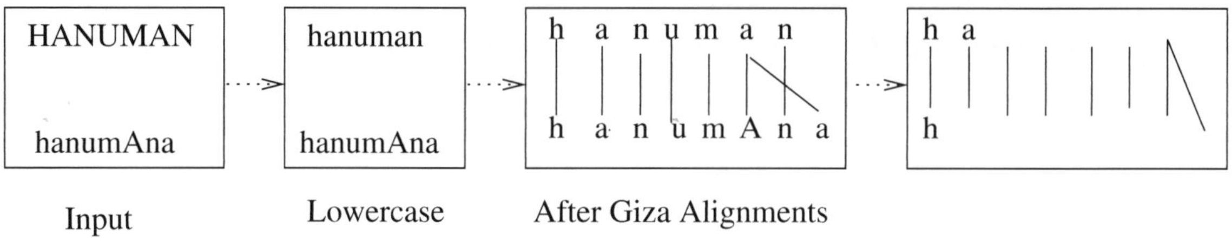

Figure 1: English-Hindi transliteration example through our system(To represent Hindi font roman script is used)

abscent in transliteration.

2. Number of token types (vocabulary) in the data is relatively very less and finite as compared to the translation data.

The work in this paper is related to the work of (Rama and Gali, 2009) who also use SMT directly to transliterate. We can model the translation problem to transliteration problem by replacing words with characters. So instead of sentences let us assume a given word is represented as a sequence of characters of the source language $F=f_1,f_2,f_3,...f_n$ which needs to be transcribed as a sequence of characters in the target language $E=e_1,e_2,e_3,...e_m$. [1]

The best possible target language sequence of characters among the possible candidate characters can be represented as:

$$E_{best} = \text{Argmax}_E \; P(E|F)$$

The above equation can be represented in terms of noisy channel model using Bayes Rule:

$$E_{best} = \text{Argmax}_E \; P(F|E) * P(E)$$

Here P(F|E) represents the transcription model where as P(E) represents the language model i.e the character n-gram of the target language. The above equation returns the best possible output sequence of characters for the given sequence of characters F.

We used some heuristics on top of Moses tool kit, which is a publicly available tool provided by (Hoang et al., 2007).

[1] F,E is used to name source and target language sequences as used in conventional machine translation notations

3 Method

3.1 Pre-processing

Firstly the data on the English side is converted to lowercase to reduce data sparsity. Each character of the words in the training and development data are separated with spaces. We also came across multi-word sequences which posed a challenge for our approach. We segmented the multi-words into separate words, such that they would be transliterated as different words.

3.2 Alignment and Post Processing

Parallel word lists are given to GIZA++ for character alignments. We observed *grow-diag-final-and* as the best alignment heuristic. From the differences mentioned above between transliteration and translation we came up with some simple heuristics to do post processing on the GIZA++ alignments.

1. As reordering of the target tokens is not allowed in transliteration. Crossing of the arcs during the alignments are removed.
   As shown in Fig 1. above.
   The second A $\rightarrow$ a is removed as it was crossing the arcs.

2. If the target character is aligned to *NULL* character on the source side then the *NULL* is removed, and the target language character is aligned to the source character aligned to previous target character.

   From Fig 1.

   n $\rightarrow$ n
   NULL $\rightarrow$ a

   to

n → na

3.3 Training and Parameter Tuning

The language models and translation models were built on the combined training and the development data. But the learning of log-linear weights during the MERT step is done using development data separately. It is obvious that the system would perform better if it was trained on the combined data. 8-gram language model and a maximum phrase length of 7 is used during training.

The transliteration systems were modeled using the minimum error rate training procedure introduced by (Och, 2003). We used BLUE score as a evaluation metric for our convenience during tuning. BLUE score is commonly used to evaluate machine translation systems and it is a function of geometric mean of n-gram precision. It was observed that improvement of the BLUE score also showed improvements in ACC.

4 Experiments and Results

Training data of 9975 words is used to build the system models, while the development data of 1974 words is used for tuning the log-linear weights for the translation engines. Our accuracies on test-data are reported in Table 1. Due to time constraints we couldn't focus on multiple correct answers in the training data, we picked just the first one for our training. Some of the translation features like word penalty, phrase penalty, reorder parameters don't play any role in transliteration process hence we didn't include them.

Before the release of the test-data we tested the system without tuning i.e. default weights were used on the development data. Later once the test-data was released the system was tuned on the development data to model the weights. We evaluated our system on ACC which accounts for Word Accuracy for top-1, Mean F-score, Mean Reciprocal Rank (MRR).

Table 1: Evaluation on Test Data

Measure	Result
ACC	0.381
Mean F-score	0.860
MRR	0.403
MAP_{ref}	0.381

5 Error Analysis

From the reference corpora we examined that majority of the errors were due to foreign origin words. As the phonetic transcription of these words is different from the other words. We also observed from error analysis that the correct target sequence of characters were occurring at lower rank in the 20-best list. We would like to see how different ranking mechanisms like SVM re-rank etc would help in boosting the correct accuracies of the system.

6 Conclusion

In this paper we show that the usage of some heuristics on top of popular phrase-based machine translation works well for the task of transliteration. First the source and target characters are aligned using GIZA++. Then some heuristics are used to modify the alignments. These modified alignments are used during estimation of the weights during minimum error rate training (MERT). Finally the Hindi characters are decoded using the beam-search based decoder. We also produced the 20-best outputs using the n-best list provided by moses toolkit. It is very interesting to see how simple heuristics helped in performing better than other systems.

References

Peter F. Brown, John Cocke, Stephen A. Della Pietra, Vincent J. Della Pietra, Fredrick Jelinek, John D. Lafferty, Robert L. Mercer, and Paul S. Roossin. 1990. A statistical approach to machine translation. *COMPUTATIONAL LINGUISTICS*, 16(2):79–85.

Eugene Charniak, Kevin Knight, and Kenji Yamada. 2003. Syntax-based language models for statistical machine translation. In *MT Summit IX. Intl. Assoc. for Machine Translation*.

David Chiang. 2005. A hierarchical phrase-based model for statistical machine translation. In *In ACL*, pages 263–270.

Andrew Finch and Eiichiro Sumita. 2008. Phrase-based machine transliteration. In *In Proc. 3rd Int'l. Joint Conf NLP, volume 1*.

Andrew Finch and Eiichiro Sumita. 2009. Transliteration by bidirectional statistical machine translation. In *NEWS '09: Proceedings of the 2009 Named Entities Workshop: Shared Task on Transliteration*, pages 52–56, Morristown, NJ, USA. Association for Computational Linguistics.

Hieu Hoang, Alexandra Birch, Chris Callison-burch, Richard Zens, Rwth Aachen, Alexandra Constantin, Marcello Federico, Nicola Bertoldi, Chris Dyer, Brooke Cowan, Wade Shen, Christine Moran, and Ondej Bojar. 2007. Moses: Open source toolkit for statistical machine translation. pages 177–180.

M. G. Abbas Malik. 2006. Punjabi machine transliteration. In *ACL-44: Proceedings of the 21st International Conference on Computational Linguistics and the 44th annual meeting of the Association for Computational Linguistics*, pages 1137–1144, Morristown, NJ, USA. Association for Computational Linguistics.

Franz Josef Och. 2003. Minimum error rate training in statistical machine translation. In *ACL '03: Proceedings of the 41st Annual Meeting on Association for Computational Linguistics*, pages 160–167, Morristown, NJ, USA. Association for Computational Linguistics.

Taraka Rama and Karthik Gali. 2009. Modeling machine transliteration as a phrase based statistical machine translation problem. In *NEWS '09: Proceedings of the 2009 Named Entities Workshop: Shared Task on Transliteration*, pages 124–127, Morristown, NJ, USA. Association for Computational Linguistics.

Tarek Sherif and Grzegorz Kondrak. 2007. Substring-based transliteration. In *Proceedings of the 45th Annual Meeting of the Association of Computational Linguistics*, pages 944–951, Prague, Czech Republic, June. Association for Computational Linguistics.

Praneeth Shishtla, V. Surya Ganesh, Sethuramalingam Subramaniam, and Vasudeva Varma. 2009. A language-independent transliteration schema using character aligned models at news 2009. In *NEWS '09: Proceedings of the 2009 Named Entities Workshop: Shared Task on Transliteration*, pages 40–43, Morristown, NJ, USA. Association for Computational Linguistics.

Harshit Surana and Anil Kumar Singh. 2009. *Digitizing The Legacy of Indian Languages*. ICFAI Books, Hyderabad.

Kenji Yamada and Kevin Knight. 2001. A syntax-based statistical translation model. pages 523–530.

Classifying Wikipedia Articles into NE's using SVM's with Threshold Adjustment

Iman Saleh
Faculty of Computers and Information, Cairo University
Cairo, Egypt
iman.saleh@fci-cu.edu.eg

Kareem Darwish
Cairo Microsoft Innovation Center
Cairo, Egypt
kareemd@microsoft.com

Aly Fahmy
Faculty of Computers and Information, Cairo University
Cairo, Egypt
a.fahmy@fci-cu.edu.eg

Abstract

In this paper, a method is presented to recognize multilingual Wikipedia named entity articles. This method classifies multilingual Wikipedia articles using a variety of structured and unstructured features and is aided by cross-language links and features in Wikipedia. Adding multilingual features helps boost classification accuracy and is shown to effectively classify multilingual pages in a language independent way. Classification is done using Support Vectors Machine (SVM) classifier at first, and then the threshold of SVM is adjusted in order to improve the recall scores of classification. Threshold adjustment is performed using beta-gamma threshold adjustment algorithm which is a post learning step that shifts the hyperplane of SVM. This approach boosted recall with minimal effect on precision.

1 Introduction

Since its launch in 2001, Wikipedia has grown to be the largest and most popular knowledge base on the web. The collaboratively authored content of Wikipedia has grown to include more than 13 million articles in 240 languages.[1] Of these, there are more than 3 million English articles covering a wide range of subjects, supported by 15 million discussion, disambiguation, and redirect pages.[2] Wikipedia provides a variety of structured, semi-structured and unstructured resources that can be valuable in areas such information retrieval, information extraction, and natural language processing. As shown in Figure 1, these resources include page redirects, disambiguation pages, informational summaries (infoboxes), cross-language links between articles covering the same topic, and a hierarchical tree of categories and their mappings to articles.

Many of the Wikipedia pages provide information about concepts and named entities (NE). Identifying pages that provide information about different NE's can be of great help in a variety of NLP applications such as named entity recognition, question answering, information extraction, and machine translation (Babych and Hartley, 2003; Dakka and Cucerzan, 2008). This paper attempts to identify multilingual Wikipedia pages that provide information about different types of NE, namely persons, locations, and organizations. The identification is done using a Support Vector Machines (SVM) classifier that is trained on a variety of Wikipedia features such as infobox attributes, tokens in text, and category links for different languages aided by cross-language links in pages. Using features from different languages helps in two ways, namely: clues such infobox attributes may exist in one language, but not in the other, and this allows for tagging pages in multiple languages simultaneously. To improve SVM classification beta-gamma threshold adjustment was used to improve recall of different NE classes and consequently overall F measure.

The separating hyperplane suggested by the SVM typically favors precision at the cost of recall and needs to be translated (via threshold adjustment) to tune for the desired evaluation metric.

Beta-gamma threshold adjustment was generally used when certain classes do not have a sufficient number of training examples, which may lead to poor SVM recall scores (Shanahan and Roma, 2003). It was used by Shanahan and Roma (2003) to binary classify a set of articles and proved to improve recall with little effect on precision.

[1] http://en.wikipedia.org/wiki/Wikipedia
[2] http://en.wikipedia.org/wiki/Special:Statistics

Proceedings of the 2010 Named Entities Workshop, ACL 2010, pages 85–92,
Uppsala, Sweden, 16 July 2010. ©2010 Association for Computational Linguistics

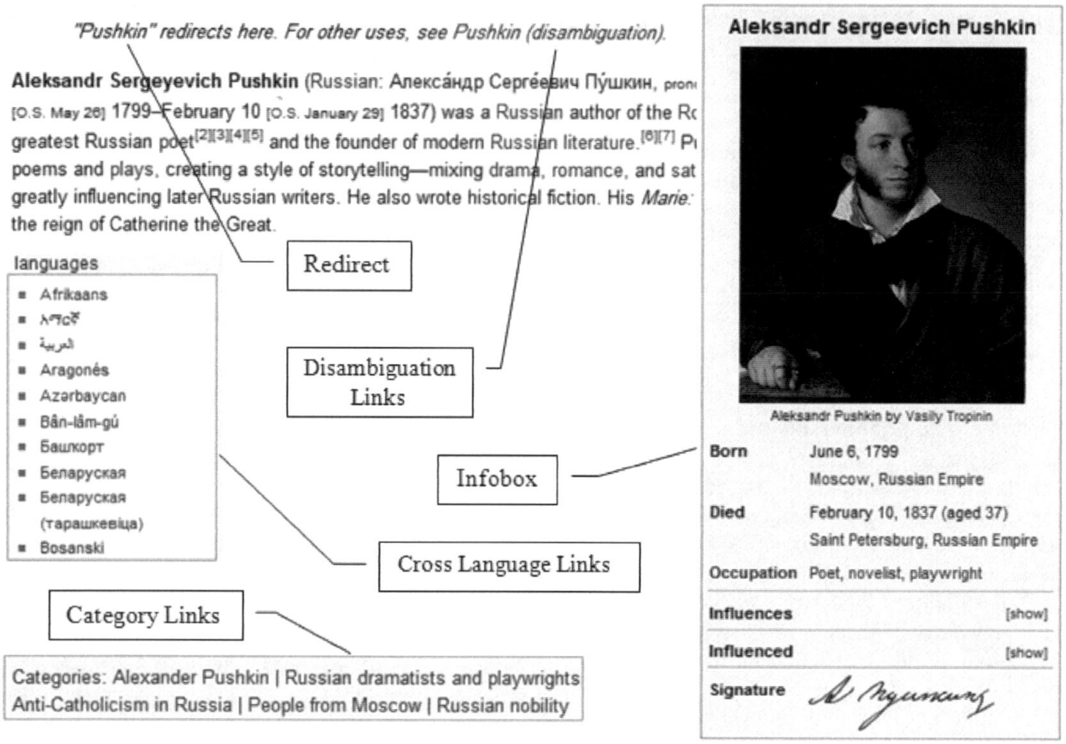

Figure 1. Sample Wikipedia article

However, the technique seems to generalize beyond cases where very few training examples are present, and it is shown in this paper to yield improvements in recall and overall F-measure in the presence of hundreds of training examples, performing better than threshold adjustment using cross validation for the specific task at hand.

The contribution of this paper lies in: introducing a language independent system that utilizes multilingual features from Wikipedia articles in different languages and can be used to effectively classify Wikipedia articles written in any language to the NE classes of types person, location, and organization; and modifying beta-gamma threshold adjustment to improve overall classification quality even when many training examples are available. The features and techniques proposed in this paper are compared to previous work in the literature.

The rest of the paper is organized as follows: Section 2 provides information about the structure and feature of Wikipedia; Section 3 surveys prior work on the problem; Section 4 describes the classification approach including features and threshold adjustment algorithm; Section 5 describes the datasets used for evaluation; Section 6 presents the results of the experiments; and Section 7 concludes the paper.

2 Wikipedia Pages

Wikipedia pages have a variety of types including:

- Content pages which constitute entries in Wikipedia (as in Figure 1). Content pages typically begin with an abstract containing a brief description of the article. They may contain semi-structured data such as infoboxes and persondata, which provide factoids about concepts or entities in pages using attribute-value pairs. Persondata structures are found only in people pages. Most of the articles in Wikipedia belong to one or more category, and the categories a page belongs to are listed in the footer of the page. As in Figure 1, the entry for Alexander Pushkin belongs to categories such as "Russian Poets" and "1799 births". Content pages provide information about common concepts or named entities of type person, location, or organization (Dakka and Cucerzan, 2008). A page in Wikipedia is linked to its translations in other languages through cross language links. These links redirects user to the same Wikipedia article written in different language.
- Category pages which lists content pages that belong to a certain category. Since

categories are hierarchical, a category page lists its parent category and sub-categories below it.

- Disambiguation pages which help disambiguate content pages with the same titles. For example, a disambiguation page for "jaguar" provides links to jaguar the cat, the car, the guitar, etc.
- Redirect pages redirect users to the correct article if the name of the article entered was not exactly the same. For example, "President Obama" is redirected to "Barak Obama".

3 Related Work

This section presents some of the effort pertaining to identifying NE pages in Wikipedia and some background on SVM threshold adjustment.

3.1 Classifying Wikipedia Articles

Toral and Munoz (2006) proposed an approach to build and maintain gazetteers for NER using Wikipedia. The approach makes use of a noun hierarchy obtained from WordNet in addition to the first sentence in an article to recognize articles about NE's. A POS tagger can be used in order to improve the effectiveness of the algorithm. They reported F-measure scores of 78% and 68% for location and person classes respectively. The work in this paper relies on using the content of Wikipedia pages only.

Watanabe et al. (2007) considered the problem of tagging NE's in Wikipedia as the problem of categorizing anchor texts in articles. The novelty of their approach is in exploiting dependencies between these anchor texts, which are induced from the HTML structure of pages. They used Conditional Random Fields (CRF) for classification and achieved F-measure scores of 79.8 for persons, 72.7 for locations, and 71.6 for organizations. This approach tags only NE's referenced inside HTML anchors in articles and not Wikipedia articles themselves.

Bhole et al. (2007) and Dakka and Cucerzan (2008) used SVM classifiers to classify Wikipedia articles. Both used a bag of words approach to construct feature vectors. In Bhole et al. (2007), the feature vector was constructed over the whole text of an article. They used a linear SVM and achieved 72.6, 70.5, and 41.6 F-measure for tagging persons, locations, and organizations respectively. For a Wikipedia article, Dakka and Cucerzan (2008) used feature vectors constructed using words in the full text of the article, the first paragraph, the abstract, the values in infoboxes, and the hypertext of incoming links with surrounding words. They reported 95% and 93% F-measure for person and location respectively. Using a strictly bag of words approach does not make use of the structure of Wikipedia articles and is compared against in the evaluation.

Richman and Schone (2008) and Nothman et al. (2008) annotated Wikipedia text with NE tags to build multilingual training data for NE taggers. The approach of Richman and Schone (2008) is based on using Wikipedia category structure to classify Wikipedia titles. Identifying NE's in other languages is done using cross language links of articles or categories of articles. Nothman et al. (2008) used a bootstrapping approach with heuristics based on the head nouns of categories and the opening sentence of an article. Evaluating the system is done by training a NE tagger using the generated training data. They reported an average 92% F-measure for all NE's.

Silberer et al. (2008) presented work on the translation of English NE to 15 different languages based on Wikipedia cross-language links with a reported precision of 95%. The resulting NE's were not classified. This paper extends the work on cross language links and uses features from multilingual pages to aid classification and to enable simultaneous tagging of entities across languages.

3.2 SVM Threshold Adjustment

Support Vector Machines (SVM) is a popular classification technique that was introduced by Vapnik (Vapnik, 1995). The technique is used in text classification and proved to provide excellent performance compared to other classification techniques such as k-nearest neighbor and naïve Bayesian classifiers. As in Figure 2, SVM attempts to find a maximum margin hyperplane that separates positive and negative examples. The separating hyperplane can be described as follows: $\langle W, X \rangle + b = 0$ or $\sum_{i=1}^{n} wi \cdot xi + b$, Where W is the normal to the hyperplane, X is an input feature vector, and b is the bias (the perpendicular distance from the origin to the hyperplane). When the number of examples for each class is not equivalent, the SVM may overfit the class that has fewer training examples. Further, the SVM training is not informed by the evaluation metric. Thus, SVM training may lead to a sub-optimal separating hyperplane. Several techniques were proposed to rectify the problem by translating the hyperplane by only adjusting bias b, which is henceforth referred to as threshold adjustment.

Some of these techniques adjust SVM threshold during learning (Vapnik 1998; Lewis 2001), while others consider threshold adjustment as a post learning step (Shanahan and Roma, 2003). One type of the later is beta-gamma threshold adjustment algorithm (Shanahan and Roma, 2003; Zhai et al., 1998), which is a post learning algorithm that has been shown to provide significant improvements for classification tasks in which very few training examples are present such as in adaptive text filtering. Such threshold adjustment allows for the tuning of an SVM to the desired measure of goodness (ex. F1 measure). A full discussion of beta-gamma threshold adjustment is provided in the experimental setup section. In the presence of many training examples, some of the training examples are set aside as a validation set to help pick an SVM threshold. Further, multi-fold cross validation is often employed.

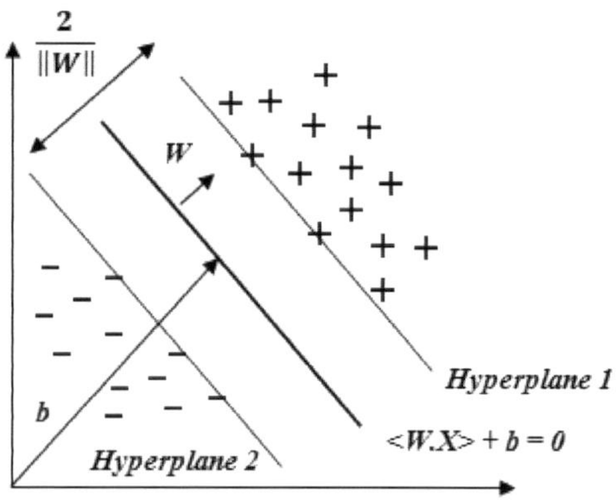

Figure 2. SVMs try to maximize the margin of separation between positive and negative examples

4 Classification Approach

Features: The classification features included content-based features such as words in page abstracts and structure-based features such category links. All the features are binary. The features are:

- Stemmed content words extracted from abstracts: an abstract for a NE may include keywords that may tell of the entity type. For example, an abstract for an NE of type person would typically include words such as "born", "pronounced", and more specific words that point to profession, role, or job (ex. president, poet, etc.).
- White space delimited attribute names from infoboxes: in the presence of infoboxes structures, the attribute names provide hints of the entity type. For example, an infobox of location may include attribute names such as "latitude", "longitude", "area", and "population".
- White space delimited words in category links for a page: category names may include keywords that would help disambiguate a NE type. For example, categories of NE of type person may include the words "births", "deaths", "people", occupation such as "poet" or "president", nationality such "American" or "Russian", etc.
- Persondata structure attributes: persondata only exist if the entity refers to a person.

The features used herein combine structural as well as content-based features from multiple languages unlike features used in the literature which were monolingual. Using multilingual features enables language independent classification of any Wikipedia article written in any language. Moreover, using primarily structural features in classification instead of the whole content of the articles allows for the effective use of multilingual pages without the need for language specific stemmers and stopword lists, the absence of which may adversely affect content based features.

Classification: Classifying Wikipedia pages was done in two steps: First training an SVM classifier; and then adjusting SVM thresholds based on beta-gamma adjustment to improve recall. Beta-gamma threshold adjustment was compared to cross-fold validation threshold adjustment. All Wikipedia articles were classified using a linear SVM. Classification was done using the Liblinear SVM package which is optimized for SVM classification problems with thousands of features (Fan et al., 2008). A variant of the beta-gamma threshold adjustment algorithm as described by (Shanahan and Roma, 2003; Zhai et al., 1998) is used to adjust the threshold of SVM. The basic steps of the algorithm are as follows:

- Divide the validation set into n folds such that each fold contains the same number of positive examples
- For each fold i,

- Classify examples in a fold and sort them in descending order based on SVM scores, where the SVM score of SVM is the perpendicular distance between an example and the separating hyperplane.
- Calculate F-measure, which is the goodness measure used in the paper, at each example.
- Determine the point of maximum F-measure and set θ_{N_i} to the SVM score at this point.
- Repeat previous steps for the set consisting of all folds other than i and set $\theta_{Max} = \theta_{N_i}$ and $\theta_{Min} = \theta_{M_i}$, where θ_{M_i} is the SVM score at the point of minimum F-measure.
- Compute $\beta_i = \frac{\theta_{N_i} - \theta_{Max}}{\theta_{Min} - \theta_{Max}}$

- $\beta = \frac{\sum \beta_i}{n}$
- The optimal threshold is obtained by interpolating between θ_{Max} and θ_{Min} obtained from the whole validation set as follows:
  $\theta_{Opt} = \alpha\, \theta_{Min} + (1 - \alpha)\, \theta_{Max}$,
  where $\alpha = \beta + (1 - \beta)e^{-\gamma M}$, M is the number of documents in the validation set, and γ is the inverse of the estimated number of documents at the point of the optimal threshold (Zhai et al., 1998). In this work, it is assigned a value that is equivalent to the inverse of the number of examples at θ_{Max}.

Since the number of training examples in Shanahan and Roma (2003) were small, n-fold cross-validation was done using the training set. In this work, the validation and training sets were non-overlapping. Further, in the work of Shanahan and Roma (2003), θ_{Min} was set to the point that yields utility = 0 as they used a filtering utility measure that can produce a utility of 0. Since no F-measure was found to equal zero in this work, minimum F-measure point was used instead.

For comparison, n-fold cross validation was used to obtain θ_{N_i} for each of the folds and then θ_{opt} as the average of all θ_{N_i}. Further, using a bag-of-words approach is used for comparison, where a feature vector in constructed based on the full text of an article.

5 Data Set

To train and test the tagging of Wikipedia pages with NE tags, a dataset of 4,936 English Wikipedia pages was developed by the authors and with split using a 60/20/20 training, validation, and testing split. The characteristics of the dataset, which is henceforth referred to as MAIN, are presented in Table 1. The English articles had links to 128 different languages, with: 16,912 articles having cross-language links; 93.3 pages on average per language; 97 languages with fewer than 100 links; with a minimum of 1 page per language (for 14 languages); and a maximum of 918 pages for French. To compare the inclusion of multilingual pages in training and testing, two variants of MAIN were used, namely: MAIN-E which has only English pages, and MAIN-EM which has English and multilingual pages from 13 languages with the most pages – Spanish, French, Finnish, Dutch, Polish, Portuguese, Italian, Norwegian, German, Danish, Hungarian, Russian, and Swedish. Other languages had too few pages. To stem text, Porter stemmer was used for English and snowball stemmers[3] were used for the other 13 languages. For all the languages, stopwords were removed. For completeness, another set was constructed to include all 128 languages to which the English pages had cross language links. This set is referred to as the MAIN-EM+ set. The authors did not have access to stemmers and stopword lists in all these languages, so simple tokenization was performed by breaking text on whitespaces and punctuation. Since many English pages don't have cross language links and most languages have too few pages, a new dataset was constructed as a subset of the aforementioned dataset such that each document in the collection has an English page with at least one cross language link to one of the 13 languages with the most pages in the bigger dataset. Table 2 details the properties of the smaller dataset, which is henceforth referred to as SUB. SUB had five variants, namely:

- SUB-E with English pages only
- SUB-EM with English and multilingual pages from the 13 languages in MAIN-EM
- SUB-M which the same as SUM-EM excluding English.
- SUB-EM+ with English pages and multilingual pages in 128 languages.
- SUB-M+ which is the same as SUB-EM+ excluding English.

The articles used in the experiments were randomly selected out of all the content articles in Wikipedia, about 3 million articles. Articles were randomly assigned to training and test sets

[3] http://snowball.tartarus.org/

and manually annotated in accordance to the CONLL – 2003 annotation guidelines[4] which are based on (Chinchor et al., 1999). Annotation was based on reading the contents of the article and then labeling it with the appropriate class. All the data, including first sentence in an article, infobox attributes, persondata attributes, and category links, were parsed from a 2010 Wikipedia XML dump.

6 Evaluation and Results

The results of classifying Wikipedia articles using SVM and threshold adjustment for MAIN-E, MAIN-EM, and MAIN-M are reported in Tables 3, 4, and 5 respectively. Tables 6, 7, 8, 9, and 10 report results for SUB-E, SUB-EM, SUB-M, SUB-EM+, and SUB-M+ respectively. In all, n is the number of cross folds used to calculate β, with n ranging between 3 and 10. The first row is the baseline scores of SVM classification without threshold adjustment. The remaining rows are the scores of SVM classification after adjusting threshold. The adjustment is performed by adding θ_{Opt} to the bias value b learned by the SVM. A t-test with 95% confidence (p-value $\leq$ 0.05) is used to determine statistical significance.

For the MAIN-E dataset, SVM threshold relaxation yielded statistically significant improvement over the baseline of using an SVM directly for location named entity. For other types of named entities improvements were not statistically significant.

Threshold adjustment led to statistically significant improvement for: all NE types for SUB-EM and SUB-EM+; for organizations for SUB-E and SUB-M+; and for locations and organization for SUB-EM. The improvements were most pronounced when recall was very low. For example, F1 measure for organization in the SUB-M dataset improved by 18 points due to a 26 point improvement in recall – though at the expense of precision.

It seems that threshold adjustment tends to benefit classification more when: using smaller training sets – as is observed when comparing the results for MAIN and SUB datasets, and when classification leads to very low recall – as indicated by organization NE for SUB datasets.

Tables 11 and 12 compare the results for the different variations of the MAIN and SUB datasets respectively. As indicated in the Tables 11 and 12, the inclusion of more and more language pages with English led to improved classification with consistent improvements in precision and recall for MAIN and consistent improvements in precision for SUB. For the SUB-M and SUB-M+ datasets, the exclusion of English led to degradation on F1 measure, with the degradation being particularly pronounced for organizations. The drop can be attributed to the loss of much valuable training examples, because there are more English pages compared to other languages. Despite the loss, proper identification of persons and locations remained high enough for many practical applications. Further, the results suggest that given more training data in the other languages, the features suggested in the paper would likely yield good classification results. Unlike the MAIN datasets, the inclusion of more languages for training and testing (from SUB-M to SUB-M+ & from SUB-EM to SUB-EM+) did not yield any improvements except for location and organization types from SUB-EM to SUB-EM+. This requires more investigation.

Tables 13 and 14 report the results of using term frequency representation of the entire page as features – a bag of words (BOWs)– as in Bhole et al. (2007). Using semi-structured data as classification features is better than using BOW representation. This could be due to the smaller number of features of higher value. In the BOW results with multilingual page inclusion, except for location NE type only in the SUB dataset, the use of term frequencies of multilingual words hurt F1-measure for the SUB and MAIN datasets. This can be attributed to the increased sparseness of the training and test data.

7 Conclusions

This paper presented a language independent method for identifying multilingual Wikipedia articles referring to named entities. An SVM was trained using multilingual features that make use of unstructured and semi-structured portions of Wikipedia articles. It was shown that using multilingual features was better than using features obtained from English articles only. Multilingual features can be used in classifying multilingual articles and is particularly useful for languages other than English, where fewer useful features are present. The number of Infobox properties and category links in English MAIN was 32,262 and 9,221 respectively, while in German there are 4,618 properties and 1,657 category links. These numbers are even lower in all other languages.

[4] http://www.cnts.ua.ac.be/conll2003/ner/annotation.txt

	Training	Validation	Test
Person	822	300	251
Locations	676	221	266
Organizations	313	113	110
Non	1085	366	414
Total	2896	1000	1040

Table 1. Characteristics of MAIN dataset: the number of Wikipedia pages in the dataset

	Training	Validation	Test
Person	332	128	95
Locations	360	115	144
Organizations	102	30	42
Non	435	150	184
Total	1229	423	465

Table 2. Characteristics of SUB dataset: the number of Wikipedia pages in the dataset

cross folds	Person			Location			Organization		
	P	R	F1	P	R	F1	P	R	F1
Baseline	98.7	90.4	94.4	94.6	85.7	89.9	**90**	**73.6**	**81.0**
n = 3	97.9	92.0	94.9	94.4	89.0	91.6	87.2	74.5	80.4
n = 4	96.7	92.0	94.3	94.4	89.0	91.6	87.2	74.5	80.4
n = 5	96.6	92.0	94.3	94.4	89.0	91.6	80.0	76.4	78.0
n =6	96.7	92.4	94.5	94.4	89.4	91.9	85.6	75.4	80.2
n =7	**96.7**	**92.8**	**94.7**	94.4	89.4	91.9	85.6	75.4	80.2
n =8	96.7	92.8	94.7	***94.0***	***90.6***	***92.3***	80.0	76.4	78.0
n =9	95.2	94.0	94.6	94.0	89.8	91.9	80.8	76.4	78.5
n = 10	94.8	94.0	94.4	94.0	90.6	92.3	77.9	80.0	78.9

Table 3. Results for MAIN-E: Best F1 bolded and italicized if significantly better than baseline.

cross folds	Person			Location			Organization		
	P	R	F1	P	R	F1	P	R	F1
Baseline	99.1	91.6	95.2	94.7	87.2	90.8	91.0	73.6	81.4
n = 3	99.7	91.2	95.2	94.7	87.2	90.8	90.1	74.5	81.6
n = 4	99.1	91.6	95.2	94.7	87.9	91.2	**90.2**	**75.4**	**82.2**
n = 5	**99.1**	**92.4**	**95.7**	94.4	89	91.6	86.4	75.4	80.6
n =6	98.3	92.4	95.3	94.7	87.9	91.2	87.4	75.4	81.0
n =7	98.3	92.4	95.3	93.7	90.2	91.9	82.3	76.4	79.2
n =8	98.3	92.8	95.5	93.7	90.2	91.9	85.7	76.4	80.8
n =9	98.3	92.8	95.5	**92.4**	**92.4**	**92.4**	82.3	76.4	79.2
n = 10	97.9	92.8	95.3	92.8	92.1	92.4	82.3	76.4	79.2

Table 4. Results for MAIN-EM: Best F1 bolded and italicized if significantly better than baseline.

cross folds	Person			Location			Organization		
	P	R	F1	P	R	F1	P	R	F1
Baseline	**99.6**	**92.0**	**95.6**	95.0	87.2	90.9	91.0	73.6	81.4
n = 3	98.3	92.4	95.3	94.3	88.3	91.2	**91.0**	**74.5**	**82.0**
n = 4	98.3	92.8	95.5	93.7	90.2	91.9	91.0	74.5	82.0
n = 5	98.3	92.8	95.5	**93.8**	**90.9**	**92.3**	89.2	75.4	81.8
n =6	97.9	93.2	95.5	93.0	91.3	92.2	88.3	75.4	81.4
n =7	95.5	93.6	94.6	93.4	90.9	92.2	87.4	75.4	81.0
n =8	95.5	93.6	94.6	91.8	92.8	92.3	85.7	76.4	80.8
n =9	95.9	93.2	94.5	92.0	92.0	92.0	84.0	76.4	80.0
n = 10	95.2	94.8	95.0	91.7	92.0	91.9	85.7	76.4	80.8

Table 5. Results for MAIN-EM+: Best F1 bolded and italicized if significantly better than baseline.

The effect of using SVM and beta-gamma threshold adjustment algorithm to improve recognizing NE's in Wikipedia was also demonstrated. The algorithm was shown to improve scores of location NE's particularly. The appropriate number of folds was found to be 8 using our dataset. Finally, the results suggest that the use of semi-structured data as classification features is significantly better than the using unstructured data only or BOWs. The paper also showed that the use of multilingual features with BOWs was not very useful.

For future work, the proposed technique can be used to create large sets of tagged Wikipedia pages in a variety of languages to aid in building parallel lists of named entities that can be used to improve MT and in training transliterator engines. Further, this work can help in building resources such gazetteers and tagged NE data in many languages for the rapid development of NE taggers in general text. Wikipedia has the advantage of covering many topics beyond those that are typically covered in news articles.

cross folds	Person			Location			Organization		
	P	R	F1	P	R	F1	P	R	F1
Baseline	100	92.6	96.2	**98.5**	**91.7**	**95**	87.0	49.0	62.5
n = 3	100	92.6	96.2	97.8	91.7	94.6	84	51.2	63.6
n = 4	100	92.6	96.2	97.8	91.7	94.6	85.2	56	67.7
n = 5	100	93.7	96.7	96.4	92.4	94.3	***87.0***	***65.8***	***75.0***
n =6	100	93.7	96.7	95.7	93.7	94.7	85.7	58.5	69.6
n =7	100	93.7	96.7	95.7	93.7	94.7	87.0	65.8	75.0
n =8	100	93.7	96.7	95.7	93.7	94.7	87.0	65.8	75.0
n =9	**100**	**94.7**	**97.3**	95.0	94.4	94.8	87.0	65.8	75.0
n = 10	100	94.7	97.3	95.0	94.4	94.8	87.0	65.8	75.0

Table 6. Results for SUB-E: Best F1 bolded and italicized if significantly better than baseline.

cross folds	Person			Location			Organization		
	P	R	F1	P	R	F1	P	R	F1
Baseline	100	91.6	95.6	99.2	88.9	93.8	100	46.3	63.3
n = 3	98.9	92.6	95.6	99.2	88.2	93.3	***100***	***53.6***	***69.8***
n = 4	98.9	92.6	95.6	98.5	91.7	95.0	92.0	56.0	69.7
n = 5	98.9	92.6	95.6	99.2	88.9	93.8	92.0	56.0	69.7
n =6	98.9	92.6	95.6	***98.5***	***93.7***	***96.0***	92.0	56.0	69.7
n =7	99.0	92.6	95.6	98.5	93.7	96.0	92.0	56.0	69.7
n =8	99.0	92.6	95.6	97.8	93.7	95.7	92.0	56.0	69.7
n =9	***98.9***	***95.7***	***97.3***	95.2	95.8	95.5	92.0	56.0	69.7
n = 10	98.9	95.7	97.3	93.2	96.5	94.9	92.0	56.0	69.7

Table 7. Results for SUB-EM: Best F1 bolded and italicized if significantly better than baseline.

References

Babych, Bogdan, and Hartley, Anthony (2003). *Improving Machine Translation quality with automatic Named Entity recognition*. 7th Int. EAMT workshop on MT and other lang. tech. tools -- EACL'03, Budapest, Hungary.

Bhole, Abhijit, Fortuna, Blaz, Grobelnik, Marko, and Mladenic, Dunja. (2007). *Extracting Named Entities and Relating Them over Time Based on Wikipedia.* Informatica (Slovenia), 31, 463-468.

Chinchor, Nancy, Brown, Erica, Ferro, Lisa, and Robinson, Patty. (1999). 1999 Named Entity Recognition Task Definition: MITRE.

Dakka, Wisam., and Cucerzan, Silviu. (2008). *Augmenting Wikipedia with Named Entity Tags.* 3rd IJCNLP, Hyderabad, India.

Fan, Rong-En, Chang, Kai-Wei, Hsieh, Cho-Jui, Wang, Xiang-Rui, and Lin, Chih-Jen. (2008). *LIBLINEAR: A Library for Large Linear Classication.* Journal of Machine Learning Research 9, 1871-1874.

Nothman, Joel, Curran, James R., and Murphy, Tara. (2008). *Transforming Wikipedia into Named Entity Training Data.* Australian Lang. Tech. Workshop.

Richman, Alexander E., and Schone, Patrick. (2008, June). *Mining Wiki Resources for Multilingual Named Entity Recognition.* ACL-08: HLT, Columbus, Ohio.

Shanahan, James G., and Roma, Norbert. (2003). *Boosting support vector machines for text classification through parameter-free threshold relaxation.* CIKM'03. New Orleans, LA, US

Silberer, Carina, Wentland, Wolodja, Knopp, Johannes, and Hartung, Matthias. (2008). *Building a Multilingual Lexical Resource for Named Entity Disambiguation, Translation and Transliteration.* LREC'08, Marrakech, Morocco.

Toral, Antonio, and Mu˜noz, Rafael (2006). *A proposal to automatically build and maintain gazetteers for Named Entity Recognition by using Wikipedia*, EACL-2008. Italy.

Vapnik, Vladimir N. (1995). *The nature of statistical learning theory*: Springer-Verlag New York, Inc.

Watanabe, Yotaro, Asahara, Masayuki, and Matsumoto, Yuji. (2007). *A Graph-Based Approach to Named Entity Categorization in Wikipedia using Conditional Random Fields.* EMNLP-CoNLL, Prague, Czech Republic

Zhai, Chengxiang, Jansen, Peter, Stoica, Emilia, Grot, Norbert, and Evans, David A. (1998). *Threshold Calibration in CLARIT Adaptive Filtering.* TREC-7, Gaithersburg, Maryland, US.

cross folds	Person			Location			Organization		
	P	**R**	**F1**	**P**	**R**	**F1**	**P**	**R**	**F1**
Baseline	100	90.5	95	99.2	90.3	94.5	100	47.6	64.5
n = 3	98.9	92.6	95.6	98.5	91.7	95	100	47.6	64.5
n = 4	98.9	92.6	95.6	98.5	91	94.6	96	57	71.6
n = 5	98.9	92.6	95.6	**98.5**	**92.4**	**95.3**	96	57	71.6
n =6	98.9	92.6	95.6	95.8	94.4	95	96	57	71.6
n =7	98.9	92.6	95.6	97	93	95	100	54.8	70.8
n =8	98.9	92.6	95.6	95.8	94.4	95	92.6	59.5	72.5
n =9	98.8	93.7	96.2	95	95	95	***96***	***59.5***	***73.5***
n = 10	***98.9***	***94.7***	***96.8***	94.5	95.8	95.2	92.6	59.5	72.5

Table 8. Results for SUB-EM+: Best F1 bolded and italicized if significantly better than baseline.

cross folds	Person			Location			Organization		
	P	**R**	**F1**	**P**	**R**	**F1**	**P**	**R**	**F1**
Baseline	97.4	77.9	86.5	97.4	78.5	86.9	100	21.9	36.0
n = 3	97.4	78.9	87.2	96.7	80.5	87.9	100	24.4	39.2
n = 4	97.5	82.0	89.0	95.3	84.0	89.3	71.4	36.6	48.4
n = 5	97.5	82.0	89.0	94.6	84.7	89.4	100	24.4	39.2
n =6	**96.3**	**83.0**	**89.3**	94.6	84.7	89.4	100	24.4	39.2
n =7	95.2	83.0	88.8	***94.6***	***86.0***	***90.2***	77.8	34	47.4
n =8	97.5	83.0	89.8	91.8	86.0	88.9	70.8	41.5	52.3
n =9	95.2	84.2	89.4	94.6	86.0	90.0	61.3	46.3	52.8
n = 10	91.2	87.4	89.2	64.9	96.5	77.6	***60.6***	***48.8***	***54.0***

Table 9. Results for SUB-M: Best F1 bolded and italicized if significantly better than baseline.

cross folds	Person			Location			Organization		
	P	**R**	**F1**	**P**	**R**	**F1**	**P**	**R**	**F1**
Baseline	97.3	76.8	85.9	97.4	77	86	100	19	32
n = 3	97.4	77.9	86.5	95	81.2	87.6	100	23.8	38.5
n = 4	97.4	77.9	86.5	95.8	78.5	86.2	91.7	26.2	40.7
n = 5	**97.4**	**80**	**87.9**	95.9	80.5	87.5	86.7	30.9	45.6
n =6	96.2	80	87.3	91	84.7	87.8	91.7	26.2	40.7
n =7	96.2	80	87.3	**92.4**	**84.7**	**88.4**	91.7	26.2	40.7
n =8	95	80	86.8	75	93.7	83.3	***79.2***	***45.2***	***57.6***
n =9	92.8	82	87	89.3	86.8	88	79.2	45.2	57.6
n = 10	90.9	84.2	87.4	65.9	97.9	78.8	79.2	45.2	57.6

Table 10. Results for SUB-M+: Best F1 bolded and italicized if significantly better than baseline.

MAIN	F1-measure		
	E	EM	EM+
Person	94.4	95.2	***95.6***
Location	89.9	90.8	**90.9**
Organization	81.0	81.4	**81.4**

Table 11. Comparing results for MAIN-{E, EM, and EM+}: Best F1 bolded and italicized if significantly better than MAIN-E

SUB	F1-Measure				
	E	EM	M	EM+	M+
Person	**96.2**	95.6	86.5	95	85.9
Location	**95**	93.8	86.9	94.5	86
Organization	62.5	63.3	36.0	**64.5**	32

Table 12. Comparing results for SUB-{E, EM, M, EM+, and M+}: Best F1 bolded

MAIN	F1-measure		
	E	EM	EM+
Person	**86.8**	85.0	84.5
Location	**87.4**	85.8	85.5
Organization	**58.0**	51.8	53.4

Table 13. Comparing results of BOWs for MAIN-{E, EM, and EM+}: Best F1 bolded

SUB	F-Measure				
	E	EM	M	EM+	M+
Person	**82.0**	80.6	68.0	79.3	61.9
Location	88.5	**90.7**	83.8	90.0	82.3
Organization	**35.6**	22.6	21.4	33.3	22.6

Table 14. Comparing results of BOWs for SUB-{E, EM, M, EM+, and M+}: Best F1 bolded

Assessing the Challenge of *Fine-Grained* Named Entity Recognition *and* Classification

Asif Ekbal, Eva Sourjikova, Anette Frank and **Simone Paolo Ponzetto**
Department of Computational Linguistics
Heidelberg University, Germany
{ekbal,sourjikova,frank,ponzetto}@cl.uni-heidelberg.de

Abstract

Named Entity Recognition and Classification (NERC) is a well-studied NLP task typically focused on coarse-grained named entity (NE) classes. NERC for more fine-grained semantic NE classes has not been systematically studied. This paper quantifies the difficulty of fine-grained NERC (FG-NERC) when performed at large scale on the people domain. We apply unsupervised acquisition methods to construct a gold standard dataset for FG-NERC. This dataset is used to benchmark methods for classifying NEs at various levels of fine-grainedness using classical NERC techniques and global contextual information inspired from Word Sense Disambiguation approaches. Our results indicate high difficulty of the task and provide a 'strong' baseline for future research.

1 Introduction

Named Entity Recognition and Classification (cf. Nadeau and Sekine (2007)) is a well-established NLP task relevant for nearly all semantic processing and information access applications. NERC has been investigated using supervised (McCallum and Li, 2003), unsupervised (Etzioni et al., 2005) and semi-supervised (Paşca et al., 2006b) learning methods. It has been investigated in multilingual settings (Tjong Kim Sang, 2002; Tjong Kim Sang and De Meulder, 2003) and special domains, e.g. biomedicine (Ananiadou et al., 2004).

The classical NERC task is confined to coarse-grained named entity (NE) classes established in the MUC (MUC-7, 1998) or CoNLL (Tjong Kim Sang, 2002) competitions, typically PERS, LOC, ORG, MISC. While most recent work concentrates on feature engineering and robust statistical models for various domains, few researchers addressed the problem of recognizing and categorizing *fine-grained* NE classes (such as *biologist, composer*, or *athlete*) in an open-domain setting.

Fine-grained NERC is expected to be beneficial for a wide spectrum of applications, including Information Retrieval (Mandl and Womser-Hacker, 2005), Information Extraction (Paşca et al., 2006a) or Question-Answering (Pizzato et al., 2006). However, manually compiling wide-coverage gazetteers for fine-grained NE classes is time-consuming and error-prone. Also, without an extrinsic evaluation, it is difficult to define a priori which classes are relevant for a particular domain or task. Finally, prior research in FG-NERC is difficult to evaluate, due to the diversity of NE classes and datasets used.

Accordingly, in the interest of a general approach, we address the challenge of capturing a *broad range* of NE classes *at various levels of conceptual granularity*. By turning FG-NERC into a widely applicable task, applications are free to choose relevant NE categories for specific needs. Also, establishing a gold standard dataset for this task enables comparative benchmarking of methods. However, the envisaged task is far from trivial, given that the set of possible semantic classes for a given NE comprises the full space of NE classes, whereas descriptive nouns may be ambiguous between a fixed set of meanings only.

The paper aims to establish a general framework for FG-NERC by addressing two goals: (i) we automatically build a gold standard dataset of NE instances classified in context with fine-grained semantic class labels; (ii) we develop strong baseline methods, to assess the aptness of standard NLP approaches for this task. The two efforts are strongly interleaved: a standardized dataset is not only essential for (comparative) evaluation, but also a prerequisite for classification approaches based on supervised learning, the most successful techniques for sequential labeling problems.

Proceedings of the 2010 Named Entities Workshop, ACL 2010, pages 93–101,
Uppsala, Sweden, 16 July 2010. ©2010 Association for Computational Linguistics

2 Related work

An early approach to FG-NERC is Alfonseca and Manandhar (2002), who identify it as a problem related to Word Sense Disambiguation (WSD). They jointly address concept hierarchy learning and instance classification using topic signatures, yet the experiments are restricted to a small ontology of 9 classes. Similarly, Fleischman and Hovy (2002) extend previous work from Fleischman (2001) on locations and address the acquisition of instances for 8 fine-grained person classes. For supervised training they compile a web corpus which is filtered using high-confident classifications from an initial classifier trained on seeds. Due to the limitations of their method to create a good sample of training data, the performance could not be generalized to held-out data.

Recent work takes the task of FG-NERC one step further by (i) extending the number of classes, (ii) relating them to reference concept hierarchies and (iii) exploring methods for building training and evaluation data, or applying weakly and unsupervised learning based on high-volume data. Tanev and Magnini (2006) selected 10 NE-subclasses of person and location using WordNet as a reference. Datasets were automatically acquired and manually filtered. They compare word and pattern-based supervised and a semi-supervised approach based on syntactic features. Giuliano & Gliozzo (2007, 2008) perform NE classification against the People Ontology, an excerpt of the WordNet hierarchy, comprising 21 people classes populated with at least 40 instances. Using minimally supervised lexical substitution methods, they cast NE classification as an ontology population task – as opposed to recognition and classification in context. In a similar setting, Giuliano (2009) explores semi-supervised classification of the People Ontology classes using latent semantic kernels, comparing models built from Wikipedia and from a news corpus. In a different line of research Paşca (2007) and Paşca and van Durme (2008) make use of query logs to acquire NEs on a large scale. While Paşca (2007) extracts NEs for 10 target classes, Paşca and van Durme (2008) combine web query logs and web documents to acquire both NE-concept pairs and concept attributes using seeds.

But while these more recent approaches all offer substantially novel contributions for many NE acquisition subtasks, none of them addresses the full task of FG-NERC, i.e., recognition and classification of NE tokens *in context*. Compared to ontology population, focusing on types, classification in raw texts needs to consider any token and cannot rely on special contexts offering indicative clues for class membership.

Bunescu and Paşca (2006) also perform disambiguation and classification of NEs in context, yet in a different setup. Disambiguation is performed into one of the known possible classes for a NE, as determined from Wikipedia disambiguation pages. Contexts for training and testing are acquired from Wikipedia pages, as opposed to general text. Disambiguation is performed using vectors of co-occurring terms and a taxonomy-based kernel that integrates word-category correlations. Evaluation is performed on the task of predicting, for a given NE in a Wikipedia page context, the correct class from among its known classes, including one experiment that included 10% of out-of-Wikipedia entities. The category space was confined to *People by occupation*, with 8,202 subclasses. Classification considered 110 broad classes, 540 highly populated classes (w/o out-of-Wikipedia entities), and 2,847 classes including less populated ones. This setup is difficult to compare given the sense granularities employed and the special Wikipedia text genre. Even though classification is performed in context, the task does not evaluate recognition.

To summarize, the field has developed robust methods for acquisition and fine-grained classification of NEs on a large scale. But, the full task of NE recognition and classification in context still remains to be addressed for a wide-coverage, fine-grained semantic class inventory that can serve as a common benchmark for future research.

3 Fine-grained NERC on a large-scale

We present experiments that assess the difficulty of open-domain FG-NERC pursued at a large scale. We concentrate on instances and classes referring to people, since it is a well-studied domain (see Section 2) and structured fine-grained information can be readily applied to a well-defined end-user task such as IR, cf. the Web People Search task (Artiles et al., 2008). Our method is general in that it requires only a (PoS tagged and chunked) corpus and a reference taxonomy to provide a concept hierarchy. Given a mapping between automatically extracted class labels and concepts in a taxonomic resource, it can be further extended to other domains, e.g. locations or the biomedical domain by leveraging open-domain taxonomies such as Yago (Suchanek et al., 2008) or WikiTaxonomy (Ponzetto and Strube, 2007). The contribution of this work is two-fold:

(i) We develop an unsupervised method for acquiring a comprehensive dataset for FG-NERC by applying linguistically motivated patterns to a corpus harvested from the Web (Section 4). Large amounts of NEs are acquired together with their contexts of occurrence and with their fine-grained class labels which are mapped to synsets in WordNet. The controlled sense inventory and the taxonomic structure offered by WordNet enables an evaluation of FG-NERC performance at different levels of concept granularity, as given by the depth at which the concepts are found. As our extraction patterns reflect a wide-spread grammatical construct, the method can be applied to many languages and extended to other domains.

(ii) Given this automatically acquired dataset, we assess the problem of FG-NERC in a systematic series of experiments, exploring the performance of NERC methods on different levels of granularities. For recognition and classification we apply standard sequential labeling techniques – i.e. a Maximum Entropy (MaxEnt) tagger (Section 5.1) – which we adapt to this hierarchical classification problem (Section 5.2). To test the hypothesis of whether a sequential labeler represents a valid choice to perform FG-NERC, we compare the latter to a MaxEnt system trained on a more semantically informed feature set, and a gloss-overlap method inspired by WSD approaches (Section 5.3).

4 Acquisition of a FG-NERC dataset

We present an unsupervised method that simultaneously acquires NEs, their semantic class and contexts of occurrence from large textual resources. In order to develop a clean resource of properly disambiguated NEs, we develop acquisition patterns for a grammatical construction that unambiguously associates proper names with their corresponding semantic class.

Pattern-based extraction of NE-concept pairs. NEs are often introduced by so-called *appositional structures* as in (1), which overtly express which semantic class (here, *painter*) the NE (*Kandinsky*) belongs to. Appositions involving proper names can be captured by extraction patterns as given in (2).

(1) ... *writings of the abstract painter Kandinsky frequently explored similarities between* ...

(2) a. [the|The]? [JJ|NN]* [NN] [NP]
the abstract painter Kandinsky

b. [NP] [,]? [a|an|the]* [JJ|NN]* [NN]
W. Kandinsky, a Russian-born painter, ..

Contexts like (2.a) provide a less noisy sequence for extraction, due to the class and instance labels being adjacent – in contrast to (2.b) where any number of modifiers can intervene between the two. Accordingly, we apply in our experiments only a restricted version of (2.a) – with a determiner – to UKWAC, an English web-based corpus (Baroni et al., 2009) that comes in a cleaned, PoS-tagged and lemmatized form. Due to its size (>2 billion tokens) and mixed genres, the corpus is ideally suited for acquiring large quantities of NEs pertaining to a broad variety of open-domain semantic classes.

Filtering heuristics. The apposition patterns are subject to noise, due to PoS-tagging errors, as well as special constructions, e.g. reduced relative clauses. The former can be controlled by frequency filters, the latter can be circumvented by using chunk boundary information[1]. A more challenging problem is to recognize whether an extracted nominal is in fact a valid semantic class for NEs. Besides, class labels can be ambiguous, so there is uncertainty as to which class an extracted entity should be assigned to. We apply two filtering strategies: we set a frequency threshold ft on the number of extracted NE tokens per class, to remove infrequent class label extractions; we then filter invalid semantic classes using information from WordNet: given the WordNet PERSON supersense, i.e. the lexicographer file for nouns denoting people, we check whether the first sense of the class label candidate is found in PERSON.

Mapping to the WordNet person domain. In order to perform a hierarchical classification of people, we need a taxonomy for the domain at hand. We achieve this by mapping the extracted class labels to WordNet synsets. In our setting, we map against all synsets found under *person#n#1*,

[1] We use YamCha (Kudo and Matsumoto, 2000) to perform phrase chunking.

which are direct hypernyms of at least one instance in WordNet ($C_{WN\_pers+Inst}$).[2] Since our goal is to map class labels to synsets (i.e. our future NE classes), we check each class label candidate against all synonyms contained in the synset. At this point we have to deal with two cases: two extracted class label candidates (synonyms such as *doctor, physician*) will map to a single synset, while ambiguous class labels (e.g. *director*) can be mapped to more than one synset. In the latter case, we heuristically choose the synset which dominates the highest number of instances in WordNet.

Mapping evaluation. We evaluated the coverage of our mapping for two sets of class labels extracted for two different frequency thresholds: $ft = 40$ and $ft = 1$. With $ft = 40$, we cover 31.1% of the synsets found under *person#n#1* in WordNet, i.e. the set of classes $C_{WN\_pers+Inst}$; conversely, 45.8% of the extracted class labels can be successfully mapped to $C_{WN\_pers+Inst}$. For threshold $ft = 1$, we are able to map to 87.9% of $C_{WN\_pers+Inst}$, with only 20.1% of extracted classes mapped to $C_{WN\_pers+Inst}$. For the remaining 79.9% of class labels (e.g. *goalkeeper, chancellor, superstar*) that have no instances in WordNet, we manually inspected 20 classes, in 20 contexts each, and established that 76% of them are appropriate NE person classes.
For threshold $ft = 40$, we obtain 153 class labels which are mapped to 146 synsets. Ten class labels are mapped to more than one synset. Using our mapping heuristic based on the majority instance class, we successfully disambiguate all of them. However, since we only map to $C_{WN\_pers+Inst}$, we introduce errors for 5 classes. E.g. 'manager' incorrectly gets mapped to *manager#n#2*, since the latter is the only synset containing instances. For these cases we manually corrected the automatic mapping.

A taxonomy for FG-NERC. We create our gold standard taxonomy of semantic classes by starting with the 146 synsets obtained from the mapping, including the 5 classes that were manually corrected. Since we concentrate on the people domain, we additionally remove 5 classes that can refer to other domains as well (e.g. *carrier, guide*). Given the remaining 141 synsets, we select the portion of WordNet rooted at *person#n#1* which contains them, together with any intervening synset found along the WordNet hierarchy. Given this WordNet excerpt, the extracted NE tokens are then appended to the respective synsets in the hierarchy. Statistics of the resulting WordNet fragment augmented with instances are given in Table 1. The taxonomy has a maximum depth of 8, and contains 213 synsets, i.e. NE classes (see column 2). 83.5% of the 31,819 extracted instances (type-level) sit in leaf nodes. The classes automatically refer back to the acquired appositional contexts. Table 1 gives statistics about the number of instances (token-level) acquired for classes at different embedding levels. In total we have at our disposal 48,512 instances (token-level) in appositional contexts. The type-token ratio is 1.52.

Level	#C	#C w/inst	#inst	#inst/C	% of inst
1	1	0	0	-	-
2	29	8	2,662	332	5.49
3	57	37	18,229	493	37.58
4	63	46	18,422	401	37.94
5	37	30	6,231	208	12.84
6	18	13	2,366	182	4.88
7	6	5	423	85	0.87
8	2	2	179	90	0.36
all	213	141	48,512	344	100

Table 1: Level-wise statistics of classes and instances across the FG-NERC person taxonomy.

Gold standard validation. To create a gold standard dataset of entities in context labeled with fine-grained classes, we first randomly select 20 classes, as well as an additional 18 which are also found in the People Ontology (Giuliano and Gliozzo, 2008). For each class, we randomly select 40 occurrences of instances in context, i.e. the words co-occurring in a window of 60 tokens before and after the instance. We asked four annotators to label these extractions for correctness, and to provide the correct label for the incorrect cases, if one was available. Only 52 contexts out of 1520 were labeled as incorrect, thus giving us 96.58% accuracy on our automatically extracted data. The manually validated dataset is used to provide a ground-truth for FG-NERC. However, the noun (e.g. *hunter*) denoting the NE class is removed from these contexts for training and testing in all experiments. This is because, due to the extraction method based on POS-patterns denoting appositions, class labels are known *a priori* to occur in the context of an instance and thus identify them with high precision.

[2] We use WordNet version 3.0. With *w#p#i* we denote the i-th sense of a word w with part of speech p. E.g., *person#n#1* is defined as { *person, individual* ... }).

5 Methodology for FG-NERC

We develop methods to perform FG-NERC using standard techniques developed for coarse-grained NERC and WSD. These are applied to our dataset from Section 4, in order to measure performance at different levels of semantic class granularity, i.e. corresponding to the depth of the semantic classes found in our WordNet fragment. We start in Section 5.1 to present a Maximum Entropy model to perform coarse-grained NERC and we extend it to perform multiclass classification in a hierarchical taxonomy (Section 5.2). We then present in Section 5.3 an alternative proposal to perform FG-NERC using global context information, as found in state-of-the-art approaches to supervised and unsupervised WSD.

5.1 NERC using a MaxEnt tagger

Our baseline system is modeled following a Maximum Entropy approach (Bender et al., 2003, *inter alia*). The MaxEnt model produces a probability for each class label t (the NE tag) of a classification instance, conditioned on its context of occurrence h. This probability is calculated by:

$$P(t|h) = \frac{1}{Z(h)} \exp\left(\sum_{j=1}^{n} \lambda_j f_j(h,t)\right) \quad (1)$$

where $f_j(h,t)$ is the j-th feature with associated weight λ_j and $Z(h)$ is a normalization constant to ensure a proper probability distribution.[3] Given a word w_i to be classified as Beginning, Inside or Outside (IOB) of a NE, we extract as features:

1. **Context words**. The words occurring within the context window $w_{i-2}^{i+2} = w_{i-2} \ldots w_{i+2}$.
2. **Word prefix and suffix**. Word prefix and suffix character sequences of length up to n.
3. **Infrequent word**. A feature that fires if w_i occurs in the training set less frequently than a given threshold (i.e. below 10 occurrences).
4. **Part-of-Speech (PoS) and chunk information**. The PoS and chunk labels of w_i.
5. **Capitalization**. A binary feature that checks whether w_i starts with a capital letter or not.
6. **Word length**. A binary feature that fires if the length of w_i is smaller than a pre-defined threshold (i.e. less than 5 characters).
7. **Digit and symbol features**. Three features check whether w_i contains digit strings, non-characters (e.g. slashes) or number expressions.
8. **Dynamic feature**. The tag t_{i-1} of the word w_{i-1} preceding w_i in the sequence w_1^n.

5.2 MaxEnt extension for FG-NERC

Extension to hierarchical classification. We apply our baseline NERC system to FG-NERC. Given a word in context, the task consists of recognizing it as a NE, and classifying it into the appropriate semantic class from our person taxonomy. We approach this as a hierarchical classification task by generating a binary classifier[4] with separate training and test sets for each node in the tree.

To perform *level-wise classification* from coarse to fine-grained classes, we need to adjust the class labels and their corresponding training and test instances for each experiment. For classification at the deepest level, each concept contains the instances of the original dataset. For classification at higher levels we leverage the semantics of the WordNet hyponym relations and expand the set of target classes (i.e. synsets) of a given level to contain all instances of hyponym synsets. Given a set I of classification instances for a given target class c, we add all instances labeled with the hyponyms of c to I. All other instances (not in that subtree) are labeled as being Outside (O-) a NE. This approach ensures that, for each node, the dataset contains two classes (NE and O) only, and implicitly 'propagates' the instances up the tree. As a result, non-leaf nodes that did not have any instance in the original dataset become populated. Also, the classification of classes at higher levels is based on larger datasets.

Extension to multiclass classification. Since we train a binary classifier for each node of the tree, we apply two methods to infer multiclass decisions from these binary classifiers, namely *level-wise* and *global* multiclass classification. In both paradigms, we combine the single decisions of the individual classifiers with the winner-takes-all strategy, using weighted voting. The weights are calculated based on the confidence value for the corresponding class, i.e., its conditional probability according to Equation (1). The output label is selected randomly in case of ties.

[3] In our implementation, we use the OpenNLP MaxEnt library (`http://maxent.sourceforge.net`).

[4] The IOB tagging scheme normally assigns three different labels, i.e. Inside (I-), Outside (O-) and Beginning (B-) of a chunk. However, our dataset does not have any instance labeled as B-, since it does not contain any adjacent NEs.

For *level-wise classification*, we combine only classifiers at the same level of embedding. Given n concepts at level l, we have n possible output labels for each word. The output label for a classification instance is determined by the highest weighted vote among all binary classifiers at level l. For *global classification* we combine all binary classifiers of the entire tree using weighted voting to determine the winning class label. The weights are calculated based on the product of confidence value and depth of the corresponding class in the tree.

5.3 FG-NERC using global contexts

FG-NERC is a more demanding task than 'classical' NERC, due to the larger amount of classes, the paucity of examples for each class, and the increasingly subtle semantic differences between these classes. For such a task contextual information is expected to be very informative – e.g. if an entity co-occurs in context with *'Nobel prize'*, this provides evidence that it is likely to be a *scientist* or *scholar*. However, the context window used by our baseline MaxEnt tagger is very local, including at most the two preceding and succeeding words. Hence, the classifier is not able to capture informative contextual clues in a larger context.

Previous work has related FG-NERC to WSD approaches (Alfonseca and Manandhar, 2002). Accordingly, we investigate two context-sensitive approaches inspired from WSD proposals, which consider a more *global context* for classification. We first define a new feature set to induce a new MaxEnt model (MaxEnt-B) which only uses lexical features from a larger context window, as used in standard supervised WSD (Lee and Ng, 2002):

1. **PoS context**. The part-of-speech occurring within the context window $pos_{i-3}^{i+3} = pos_{i-3} \ldots pos_{i+3}$.
2. **Local collocation**. Local collocations C_{nm} surrounding w_i. We use $C_{-2,-1}$ and $C_{1,2}$.
3. **Content words in surrounding context**. We consider all unigrams in contexts $w_{i-3}^{i+3} = w_{i-3} \ldots w_{i+3}$ of w_i (crossing sentence boundaries) for the entire training data. We convert tokens to lower case, remove stopwords, numbers and punctuation symbols. We define a feature vector of length 10 using the 10 most frequent content words. Given a classification instance, the feature corresponding to token t is set to 1 iff the context w_{i-3}^{i+3} of w_i contains t.

In addition, we use a Lesk-like method (Lesk, 1986) which labels instances in context with the WordNet synset whose gloss has the maximum overlap with the glosses of the senses of its words in context. Given the small context provided by the WordNet glosses, we follow Banerjee and Pedersen (2003) and expand these to also include the words from the glosses of the hypernym and hyponym synsets.

6 Experiments

6.1 Benchmarking on coarse-grained NERC

We benchmark the performance of our baseline MaxEnt classifier using the feature set from Section 5.1 (MaxEnt-A henceforth) on the CoNLL-2003 shared task dataset (Tjong Kim Sang and De Meulder, 2003), the *de-facto* standard for evaluating coarse-grained NERC systems.

In MaxEnt modeling, feature selection is a crucial problem and key to improving classification performance. MaxEnt, however, does not provide methods for automatic feature selection. We therefore experimented with various combinations of features standardly used for NERC (1-8 of Section 5.1). Model parameters are computed with 200 iterations without feature frequency cutoff. The best configuration is found by optimizing the F_1 measure on the development data with various feature representations. The chosen features are: 1, 2 (with $n = 3$), 4, 5, 6, 7 and 8. Evaluation on the test set is performed blindly, using this feature set. The results are presented in Table 2.

The MaxEnt labeler achieves performance comparable with the CoNLL-2003 task participants, ranking 12th among the 16 systems participating in the task, with a 2 point margin off the F_1 of the most similar system of Bender et al. (2003) and 7 points below the best-performing system (Florian et al., 2003). The former used a relatively complex set of features and different gazetteers extracted from unannotated data. The latter combined four diverse classifiers, namely a robust linear classifier, maximum entropy, transformation-based learning and a hidden Markov model. They used different feature sets, unannotated data and an additional NE tagger. In comparison, our NERC system is simpler and based on a small set of features that can be easily obtained for many languages. Besides, it does not make use of any external resources and still shows state-of-the-art performance on the overall data.

	Recall	Precision	$F_{\beta=1}$
PER	83.02%	81.40%	82.21%
LOC	88.47%	88.19%	88.23%
ORG	77.20%	68.03%	72.23%
MISC	81.20%	83.92%	82.54%
Overall	83.11%	80.47%	81.77%

Table 2: Results on the CoNLL-2003 test data.

Set	# tokens	# NEs
Training	2,431,041	38,810
Development	478,871	9,702
Test	181,490	1,520

Table 3: Statistics for training, dev and test sets.

6.2 Evaluating FG-NERC

Experimental setting. For the task of FG-NERC, we compare the performance of MaxEnt-A with the MaxEnt-B model from Section 5.3 and the Lesk method. The data is partitioned into training and development sets by randomly selecting 80%-20% of the contexts in which the NEs occur. We use the held-out, manually validated gold standard from Section 4 for blind evaluation. Statistics for the dataset are reported in Table 3.

We build a MaxEnt model for each FG-NE class, using the features that performed best on the CoNLL task, *except* the digit and dynamic NE features (MaxEnt-A), and context features 1-3 of Section 5.3 (MaxEnt-B). Model parameters are computed in the same way as for coarse-grained NERC. Table 3 shows that our training set is highly unbalanced. The ratio between positive (NEs) and negative examples (i.e. O classification instances) at the topmost level is 63:1. Also, with increasing levels of fine-grainedness, the number of negative (-O) NE classes is increasing for each binary classifier. We observed on the development set that this skewed distribution heavily biases the classifiers towards the negative category, and accordingly investigated sampling techniques to make the ratio of positive and negative examples more balanced. We experiment with a sampling strategy that over-samples the positive examples and under-samples the negative ones. We define various ratios of over-sampling depending upon the number of positive examples in the original training set. Table 4 lists the factors (f) of over-sampling applied to the original positive samples (P), with minimum and maximum sizes of the ob-

factor f	size of P	min P'	max P'
$20 \times P$	1 – 2K	20	40K
$15 \times P$	2K – 5K	30K	75K
$10 \times P$	5K – 10K	50K	100K
$5 \times P$	10K – 20K	50K	100K
$2 \times P$	20K – 50K	40K	100K
P	50K – ...	50K	>50K

Table 4: Oversampling of positive samples.

Level	MaxEnt-A			MaxEnt-B		
	R	P	F_1	R	P	F_1
1	98.7	85.0	91.4	95.1	83.0	88.6
2	96.0	65.5	77.9	48.1	46.3	47.2
3	95.3	54.3	69.3	43.3	41.1	42.2
4	86.8	52.8	65.6	41.1	37.2	39.1
5	90.4	45.9	60.9	49.2	21.5	29.9
6	91.6	36.9	52.6	51.7	13.2	21.1
7	89.5	31.8	46.9	42.2	10.2	16.4
8	100.0	19.9	66.7	87.1	8.1	14.7
global	85.1	43.2	57.3	61.9	26.6	37.2
hierarchical	87.7	44.8	59.4	64.5	29.5	40.5

Table 6: Level-wise NE recognition & classification evaluation (in %).

tained oversampled sets P' for different ranges of original sizes of P.[5] Oversampling is done without replacement. The number of negative instances is always downsampled on the basis of P' to yield a 1:5 ratio of positive and negative samples, a ratio we estimated from the CoNLL-2003 data.

Level-wise evaluation results on the *FG-NE classification-only (NEC) task* for the MaxEnt classifiers and Lesk are given in Table 5. Table 6 reports results for the evaluation of the MaxEnt model performing *both classification and recognition*. As for coarse-grained NERC, we evaluate using the standard metrics of recall (R), precision (P) and balanced F-measure (F_1). As baseline, we use a majority class assignment – i.e. at each level, we label all instances with the most frequent class label. For *global FG-NE classification*, reported in Table 5, the original fine-grained classes are considered, across the entire class hierarchy. Global evaluation is performed by counting exact label predictions on the entire hierarchy (*global*) and using the evaluation metric of Melamed and Resnik (2000, *hierarchical*). As baseline we assume the most frequent class label in the training set.

Discussion. All methods perform reasonably well, indicating the feasibility of the task. For the MaxEnt models, Table 5 shows a general high recall and decreasing precision as we move down the hierarchy. Degradation in the overall F_1 score is

[5]Sampling ratios are determined on the development set.

Level	Baseline			MaxEnt-A			MaxEnt-B			Lesk		
	R	P	F_1	R	P	F_1	R	P	F_1	R	P	F_1
1	100.0	100.0	100.0	100.0	100.0	100.0	100.0	100.0	100.0	100.0	100.0	100.0
2	28.4	25.9	27.1	85.8	88.6	87.0	79.5	84.9	82.2	16.4	19.7	17.9
3	27.9	23.1	25.2	83.9	88.1	85.9	75.5	79.8	77.5	16.2	16.2	16.2
4	18.8	20.4	19.5	74.6	85.0	79.5	65.4	71.3	68.2	11.3	11.3	11.3
5	25.8	19.0	21.9	78.8	83.4	80.9	78.6	74.1	76.3	13.5	14	13.8
6	24.7	7.8	11.9	88.5	73.6	80.4	78.7	74.1	75.7	33.2	37.5	35.2
7	19.1	5.34	8.3	79.2	76.5	77.8	78.1	72.7	75.3	49.4	49.4	49.4
8	34.2	2.9	5.5	82.8	73.8	78.1	81.1	71.1	75.8	0.1	0.1	0.1
global	34.6	18.5	24.1	81.1	84.2	82.6	78.0	74.2	76.6	36.5	38.6	37.5
hierarchical	33.0	21.2	25.8	83.5	86.2	84.8	78.2	77.8	78.1	36.6	38.7	37.6

Table 5: Level-wise evaluation of fine-grained NE classification techniques (in %).

given by the increasingly limited amount of class instances found towards the low regions of the tree (down to an average of 85 and 90 instances per class for levels 7 and 8, respectively) (cf. Table 1). The 'classical' feature set (MaxEnt-A) yields better performance compared to the semantic feature set (MaxEnt-B). However MaxEnt-B still achieves a respectable performance, given that it contains a few semantic features only.

The MaxEnt classifiers achieve a far better performance than Lesk. This is in-line with previous findings in WSD, namely unsupervised fine-grained disambiguation methods rarely performing above the baseline, and suggests that Lesk can be merely used as a 'strong' baseline. Error analysis showed that it performs poorly due to the limited context provided by the WordNet glosses, and the limited impact of gloss expansions deriving from the low connectivity between synsets.

Comparison of Tables 5 and 6 shows that performance decreases considerably for a classifier that not only assigns fine-grained classes, but also detects which tokens actually are NEs. As for the classification-only task, the performance decreases as one moves to lower levels. This indicates that the complexity of the task is proportional to the fine-grainedness of the class inventory. MaxEnt-B, lacking 'classical' NER features, shows dramatic losses, compared to MaxEnt-A.

Comparison to other work. We compared the performance of our system based on global classification (one vs. rest) against the figures reported for individual categories in Giuliano (2009). The MaxEnt-A system compares favorably, although it considers (i) more classes at each level – i.e. 213 vs. 21 – and (ii) classifies NEs at finer-grained levels – i.e. 8 vs. 4 maximum depth in the respective WordNet fragments. We achieve overall micro average R, P and F_1 values of 87.5%, 85.7% and 86.6%, respectively, compared to Giuliano's 79.6%, 80.9% and 80.2%. Due to the different setups and data used, these figures do not offer a basis for true comparison. However, the figures suggest that our system achieves respectable performance on a more complex classification problem.

7 Conclusions

We presented a method to perform FG-NERC on a large scale. Our contribution lies in the definition of a benchmarking setup for this task in terms of gold standard datasets and strong baseline methods provided by a MaxEnt classifier. We proposed a pattern-based approach for the acquisition of fined-grained NE semantic classes and instances. This corpus-based method relies only on the availability of large text corpora, such as the WaCky corpora, in contrast to resources difficult to obtain, such as query-logs (Paşca and van Durme, 2008). It makes use of a very large Web corpus to extract instances from open-domain contexts – in contrast to standard NERC approaches, which are tailored for newswire data and do not generalize well across domains. Our gold standard training and test datasets are currently based only on appositional patterns[6]. Therefore, it does not include the full spectrum of constructions in which instances can be found in context. Future work will investigate semi-supervised and heuristics (e.g. 'one sense per discourse') methods to expand the data with examples from follow-up mentions, e.g. co-occurring in the same document.

Our MaxEnt models still perform very local classification decisions, relying on separate models for each semantic class. We accordingly plan to explore both global models operating on the overall hierarchy, and more informative feature sets.

[6]The data are available for research purposes at http://www.cl.uni-heidelberg.de/fgnerc.

References

Enrique Alfonseca and Suresh Manandhar. 2002. An unsupervised method for general named entity recognition and automated concept discovery. In *Proc. of GWC-02*.

S. Ananiadou, C. Friedman, and J.I. Tsujii. 2004. Special issue on named entity recognition in biomedicine. *Journal of Biomedical Informatics*, 37(6).

Javier Artiles, Satoshi Sekine, and Julio Gonzalo. 2008. Web people search. In *Proc. of LREC '08*.

Satanjeev Banerjee and Ted Pedersen. 2003. Extended gloss overlap as a measure of semantic relatedness. In *Proc. of IJCAI-03*, pages 805–810.

Marco Baroni, Silvia Bernardini, Adriano Ferraresi, and Eros Zanchetta. 2009. The wacky wide web: A collection of very large linguistically processed web-crawled corpora. *Journal of Language Resources and Evaluation*, 43(3):209–226.

Oliver Bender, Franz Josef Och, and Hermann Ney. 2003. Maximum entropy models for named entity recognition. In *Proc. of CoNLL-03*, pages 148–151.

Razvan Bunescu and Marius Paşca. 2006. Using encyclopedic knowledge for named entity disambiguation. In *Proc. of EACL-06*, pages 9–16.

Oren Etzioni, Michael Cafarella, Doug Downey, Ana-Maria Popescu, Tal Shaked, Stephen Soderland, Daniel S. Weld, and Alexander Yates. 2005. Unsupervised named-entity extraction from the web: an experimental study. *Artificial Intelligence*, 165(1):91–134.

Michael Fleischman and Eduard Hovy. 2002. Fine grained classification of named entities. In *Proc. of COLING-02*, pages 1–7.

Michael Fleischman. 2001. Automated subcategorization of named entities. In *Proc. of the ACL 2001 Student Workshop*.

Radu Florian, Abe Ittycheriah, Hongyan Jing, and Tong Zhang. 2003. Named entity recognition through classifier combination. In *Proc. of CoNLL-03*, pages 168–171.

Claudio Giuliano and Alfio Gliozzo. 2007. Instance based lexical entailment for ontology population. In *Proc. of ACL-07*, pages 248–256.

Claudio Giuliano and Alfio Gliozzo. 2008. Instance-based ontology population exploiting named-entity substitution. In *Proc. of COLING-ACL-08*, pages 265–272.

Claudio Giuliano. 2009. Fine-grained classification of named entities exploiting latent semantic kernels. In *Proc. of CoNLL-09*, pages 201–209.

Taku Kudo and Yuji Matsumoto. 2000. Use of Support Vector Machines for chunk identification. In *Proc. of CoNLL-00*, pages 142–144.

Yoong Keok Lee and Hwee Tou Ng. 2002. An empirical evaluation of knowledge sources and learning algorithms for word sense disambiguation. In *Proc. of EMNLP-02*, pages 41–48.

Michael Lesk. 1986. Automatic sense disambiguation using machine readable dictionaries: how to tell a pine cone from an ice cream cone. In *Proceedings of the ACL-SIGDOC Conference*, pages 24–26.

Thomas Mandl and Christa Womser-Hacker. 2005. The effect of named entities on effectiveness in cross-language information retrieval evaluation. In *Proc. of ACM SAC 2005*, pages 1059–1064.

Andrew McCallum and Andrew Li. 2003. Early results for named entity recognition with conditional random fields, features induction and web-enhanced lexicons. In *Proc. of CoNLL-03*, pages 188–191.

Dan Melamed and Philip Resnik. 2000. Tagger evaluation given hierarchical tag sets. *Computers and the Humanities*, pages 79–84.

MUC-7. 1998. *Proceedings of the Seventh Message Understanding Conference (MUC-7)*. Morgan Kaufmann, San Francisco, Cal.

David Nadeau and Satoshi Sekine. 2007. A survey of named entity recognition and classification. *Journal of Linguisticae Investigationes*, 30(1).

Marius Paşca and Benjamin van Durme. 2008. Weakly-supervised acquisition of open-domain classes and class attributes from web documents and query logs. In *Proc. of ACL-08*, pages 19–27.

M. Paşca, D. Lin, J. Bigham, A. Lifchits, and A. Jain. 2006a. Names and similarities on the web: Fact extraction in the fast lane. In *Proc. of COLING-ACL-06*, pages 809–816.

Marius Paşca, Dekang Lin, Jeffrey Bigham, Andrei Lifchits, and Alpa Jain. 2006b. Organizing and searching the world wide web of facts – Step one: The one-million fact extraction challenge. In *Proc. of AAAI-06*, pages 1400–1405.

Marius Paşca. 2007. Weakly-supervised discovery of named entities using web search queries. In *Proc. of CIKM-2007*, pages 683–690.

Luiz Augusto Pizzato, Diego Molla, and Cécile Paris. 2006. Pseudo relevance feedback using named entities for question answering. In *Proc. of ALTW-2006*, pages 83–90.

Simone Paolo Ponzetto and Michael Strube. 2007. Deriving a large scale taxonomy from Wikipedia. In *Proc. of AAAI-07*, pages 1440–1445.

Fabian M. Suchanek, Gjergji Kasneci, and Gerhard Weikum. 2008. YAGO: A Large Ontology from Wikipedia and WordNet. *Elsevier Journal of Web Semantics*, 6(3):203–217.

Hristo Tanev and Bernardo Magnini. 2006. Weakly supervised approaches for ontology population. In *Proc. of EACL-06*, pages 17–24.

Erik F. Tjong Kim Sang and Fien De Meulder. 2003. Introduction to the CoNLL-2003 Shared Task: Language-independent Named Entity Recognition. In *Proc. of CoNLL-03*, pages 127–132.

Erik F. Tjong Kim Sang. 2002. Introduction to the CoNLL-2002 Shared Task: Language-independent Named Entity Recognition. In *Proc. of CoNLL-02*, pages 155–158.

Using Deep Belief Nets for Chinese Named Entity Categorization

Yu Chen[1], You Ouyang[2], Wenjie Li[2], Dequan Zheng[1], Tiejun Zhao[1]
[1]School of Computer Science and Technology, Harbin Institute of Technology, China
{chenyu, dqzheng, tjzhao}@mtlab.hit.edu.cn
[2]Department of Computing, The Hong Kong Polytechnic University, Hong Kong
{csyouyang, cswjli}@comp.polyu.edu.hk

Abstract

Identifying named entities is essential in understanding plain texts. Moreover, the categories of the named entities are indicative of their roles in the texts. In this paper, we propose a novel approach, Deep Belief Nets (DBN), for the Chinese entity mention categorization problem. DBN has very strong representation power and it is able to elaborately self-train for discovering complicated feature combinations. The experiments conducted on the Automatic Context Extraction (ACE) 2004 data set demonstrate the effectiveness of DBN. It outperforms the state-of-the-art learning models such as SVM or BP neural network.

1 Introduction

Named entities (NE) are defined as the names of existing objects, such as persons, organizations and etc. Identifying NEs in plain texts provides structured information for semantic analysis. Hence the named entity recognition (NER) task is a fundamental task for a wide variety of natural language processing applications, such as question answering, information retrieval and etc. In a text, an entity may either be referred to by a common noun, a noun phrase, or a pronoun. Each reference of the entity is called a mention. NER indeed requires the systems to identify these entity mentions from plain texts. The task can be decomposed into two sub-tasks, i.e., the identification of the entities in the text and the classification of the entities into a set of pre-defined categories. In the study of this paper, we focus on the second sub-task and assume that the boundaries of all the entity mentions to be categorized are already correctly identified.

In early times, NER systems are mainly based on handcrafted rule-based approaches. Although rule-based approaches achieved reasonably good results, they have some obvious flaws. First, they require exhausted handcraft work to construct a proper and complete rule set, which partially expressing the meaning of entity. Moreover, once the interest of task is transferred to a different domain or language, rules have to be revised or even rewritten. The discovered rules are indeed heavily dependent on the task interests and the particular corpus. Finally, the manually-formatted rules are usually incomplete and their qualities are not guaranteed.

Recently, more attentions are switched to the applications of machine learning models with statistic information. In this camp, entity categorization is typically cast as a multi-class classification process, where the named entities are represented by feature vectors. Usually, the vectors are abstracted by some lexical and syntactic features instead of semantic feature. Many learning models, such as Support Vector Machine (SVM) and Neural Network (NN), are then used to classify the entities by their feature vectors.

Entity categorization in Chinese attracted less attention when compared to English or other western languages. This is mainly because the unique characteristics of Chinese. One of the most common problems is the lack of boundary information in Chinese texts. For this problem, character-based methods are reported to be a possible substitution of word-based methods. As to character-based methods, it is important to study the implicit combination of characters.

In our study, we explore the use of Deep Belief Net (DBN) in character-based entity categorization. DBN is a neural network model which is developed under the deep learning architecture. It is claimed to be able to automatically learn a deep hierarchy of the input features with increasing levels of abstraction for the complex problem. In our problem, DBN is used to automatically discover the complicated composite effects of the characters to the NE categories from the input data. With DBN, we need not to manually construct the character combination features for expressing the semantic relationship among characters in entities. Moreover, the deep structure of DBN enables the possibility of discovering very sophisticated

Proceedings of the 2010 Named Entities Workshop, ACL 2010, pages 102–109,
Uppsala, Sweden, 16 July 2010.

combinations of the characters, which may even be hard to discover by human.

The rest of this paper is organized as follow. Section 2 reviews the related work on name entity categorization. Section 3 introduces the methodology of the proposed approach. Section 4 provides the experimental results. Finally, section 5 concludes the whole paper.

2 Related work

Over the past decades, NER has evolved from simple rule-based approaches to adapted self-training machine learning approaches.

As early rule-based approaches, MacDonald (1993) utilized local context, which implicate internal and external evidence, to aid on categorization. Wacholder (1997) employed an aggregation of classification method to capture internal rules. Both used hand-written rules and knowledge bases. Later, Collins (1999) adopted the AdaBoost algorithm to find a weighted combination of simple classifiers. They reported that the combination of simple classifiers can yield some powerful systems with much better performances. As a matter of fact, these methods all need manual studies on the construction of the rule set or the simple classifiers.

Machine learning models attract more attentions recently. Usually, they train classification models based on context features. Various lexical and syntactic features are considered, such as N-grams, Part-Of-Speech (POS), and etc. Zhou and Su (2002) integrated four different kinds of features, which convey different semantic information, for a classification model based on the Hidden Markov Model (HMM). Koen (2006) built a classifier with the Conditional Random Field (CRF) model to classify noun phrases in a text with the WordNet SynSet. Isozaki and Kazawa (2002) studied the use of SVM instead.

There were fewer studies in Chinese entity categorization. Guo and Jiang (2005) applied Robust Risk Minimization to classify the named entities. The features include seven traditional lexical features and two external-NE-hints based features. An important result they reported is that character-based features can be as good as word-based features since they avoid the Chinese word segmentation errors. In (Jing et al., 2003), it was further reported that pure character-based models can even outperform word-based models with character combination features.

Deep Belief Net is introduced in (Hinton et al., 2006). According to their definition, DBN is a deep neural network that consists of one or more Restricted Boltzmann Machine (RBM) layers and a Back Propagation (BP) layer. This multi-layer structure leads to a strong representation power of DBN. Moreover, DBN is quite efficient by using RBM to implement the middle layers, since RBM can be learned very quickly by the Contrastive Divergence (CD) approach. Therefore, we believe that DBN is very suitable for the character-level Chinese entity mention categorization approach. It can be used to solve the multi-class categorization problem with just simple binary features as the input.

3 Deep Belief Network for Chinese Entity Categorization

3.1 Problem Formalization

An Entity mention categorization is a process of classifying the entity mentions into different categories. In this paper, we assume that the entity mentions are already correctly detected from the texts. Moreover, an entity mention should belong to one and only one predefined category. Formally, the categorization function of the name entities is

$$f(V(e_i)) \rightarrow C \quad (1)$$

where e_i is an entity mention from all the mention set E, $V(e_i)$ is the binary feature vector of e_i, $C=\{C_1, C_2, \ldots, C_M\}$ is the pre-defined categories. Now the question is to find a classification function $f: R^{|D|} \rightarrow C$ which maps the feature vector $V(e_i)$ of an entity mention to its category. Generally, this classification function is learned from training data consisting of entity mentions with labeled categories. The learned function is then used to predict the category of new entity mentions by their feature vectors.

3.2 Character-based Features

As mentioned in the introduction, we intend to use character-level features for the purpose of avoiding the impact of the Chinese word segmentation errors. Denote the character dictionary as $D=\{d_1, d_2, \ldots, d_N\}$. To an e, it's feature vector is $V(e)=\{v_1, v_2, \ldots, v_N\}$. Each unit v_i can be valued as Equation 2.

$$v_i = \begin{cases} 1 & d_i \in e \\ 0 & d_i \notin e \end{cases} \quad (2)$$

For example, there is an entity mention 克林顿 'Clinton'. So its feature vector is a vector with the same length as the character dictionary, in which all the dimensions are 0 except the three dimensions standing for 克, 林, and 顿. The representation is clearly illustrated in Figure 1 below. Since our objective is to test the effectiveness of DBN for this task. Therefore, we do not involve any other feature.

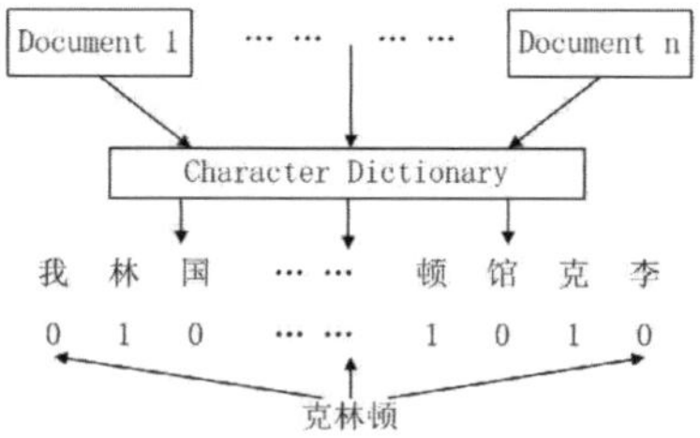

Fig. 1. Generating the character-level features

Characters compose the named entity and express its meaning. As a matter of fact, the composite effect of the characters to the mention category is quite complicated. For example, 老李 'Mr. Li' and 老挝 'Laos' both have character 老, but 老李 'Mr. Li' indicates a person but 老挝 'Laos' indicates a country. These are totally different NEs. Another example is 巴拉圭首都 'Capital of Paraguay' and 雅松森 'Asuncion'. They are two entity mentions point to the same entity despite that the two entities do not have any common characters. In such case, independent character features are not sufficient to determine the categories of the entity mentions. So we should also introduce some features which are able to represent the combinational effects of the characters. However, such kind of features is very hard to discover. Meanwhile, a complete set of combinations is nearly impossible to be found manually due to the exponential number of all the possible combinations. As in our study, we adopt DBN to automatically find the character combinations.

3.3 Deep Belief Nets

Deep Belief Network (DBN) is a complicated model which combines a set of simple models that are sequentially connected (Ackley, 1985). This deep architecture can be viewed as multiple layers. In DBN, upper layers are supposed to represent more "abstract" concepts that explain the input data whereas lower layers extract "low-level features" from the data. DBN often consists of many layers, including multiple Restricted Boltzmann Machine (RBM) layers and a Back Propagation (BP) layer.

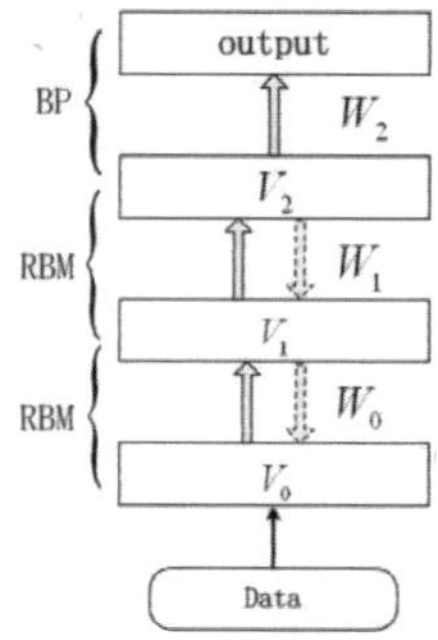

Fig. 2. The structure of a DBN.

As illustrated in Figure 2, when DBN receives a feature vector, the feature vector is processed from the bottom to the top through several RBM layers in order to get the weights in each RBM layer, maintaining as many features as possible when they are transferred to the next layer. RBM deals with feature vectors only and omits the label information. It is unsupervised. In addition, each RBM layer learns its parameters independently. This makes the parameters optimal for the relevant RBM layer but not optimal for the whole model. To solve this problem, there is a supervised BP layer on top of the model which fine-tunes the whole model in the learning process and generates the output in the inference process. After the processing of all these layers, the final feature vector consists of some sophisticated features, which reflect the structured information among the original features. With this new feature vector, the classification performance is better than directly using the original feature vector.

None of the RBM is capable of guaranteeing that all the information conveyed to the output is accurate or important enough. However the learned information produced by preceding RBM layer will be continuously refined through the next RBM layer to weaken the wrong or insignificant information in the input. Each layer can detect feature in the relevant spaces. Multiple layers help to detect more features in different spaces. Lower layers could support object detection by spotting low-level features indicative of object parts. Conversely, information about objects in the higher layers could resolve lower-level ambiguities. The units in the final layer share more information from the data. This increases the representation power of the whole model. It is certain that more layers mean more computation time.

DBN has some attractive features which make it very suitable for our problem.

1) The unsupervised process can detect the structures in the input and automatically obtain better feature vectors for classification.
2) The supervised BP layer can modify the whole network by back-propagation to improve both the feature vectors and the classification results.
3) The generative model makes it easy to interpret the distributed representations in the deep hidden layers.
4) This is a fast learning algorithm that can find a fairly good set of parameters quickly and can ensure the efficiency of DBN.

3.3.1 Restricted Boltzmann Machine (RBM)

In this section, we will introduce RBM, which is the core component of DBN. RBM is Boltzmann Machine with no connection within the same layer. An RBM is constructed with one visible layer and one hidden layer. Each visible unit in the visible layer V is an observed variable v_i while each hidden unit in the hidden layer H is a hidden variable h_j. Its joint distribution is

$$p(v,h) \propto \exp(-E(v,h)) = e^{h^T Wv + b^T x + c^T h} \quad (3)$$

In RBM, the parameters that need to be estimated are $\theta = (W,b,c)$ and $(v,h) \in \{0,1\}^2$.

To learn RBM, the optimum parameters are obtained by maximizing the above probability on the training data (Hinton, 1999). However, the probability is indeed very difficult in practical calculation. A traditional way is to find the gradient between the initial parameters and the respect parameters. By modifying the previous parameters with the gradient, the expected parameters can gradually approximate the target parameters as

$$W^{(\tau+1)} = W^{(\tau)} + \eta \frac{\partial P(v^0)}{\partial W}\bigg|_{W^\tau} \quad (4)$$

where η is a parameter controlling the leaning rate. It determines the speed of W converging to the target.

Traditionally, the Markov chain Monte Carlo method (MCMC) is used to calculate this kind of gradient.

$$\frac{\partial \log p(v,h)}{\partial w} = \langle h^0 v^0 \rangle - \langle h^\infty v^\infty \rangle \quad (5)$$

where $\log p(v,h)$ is the log probability of the data. $\langle h^0 v^0 \rangle$ denotes the multiplication of the average over the data states and its relevant sample in hidden unit. $\langle h^\infty v^\infty \rangle$ denotes the multiplication of the average over the model states in visible unit and its relevant sample in hidden unit.

However, MCMC requires estimating an exponential number of terms. Therefore, it typically takes a long time to converge to $\langle h^\infty v^\infty \rangle$. Hinton (2002) introduced an alternative algorithm, i.e., the contrastive divergence (CD) algorithm, as a substitution. It is reported that CD can train the model much more efficiently than MCMC. To estimate the distribution $p(x)$, CD considers a series of distributions { $p_n(x)$ } which indicate the distributions in n steps. It approximates the gap of two different Kullback-Leiler divergences (Kullback, 1987) as

$$CD_n = KL(p_0 \| p_\infty) - KL(p_n \| p_\infty) \quad (6)$$

Maximizing the log probability of the data is exactly the same as minimizing the Kullback–Leibler divergence between the distribution of the data p_0 and the equilibrium distribution p_∞ defined by the model. In each step, the gap is approximately minimized so that we can obtain the final distribution which has the smallest Kullback-Leiler divergence with the fantasy distribution.

After n steps, the gradient can be estimated and used in Equation 4 to adjust the weights of RBM. In our experiments, we set n to be 1. It means that in each step of gradient calculation, the estimate of the gradient is used to adjust the weight of RBM. In this case, the estimate of the gradient is just the gap between the products of the visual layer and the hidden layer, i.e.,

$$\frac{\partial \log p(v,h)}{\partial W} = \langle h^0 v^0 \rangle - \langle h^1 v^1 \rangle \quad (7)$$

Figure 3 below illustrates the process of learning RBM with CD-based gradient estimation.

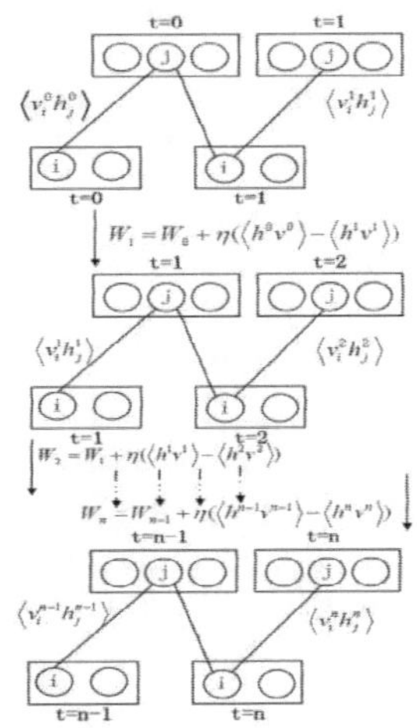

Fig. 3. Learning RBM with CD-based gradient estimation

3.3.2 Back-propagation (BP)

The RBM layers provide an unsupervised analysis on the structures of data set. They automatically detect sophisticated feature vectors. The last layer in DBN is the BP layer. It takes the output from the last RBM layer and applies it in the final supervised learning process. In DBN, not only is the supervised BP layer used to generate the final categories, but it is also used to fine-tune the whole network. Specifically speaking, when the parameters in BP layer are changed during its iterating process, the changes are passed to the other RBM layers in a top-to-bottom sequence.

The BP algorithm has a feed-forward step and a back-propagation step. In the feed-forward step, the input values are propagated to obtain the output values. In the back-propagation step, the output values are compared to the real category labels and used them to modify the parameters of the model. We consider the weight w_{ij} which indicates the edge pointing from the *i*-th node in one RBM layer to the *j*-th node in its upper layer. The computation in feed-forward is $o_i w_{ij}$, where o_i is the stored output for the unit *i*. In the back-propagation step, we compute the error *E* in the upper layers and also the gradient with respect to this error, i.e., $\partial E / \partial o_i w_{ij}$. Then the weight w_{ij} will be adjusted by the gradient descent.

$$\Delta w_{ij} = -\gamma o_i \frac{\partial E}{\partial o_i w_{ij}} = -\gamma o_i \delta_j \qquad (8)$$

where $-\gamma$ is used to control the length of the moving step.

3.3.3 DBN-based Entity Mention Categorization

For each entity mention, it is represented by the character feature vector as introduced in section 3.2 and then fed to DBN. The training procedure can be divided into two phases. The first phase is the parameter estimation process of the RBMs on all the inputted feature vectors. When a feature vector is fed to DBN, the first RBM layer is adjusted automatically according to this vector. After the first RBM layer is ready, its output becomes the input of the second RBM layer. The weights of the second RBM layer are also adjusted. The similar procedure is carried out on all the RBM layers. Then DBN will operates in the second phase, the back-propagation algorithm. The labeled categories of the entity mention are used to tune the parameters of the BP layer. Moreover, the changes of the BP layer are also fed back to the RBM layers. The procedure will iterate until the terminating condition is met. It can be a fixed number of iterations or a pre-given precision threshold. Once the weights of all the layers in DBN are obtained, the estimated model could be used to prediction.

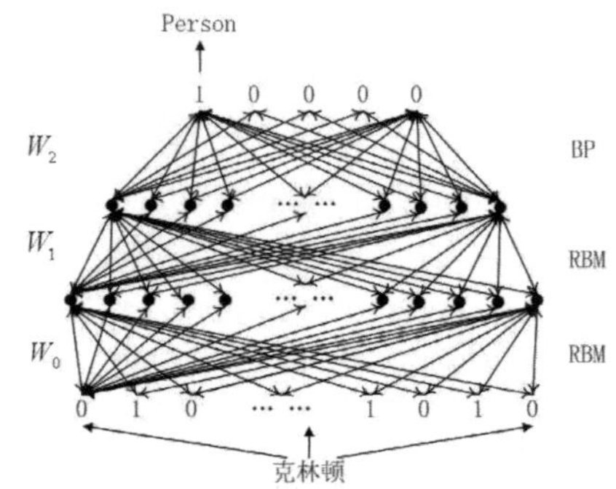

Fig. 4. The mention categorization process of DBN

Figure 4 illustrates the classification process of DBN. In prediction, for an entity mention *e*, we first calculate its feature vector *V*(*e*) and used as the input of DBN. *V*(*e*) is passed through all the layers to get the outputs for all RBM layers and last back-propagation layer. In the *i*th RBM layer, the dimensions in the input vector $V_{input\_i}(e)$ are combined to yield the dimensions of the next feature vector $V_{output\_i}(e)$ as input of the next layer. After the feature vector *V*(*e*) goes through all the RBM layers, it is indeed transformed to another feature vector *V'*(*e*) which consists of complicated combinations of the original character features and contains rich structured information between the characters. This feature vector is then fed into the BP layer to get the final category *c*(*e*).

4 Experiments

4.1 Experiment Setup

In our experiment, we use the ACE 2004 corpus to evaluate our approach. The objective of this study is that the correctly detected Chinese entity mentions categorization using DBN from the text and figure out the suitability of DBN on this task. Moreover, an entity mention should belong to one and only one category.

According to the guideline of the ACE04 task, there are five categories for consideration in total, i.e., Person, Organization, Geo-political entity, Location, and Facility. Moreover, each entity mention is expressed in two forms, i.e., the head and the extent. For example, 美国总统克林顿 'President Clinton of USA' is the extent of an entity mention and 克林顿 'Clinton' is the corresponding head. The two phrases both point to a named entity whose name is Clinton and he is the president of USA. Here we make the "breakdown" strategy mentioned in Li et al. (2007) that only the entity head is considered to generate the feature vector, considering that the information from the entity head refines the name entity. Although the entity extent includes more information, it also brings many noises which may make the learning process much more difficult.

In our experiments, we test the machine learning models under a 4-flod cross-validation. All entity mentions are divided into four parts randomly where three parts are used for training and one for test. In total, 7746 mentions are used for training and 2482 mentions are used for testing at each round. Precision is chosen as the evaluation criterion, calculated by the proportion of the number of correctly categorized instances and the number of total instances. Since all the instances should be classified, the recall value is equal to the precision value.

4.2 Evaluation on Named Entity categorization

First of all, we provide some statistics of the data set. The distribution of entity mentions in each category is given in table 1. The size of the character dictionary in the corpus is 1185, so does the dimension of each feature vector.

Type	Quantity
Person	4197
Organization	1783
Geo-political entity	287
Location	3263
Facility	399

Table 1. Number of entity mentions in each category

In the first experiment, we compare the performance of DBN with some popular classification algorithms, including Support Vector Machine (labeled by SVM) and a traditional BP neutral network (labeled by NN (BP)). To implement the models, we use the LibSVM toolkit[1] for SVM and the neural neutral network toolbox in Matlab[2] for BP. The DBN in this experiment includes two RBM layers and one BP layer. Results of the first experiment are given in Table 2.

Learning Model	Precision
DBN	91.45%
SVM	90.29%
NN(BP)	87.23%

Table 2. Performances of the systems with different classification models

In this experiment, the DBN has three RBM layers and one BP layer. And the numbers of units in each RBM layer are 900, 600 and 300 respectively. NN (BP) has the same structure as DBN. As for SVM, we choose the linear kernel with the penalty parameter C=1 and set the other parameters as default after comparing different kernels and parameters.

In the results, DBN achieved better performance than both SVM and BP neural network. This clearly proved the advantages of DBN. The deep architecture of DBN yields stronger representation power which makes it able to detect more complicated and efficient features, thus better performance is achieved.

In the second experiment, we intend to examine the performance of DBN with different number of RBM layers, from one RBM layer plus one BP layer to three RBM layers plus one BP layer. The amount of the units in the first RBM layer is set 900 and the amount in the second RBM layer is 600, if the second layer exists. As for the third RBM layers, the amount of units is set to 300.

Construction of Neural Network	Precision
Three RBMs and One BP	91.45%
Two RBMs and One BP	91.42%
One RBM and one BP	91.05%

Table 3. Performance of DBNs with different number s of RBM layers

Results in Table 3 show that the performance tends to be better when more RBM layers are incorporated. More RBM layers do enhance the representation power of DBN. However, it is also noted that the improvement is not significant from two layers to three layers. The reason may

[1] available at http://www.csie.ntu.edu.tw/~cjlin/libsvm/
[2] available at http://www.mathworks.com/access/helpdesk/help/toolbox/nnet/backprop.html

be that two-RBM DBN already has enough representation power for modeling this data set and thus one more RBM layer brings insignificant improvement. It is also mentioned in Hinton (2006) that more than three RBM layers are indeed not necessary. Another important result in Table 3 is that the DBN with One RBM and one BP performs much better than the neutral network with only BP in Table 1. This clearly showed the effectiveness of feature combination by the RBM layer again.

As to the amount of units in each RBM layer, it is manually fixed in upper experiments. This number certainly affects the representation power of an RBM layer, consequently the representation power of the whole DBN. In this set of experiment, we intend to study the effectiveness of the unit size to the performance of DBN. A series of DBNs with only one RBM layer and different unit numbers for this RBM layer is evaluated. The results are provided in Table 4 below.

Construction of Neural Network	Precision
one RBM(300 units) + one BP	90.61%
one RBM(600 units) + one BP	90.69%
one RBM(900 units) + one BP	91.05%
one RBM(1200 units) + one BP	90.98%
one RBM(1500 units) + one BP	90.61%
one RBM(1800 units) + one BP	90.57%

Table 4. Performance of One-RBM DBNs with different number of units

Based on the results, we can see that the performance is quite stable with different unit numbers. But the numbers that are closer to the original feature size seem to be some better. This could suggest that we should not decrease or increase the dimension of the vector feature too much when casting the vector transformation by RBM layers.

Finally, we show the results of the individual categories. For each category, the Precision-Recall-F values are provided in table 5, in which the *F*-measure is calculated by

$$F\text{-measure}=\frac{2*\text{Precision}*\text{Recall}}{\text{Precision}+\text{Recall}} \quad (9)$$

Type	P	R	*F*
Person	91.26%	96.26%	93.70%
Organization	89.86%	89.04%	89.45%
Location	77.58%	59.21%	76.17%
Geo-political entity	93.60%	91.89%	92.74%
Facility	77.43%	63.72%	69.91%

Table 5. Performances of the system on each category

5 Conclusions

In this paper we presented our recent work on applying a novel machine learning model, the Deep Belief Nets, on Chinese entity mention categorization. It is demonstrated that DBN is very suitable for character-level mention categorization approaches due to its strong representation power and the ability on discovering complicated feature combinations. We conducted a series of experiments to prove the benefits of DBN. Experimental results clearly showed the advantages of DBN that it obtained better performance than existing approaches such as SVM and traditional BP neutral network.

References

David Ackley, Geoffrey Hinton, and Terrence Sejnowski. 1985. A learning algorithm for Boltzmann machines. *Cognitive Science*. 9.

David MacDonald. 1993. Internal and external evidence in the identification and semantic categorization of proper names. *Corpus Processing for Lexical Acquisition*, MIT Press, 61-76.

Geoffrey Hinton. 1999. Products of experts. In Proceedings of the Ninth International. *Conference on Artificial Neural Networks (ICANN)*. Vol. 1, 1–6.

Geoffrey Hinton. 2002. Training products of experts by minimizing contrastive divergence. *Neural Computation*, 14, 1771–1800.

Geoffrey Hinton, Simon Osindero, and Yee-Whey Teh. 2006. A fast learning algorithm for deep belief nets. *Neural Computation*. 18, 1527–1554 .

GuoDong Zhou and Jian Su. 2002. Named entity recognition using an hmm-based chunk tagger. *In proceedings of ACL*. 473-480.

Hideki Isozaki and Hideto Kazawa. 2002. Efficient support vector classifiers for named entity recognition. *In proceedings of IJCNLP*. 1-7.

Honglei Guo, Jianmin Jiang, Guang Hu and Tong Zhang. 2005. Chinese named entity recognition based on multilevel linguistics features. *In proceedings of IJCNLP*. 90-99.

Jing, Hongyan, Radu Florian, Xiaoqiang Luo, Tong Zhang and Abraham Ittycheriah. 2003. How to get a Chinese name (entity): Segmentation and combination issues. *In proceedings of EMNLP*. 200-207.

Koen Deschacht and Marie-Francine Moens. 2006, Efficient Hierarchical Entity Classifier Using Conditional Random Field. *In Proceedings of the*

2nd Workshop on Ontology Learning and Population. 33-40.

Michael Collins and Yoram Singer. 1999. Unsupervised models for named entity classification. *In Proceedings of EMNLP'99.*

Nina Wacholder, Yael Ravin and Misook Choi. 1997. Disambiguation of Proper Names in Text. *In Proceedings of the Fifth Conference on Applied Natural Language Processing.*

Solomon Kullback. 1987. Letter to the Editor: The Kullback-Leibler distance. *The American Statistician* 41 (4): 340–341.

Wenjie Li and Donglei Qian. 2007. Detecting, Categorizing and Clustering Entity Mentions in Chinese Text, *in Proceedings of the 30th Annual International ACM SIGIR Conference (SIGIR'07).* 647-654.

Yoshua Bengio and Yann LeCun. 2007. Scaling learning algorithms towards ai. *Large-Scale Kernel Machines.* MIT Press.

Simplified Feature Set for Arabic Named Entity Recognition

Ahmed Abdul-Hamid, Kareem Darwish
Cairo Microsoft Innovation Center
Cairo, Egypt
{ahmedab,kareemd}@microsoft.com

Abstract

This paper introduces simplified yet effective features that can robustly identify named entities in Arabic text without the need for morphological or syntactic analysis or gazetteers. A CRF sequence labeling model is trained on features that primarily use character n-gram of leading and trailing letters in words and word n-grams. The proposed features help overcome some of the morphological and orthographic complexities of Arabic. In comparing to results in the literature using Arabic specific features such POS tags on the same dataset and same CRF implementation, the results in this paper are lower by 2 F-measure points for locations, but are better by 8 points for organizations and 9 points for persons.

1 Introduction

Named entity recognition (NER) continues to be an important part of many NLP applications such as information extraction, machine translation, and question answering (Benajiba et al., 2008). NER is concerned with identifying sequences of words referring to named entities (NE's) such as persons, locations, and organizations. For example, in the word sequence "Alan Mulally, CEO of Detroit based Ford Motor Company," Alan Mulally, Detroit, and Ford Motor Company would be identified as a person, a location, and an organization respectively.

Arabic is a Semitic language that present interesting morphological and orthographic challenges that may complicate NER. Some of these challenges include:

- Coordinating conjunctions, prepositions, possessive pronouns, and determiners are typically attached to words as prefixes or suffixes.
- Proper names are often common language words. For example, the proper name "Iman" also means faith.
- Lack capitalization of proper nouns.

The paper introduces a simplified set of features that can robustly identify NER for Arabic without the need for morphological or syntactic analysis. The proposed features include: word leading and trailing character n-gram features that help handle prefix and suffix attachment; word n-gram probability based features that attempt to capture the distribution of NE's in text; word sequence features; and word length.

The contributions of this paper are as follows:

1. Identifying simplified features that work well for Arabic without gazetteers and without morphological and syntactic features, leading to improvements over previously reported results.
2. Using leading and trailing character n-grams in words, which help capture valuable morphological and orthographic clues that would indicate or counter-indicate the presence of NE's.
3. Incorporating word language modeling based features to capture word associations and relative distribution of named entities in text.

Conditional Random Fields (CRF) sequence labeling was used in identifying NE's, and the experiments were performed on two standard Arabic NER datasets.

The rest of the paper is organized as follows: Section 2 surveys prior work on Arabic NER; Section 3 introduces the proposed features and motivates their use; Section 4 describes experimental setup and evaluation sets; Section 5 reports on experimental results; and Section 6 concludes the paper.

2 Background

Much work has been done on NER with multiple evaluation forums dedicated to information extraction in general and to NER in specific. Nadeau and Sekine (2009) surveyed lots of work on NER for a variety of languages and using a myriad of techniques. Significant work has been conducted by Benajiba and colleagues on Arabic NER (Benajiba and Rosso, 2008; Benajiba et al., 2008; Benajiba and Rosso, 2007; Benajiba et al.,

Proceedings of the 2010 Named Entities Workshop, ACL 2010, pages 110–115,
Uppsala, Sweden, 16 July 2010.

2007). Benajiba et al. (2007) used a maximum entropy based classification trained on a feature set that include the use of gazetteers and a stop-word list, appearance of a NE in the training set, leading and trailing word bigrams, and the tag of the previous word. They reported 80%, 37%, and 47% F-measure for locations, organizations, and persons respectively. Benajiba and Rosso (2007) improved their system by incorporating POS tags to improve NE boundary detection. They reported 87%, 46%, and 52% F-measure for locations, organizations, and persons respectively. Benajiba and Rosso (2008) used CRF sequence labeling and incorporated many language specific features, namely POS tagging, base-phrase chunking, Arabic tokenization, and adjectives indicating nationality. They reported that tokenization generally improved recall. Using POS tagging generally improved recall at the expense of precision, leading to overall improvement in F-measure. Using all their suggested features they reported 90%, 66%, and 73% F-measure for location, organization, and persons respectively. In Benajiba et al. (2008), they examined the same feature set on the Automatic Content Extraction (ACE) datasets using CRF sequence labeling and Support Vector Machine (SVM) classifier. They did not report per category F-measure, but they reported overall 81%, 75%, and 78% macro-average F-measure for broadcast news and newswire on the ACE 2003, 2004, and 2005 datasets respectively. Huang (2005) used an HMM based NE recognizer for Arabic and reported 77% F-measure on the ACE 2003 dataset. Farber et al. (2008) used POS tags obtained from an Arabic morphological analyzer to enhance NER. They reported 70% F-measure on the ACE 2005 dataset. Shaalan and Raza (2007) reported on a rule-based system that uses hand crafted grammars and regular expressions in conjunction with gazetteers. They reported upwards of 93% F-measure, but they conducted their experiments on non-standard datasets, making comparison difficult.

McNamee and Mayfield (2002) explored the training of an SVM classifier using many language independent binary features such as leading and trailing letters in a word, word length, presence of digits in a word, and capitalization. They reported promising results for Spanish and Dutch. In follow on work, Mayfield et al. (2003) used thousands of language independent features such character n-grams, capitalization, word length, and position in a sentence, along with language dependent features such as POS tags and BP chunking. For English, they reported 89%, 79%, and 91% F-measure for location, organization, and persons respectively.

The use of CRF sequence labeling has been increasing over the past few years (McCallum and Li, 2003; Nadeau and Sekine, 2009) with good success (Benajiba and Rosso, 2008). Though, CRF's are not guaranteed to be better than SVM's (Benajiba et al., 2008).

3 NER Features

For this work, a CRF sequence labeling was used. The advantage of using CRF is that they combine HMM-like generative power with classifier-like discrimination (Lafferty et al., 2001; Sha and Pereira, 2003). When a CRF makes a decision on the label to assign to a word, it also accounts for the previous and succeeding words. The CRF was trained on a large set of surface features to minimize the use of Arabic morphological and syntactic features. Apart from stemming two coordinating conjunctions, no other Arabic specific features were used.
The features used were as follows:

- Leading and trailing character bigrams (**6bi**). For a given word composed of the letter sequence l_0^n, where l_0 and l_n are a start and end word markers respectively, the first three bigrams (l_0^1, l_1^2, and l_2^3) and last three bigrams (l_{n-3}^{n-2}, l_{n-2}^{n-1}, and l_{n-1}^{n}) were used as features. Using leading and trailing character bigrams of a word was an attempt to account for morphological and orthographic complexities of Arabic and to capture surface clues that would indicate the presence of a NE or not. For example, plural forms of common words in Arabic are often obtained by attaching the suffixes *wn*[1] (ون) or *yn* (ين) for masculine nouns and *At* (ات) for feminine nouns. Presence of such plural form markers would generally indicate a plural noun, but would counter-indicate a NE. Also, verbs in present tense start with the letters *A* (ا), *t* (ت), *y* (ي), and *n* (ن). These would contribute to concluding that a word may not be a NE. Further, coordinate conjunctions, such as *f* (ف) and *w* (و), and prepositions, such as *b* (ب), *k* (ك), and *l* (ل), composed of single letters are often attached as prefixes to words. Accounting for them may help overcome some of the problems associated with not

[1] Arabic letters are presented using the Buckwalter transliteration scheme

stemming. Further, the determiner *Al* (ال) may be a good indicator for proper nouns particularly in the case of organizations. This would be captured by the second bigram from the head of the word. If the determiner is preceded by a coordinating conjunction, the third bigram from the head of the word would be able to capture this feature.

- Leading and trailing character trigrams (**6tri**). For a given word composed of the letter sequence l_0^n, where l_0 and l_n are a start and end word markers respectively, the first three trigrams (l_0^2, l_1^3, and l_2^4) and last three trigrams (l_{n-4}^{n-2}, l_{n-3}^{n-1}, and l_{n-2}^{n}) were used as features. The rationale for using these features is very similar to that of using character bigrams. The added value of using character trigrams, is that they would allow for the capture of combinations of prefixes and suffixes. For example, a word may begin with the prefixes *w+Al* (و+ال), which are a coordinating conjunction and determiner respectively.
- Leading and trailing character 4-grams (**6quad**). For a given word composed of the letter sequence l_0^n, where l_0 and l_n are a start and end word markers respectively, the first three 4 grams (l_0^3, l_1^4, and l_2^5) and last three 4 grams (l_{n-5}^{n-2}, l_{n-4}^{n-1}, and l_{n-3}^{n}) were used as features. Similar to leading and trailing trigrams, these features can capture combinations of prefixes and suffixes.
- Word position (**WP**). The feature captures the relative position of a word in a sentence as follows:

$$WP = \frac{Absolute\ position}{Sentence\ length}$$

Typically, Arabic is a VSO language. Thus, NE's in specific and nouns in general do not start sentences.

- Word length (**WL**). The feature captures the length of named entities, as some NE's, particularly transliterated NE's, may be longer than regular words.
- Word unigram probability (**1gP**). This is simply the unigram probability of word. Accounting for unigram probability would help exclude common words. Also, named entities are often out-of-vocabulary words.
- Word with previous and word with succeeding word-unigram ratio (**1gPr**). Given a word w_i, these two features are computed as:

$$1gPr_1 = \frac{p(w_i)}{p(w_{i-1})}$$

$$1gPr_2 = \frac{p(w_{i+1})}{p(w_i)}$$

This feature would potentially capture major shifts between word probabilities. For example, a named entity is likely to have much lower probability compared to the word before it and the word after it.

- Features that account for dependence between words in a named entity. Popular NE's are likely collocations, and words that make up named entities don't occur next to each other by chance. These features are as follows:
  - Word with previous and word with succeeding word bigram (**2gP**). For a given word w_i, the two bigram probabilities are $p(w_{i-1}w_i)$ and $p(w_iw_{i+1})$. Words composing named entities are likely conditionally dependent.
  - *t*-test between a word and the word that precedes and succeeds it (**T**). Given a word sequence w_i and w_{i+1}:

$$t = \frac{\bar{x} - \mu}{\sqrt{\frac{s^2}{N}}}$$

    Wher$\bar{x} = p(w_i\, w_{i+1})$, $= p(w_i) * p(w_{i+1})$, $s^2 \approx \bar{x}$, and *N* is the number of words in the corpus (Manning and Schutze, 1999).
  - Mutual information between a word and the word that precedes and succeeds it (**MI**). Given a word sequence w_i and w_{i+1}:
    $MI = log_2 \left[\frac{\bar{x}}{\mu}\right]$, where $\bar{x}$ and μ are identical to those in the t-test.
- Character n-gram probability (**3gCLM**). Given character trigram language models for locations, persons, organizations, and non-NE's, the four features are just the character language model probabilities using the four different language models. The motivation for these features stem from the likelihood that NE's may have a different distribution of characters particularly for person names. This stems from the fact that many NE's are transliterated names.

4 Experimental Setup

4.1 Datasets

For this work, the NE's of interest were persons, locations, and organizations only. Two datasets were used for the work in this paper. The first was a NE tagged dataset developed by Binajiba et al. (2007). The Binajiba dataset is composed of newswire articles totaling more than 150,000 words. The number of different NE's in the collection are:

Locations (LOC)	878
Organizations (ORG)	342
Persons (PER)	689

The second was the Arabic Automatic Content Extraction (ACE) 2005 dataset. The ACE dataset is composed of newswire, broadcast news, and weblogs. For experiments in this work, the weblogs portion of the ACE collection was excluded, because weblogs often include colloquial Arabic that does not conform to modern standard Arabic. Also, ACE tags contain many subcategories. For example, locations are tagged as regions, bodies of water, states, etc. All sub-tags were ignored and were conflated to the base tags (LOC, ORG, PER). Further, out of the 40 subentity types, entities belonging to the following 13 ACE sub-entity types were excluded because they require anaphora resolution or they refer to non-specific NE's: nominal, pronominal, kind of entity (as opposed to a specific entity), negatively quantified entity, underspecified entity, address, boundary (eg. border), celestial object (comet), entertainment venue (eg. movie theater), sport (eg. football), indeterminate (eg. human), vehicle, and weapon. The total number of words in the collection is 98,530 words (66,590 from newswire and 31,940 from broadcast news). The number of NE's is as follows:

Locations (LOC)	867
Organizations (ORG)	269
Persons (PER)	524

Since both collections do not follow the same tagging conventions, training and testing were conducted separately for each collection. Each collection was 80/20 split for training and testing.

4.2 Data Processing and Sequence Labeling

Training and testing were done using CRF++ which is a CRF sequence label toolkit. The following processing steps of Arabic were performed:

- The coordinating conjunctions *w* (و) and *f* (ف), which always appear as the first prefixes in a word, were optionally stemmed. *w* and *f* were stemmed using an in-house Arabic stemmer that is a reimplementation of the stemmer proposed by Lee et al. (2003). However, stemming *w* or *f* could have been done by stemming the *w* or *f* and searching for the stemmed word in a large Arabic corpus. If the stemmed word appears more than a certain count, then stemming was appropriate.
- The different forms of *alef* (*A* (ا), | (آ), > (أ), and < (إ)) were normalized to *A* (ا), *y* (ي) and *Y* (ى) were normalized to *y* (ي), and *p* (ة) was mapped to *h* (ه).

4.3 Evaluation

The figures of merit for evaluation were precision, recall, and F-measure ($\beta = 1$), with evaluation being conducted at the phrase level. Reporting experiments with all the different combinations of features would adversely affect the readability of the paper. Thus, to ascertain the contribution of the different features, a set of 15 experiments are being reported for both datasets. The experiments were conducted using raw Arabic words (**3w**) and stems (**3s**). Using the short names of features (bolded after feature names in section 3), the experiments were as follows:

- 3w
- 3w_6bi
- 3w_6bi_6tri
- 3w_6bi_6tri_6quad
- 3w_6bi_6tri_6quad_WL
- 3w_6bi_6tri_6quad_WP
- 3s
- 3s_6bi_6tri_6quad
- 3s_6bi_6tri_6quad_1gP
- 3s_6bi_6tri_6quad_1gPr_1gP
- 3s_6bi_6tri_6quad_2gP
- 3s_6bi_6tri_6quad_3gCLM
- 3s_6bi_6tri_6quad_MI
- 3s_6bi_6tri_6quad_T
- 3s_6bi_6tri_6quad_T_MI

5 Experimental Results

Table 1 lists the results for the Benajiba and ACE datasets respectively. Tables 2 and 3 report the best obtained results for both datasets. The results include precision (**P**), recall (**R**), and F-measure (**F**) for NE's of types location (LOC), organization (ORG), and person (PER). The best results for P, R, and F are bolded in the tables.

In comparing the base experiments **3w** and **3s** in which the only the surface forms and the stems were used respectively, both produced the highest precision. However, **3s** improved recall over **3w** by 7, 13, and 14 points for LOC, ORG, and PER respectively on the Benajiba dataset. Though using **3s** led to a drop in P for ORG compared to **3w**, it actually led to improvement in P for PER. Similar results were observed for the ACE dataset, but the differences were less pronounced with 1% to 2% improvements in recall. However, when including the **6bi**, **6tri**, and **6quad** features the difference between using words or stems dropped to about 1 point in recall and nearly no difference in precision. This would indicate the effectiveness of using leading and trailing character n-grams in overcoming morphological and orthographic complexities.

		Benajiba			ACE		
Run Name	Type	P	R	F	P	R	F
3w	LOC	**96**	59	73	88	59	71
	ORG	**92**	36	51	**87**	50	63
	PER	90	32	48	**94**	47	63
3w_6bi	LOC	92	75	82	85	72	78
	ORG	83	57	67	76	54	63
	PER	87	68	76	89	70	78
3w_6bi_6tri	LOC	93	79	86	87	77	**82**
	ORG	82	61	70	77	56	65
	PER	89	72	80	89	**73**	80
3w_6bi_6tri_6quad	LOC	93	**83**	87	87	77	81
	ORG	84	64	72	77	55	65
	PER	90	73	81	92	71	80
3w_6bi_6tri_6quad_WL	LOC	93	82	87	87	**78**	**82**
	ORG	83	64	73	79	56	65
	PER	89	73	80	93	71	**81**
3w_6bi_6tri_6quad_WP	LOC	91	82	86	88	77	82
	ORG	83	62	71	77	**59**	**67**
	PER	89	74	81	91	70	79
3s	LOC	**96**	66	78	**89**	60	72
	ORG	88	49	63	86	52	65
	PER	**93**	46	61	92	49	64
3s_6bi_6tri_6quad	LOC	93	**83**	**88**	87	77	**82**
	ORG	84	63	72	78	58	**67**
	PER	90	74	81	91	70	80
3s_6bi_6tri_6quad_1gP	LOC	93	**83**	**88**	87	77	**82**
	ORG	84	64	73	79	57	66
	PER	90	**75**	**82**	93	70	80
3s_6bi_6tri_6quad_1gPr_1gP	LOC	93	81	87	87	77	81
	ORG	85	60	70	82	55	66
	PER	91	72	81	93	69	79
3s_6bi_6tri_6quad_2gP	LOC	93	81	87	88	77	**82**
	ORG	85	61	71	82	56	**67**
	PER	89	74	81	90	69	78
3s_6bi_6tri_6quad_3gCLM	LOC	93	82	87	87	76	81
	ORG	84	**65**	**74**	78	56	66
	PER	90	74	81	93	71	**81**
3s_6bi_6tri_6quad_MI	LOC	93	81	86	87	77	**82**
	ORG	84	59	69	82	56	66
	PER	90	72	80	93	70	80
3s_6bi_6tri_6quad_T	LOC	93	81	87	87	76	81
	ORG	85	61	71	82	55	66
	PER	90	72	80	93	69	79
3s_6bi_6tri_6quad_T_MI	LOC	93	80	86	87	76	81
	ORG	85	57	68	82	54	65
	PER	91	71	80	93	67	78

Table 1: NER results for the Benajiba and ACE datasets

	P	R	F
LOC	93	83	88
ORG	84	64	73
PERS	90	75	82
Avg.	89	74	81

Table 2: Best results on Benajiba dataset (Run name: 3s_6bi_6tri_6quad_1gP)

	P	R	F
LOC	87	77	82
ORG	79	56	65
PERS	93	71	81
Avg.	88	70	76

Table 3: Best results on ACE dataset (Run name: 3w_6bi_6tri_6quad_WL)

	P	R	F
LOC	93	87	90
ORG	84	54	66
PERS	80	67	73
Avg.	86	69	76

Table 4: The results in (Benajiba and Rosso, 2008) on Benajiba dataset

The **3s_6bi_6tri_6quad** run produced nearly the best F-measure for both datasets, with extra features improving overall F-measure by at most 1 point.

Using t-test **T** and mutual information **MI** did not yield any improvement in either recall or precision, and often hurt overall F-measure. As highlighted in the results, the 1gP, 2gP, WL, WP, and 3gCLM typically improved recall slightly, often leading to 1 point improvement in overall F-measure.

To compare to results in the literature, Table 4 reports the results obtained by Benajiba and Rosso (2008) on the Benajiba dataset using the CRF++ implementation of CRF sequence labeling trained on a variety of Arabic language specific features. The comparison was not done on their results on the ACE 2005 dataset due to potential difference in tags. The averages in Tables 2, 3, and 4 are macro-averages as opposed to micro-averages reported by Benajiba and Rosso (2008). In comparing Tables 2 and 4, the features suggested in this paper reduced F-measure for locations by 2 points, but improved F-measure for organizations and persons by 8 points and 9 points respectively, due to improvements in both precision and recall.

The notable part of this work is that using a simplified feature set outperforms linguistic features. As explained in Section 3, using leading and trailing character n-grams implicitly capture morphological and syntactic features that typically used for Arabic lemmatization and POS tagging (Diab, 2009). The improvement over using linguistic features could possibly be attributed to the following reasons: not all prefixes and suffixes types equally help in identifying named entities (ex. appearance of a definite article or not); not all prefixes and suffix surface forms equally help (ex. appearance of the coordinating conjunction *w* "و" vs. *f* "ف"); and mistakes in stemming and POS tagging. The lag in recall for locations behind the work of Benajiba and Rosso (2008) could be due to the absence of location gazetteers.

6 Conclusion and Future Work

This paper presented a set of simplified yet effective features for named entity recognition in Arabic. The features helped overcome some of the morphological and orthographic complexities of Arabic. The features included the leading and trailing character n-grams in words, word association features such as t-test, mutual information, and word n-grams, and surface features such word length and relative word position in a sentence. The most important features were leading and trailing character n-grams in words. The proposed feature set yielded improved results over those in the literature with as much as 9 point F-measure improvement for recognizing persons.

For future work, the authors would like to examine the effectiveness of the proposed feature set on other morphologically complex languages, particularly Semitic languages. Also, it is worth examining the combination of the proposed features with morphological features.

References

Y. Benajiba, M. Diab, and P. Rosso. 2008. *Arabic Named Entity Recognition using Optimized Feature Sets*. Proceedings of the 2008 Conference on Empirical Methods in Natural Language Processing, pages 284–293, Honolulu, October 2008.

Y. Benajiba and P. Rosso. 2008. *Arabic Named Entity Recognition using Conditional Random Fields*. In Proc. of Workshop on HLT & NLP within the Arabic World, LREC'08.

Y. Benajiba, P. Rosso and J. M. Benedí. 2007. *ANERsys: An Arabic Named Entity Recognition system based on Maximum Entropy*. In Proc. of CICLing-2007, Springer-Verlag, LNCS(4394), pp. 143-153.

Y. Benajiba and P. Rosso. 2007. *ANERsys 2.0: Conquering the NER task for the Arabic language by combining the Maximum Entropy with POS-tag information*. In Proc. of Workshop on Natural Language-Independent Engineering, IICAI-2007.

M. Diab. 2009. *Second Generation Tools (AMIRA 2.0): Fast and Robust Tokenization, POS tagging, and Base Phrase Chunking*. Proceedings of the Second International Conference on Arabic Language Resources and Tools, 2009.

B. Farber, D. Freitag, N. Habash, and O. Rambow. 2008. *Improving NER in Arabic Using a Morphological Tagger*. In Proc. of LREC'08.

F. Huang. 2005. *Multilingual Named Entity Extraction and Translation from Text and Speech*. Ph.D. Thesis. Pittsburgh: Carnegie Mellon University.

J. Lafferty, A. McCallum, and F. Pereira. 2001. *Conditional random fields: Probabilistic models for segmenting and labeling sequence data*, In Proc. of ICML, pp.282-289, 2001.

Young-Suk Lee, Kishore Papineni, Salim Roukos, Ossama Emam, Hany Hassan. 2003. *Language Model Based Arabic Word Segmentation*. ACL 2003: 399-406

C. Manning and H. Schutze. 1999. *Foundations of Statistical Natural Language Processing*. Cambridge, Massachusetts: The MIT Press.

J. Mayfield, P. McNamee, and C. Piatko. 2003. *Named Entity Recognition using Hundreds of Thousands of Features*. HLT-NAACL 2003-Volume 4, 2003.

A. McCallum and W. Li. 2003. *Early Results for Named Entity Recognition with Conditional Random Fields, Features Induction and Web-Enhanced Lexicons*. In Proc. Conference on Computational Natural Language Learning.

P. McNamee and J. Mayfield. 2002. *Entity extraction without language-specific*. Proceedings of CoNLL, 2002.

D. Nadeau and S. Sekine. 2009. *A survey of named entity recognition and classification*. Named entities: recognition, classification and use, ed. S. Sekine and E. Ranchhod, John Benjamins Publishing Company.

F. Sha and F. Pereira. 2003. *Shallow parsing with conditional random fields*, In Proc. of HLT/NAACL-2003.

K. Shaalan and H. Raza. 2007. Person Name Entity Recognition for Arabic. Proceedings of the 5th Workshop on Important Unresolved Matters, pages 17–24, Prague, Czech Republic, June 2007.

Think Globally, Apply Locally: Using Distributional Characteristics for Hindi Named Entity Identification

Shalini Gupta   Pushpak Bhattacharyya
Department of Computer Science and Engineering
IIT Bombay
Mumbai, India.
{shalini, pb}@cse.iitb.ac.in

Abstract

In this paper, we present a novel approach for Hindi Named Entity Identification (NEI) in a large corpus. The key idea is to harness the global distributional characteristics of the words in the corpus. We show that combining the global distributional characteristics along with the local context information improves the NEI performance over statistical baseline systems that employ only local context. The improvement is very significant (about 10%) in scenarios where the test and train corpus belong to different genres. We also propose a novel measure for NEI based on term informativeness and show that it is competitive with the best measure and better than other well known information measures.

1 Introduction

NER is the task of identifying and classifying words in a document into predefined classes like person, location, organization, *etc.* It has many applications in Natural Language Processing (NLP) NER can be divided into two sub-tasks, Named Entity Identification (NEI) and Named Entity Classification (NEC). In this paper, we focus on the first step, *i.e.*, Named Entity Identification. NEI is useful in applications where a list of Named Entities (NEs) is required. Machine Translation needs identification of named entities, so that they can be transliterated.

For Indian languages, it is tough to identify named entities because of the lack of capitalization. Many approaches based on MEMM (Saha et al., 2008b), CRFs (Li and McCallum, 2003) and hybrid models have been tried for Hindi Named Entity Recognition. These approaches use only the local context for tagging the text. Many applications need entity identification in large corpora. When such a large corpus is to be tagged, one can use the global distributional characteristics of the words to identify the named entities. The state-of-the-art methods do not take advantage of these characteristics. Also, the performance of these systems degrades when the training and test corpus are from different domain or different genre. We present here our approach-*Combined Local and Global Information for Named Entity Identification* (CLGIN) which combines the global characteristics with the local context for Hindi Named Entity Identification. The approach comprises of two steps: (i) *Named Entity Identification using Global Information* (NGI) which uses the global distributional characteristics along with the language cues to identify NEs and (ii) Combining the tagging from step 1 with the MEMM based statistical system. We consider the MEMM based statistical system (S-MEMM) as the Baseline. Results show that the CLGIN approach outperforms the baseline S-MEMM system by a margin of about 10% when the training and test corpus belong to different genre and by a margin of about 2% when both, training and test corpus are similar. NGI also outperforms the baseline, in the former case, when training and test corpus are from different genre. Our contributions in this paper are:

- Developing an approach of harnessing the global characteristics of the corpus for Hindi Named Entity Identification using information measures, distributional similarity, lexicon, term co-occurrence and language cues
- Demonstrating that combining the global characteristics with the local contexts improves the accuracy; and with a very significant amount when the train and test corpus are not from same domain or similar genre
- Demonstrating that the system using only the

Proceedings of the 2010 Named Entities Workshop, ACL 2010, pages 116–125,
Uppsala, Sweden, 16 July 2010.

global characteristics is also quite comparable with the existing systems and performs better than them, when train and test corpus are unrelated

- Introducing a new scoring function, which is quite competitive with the best measure and better than other well known information measures

Approach	Description
S-MEMM (Baseline)	MEMM based statistical system without inserting global information
NGI	Uses global distributional characteristics along with language information for NE Identification
CLGIN	Combines the global characteristics derived using NGI with S-MEMM

Table 1: Summary of Approaches

2 Related Work

There is a plethora of work on NER for English ranging from supervised approaches like HMMs(Bikel et al., 1999), Maximum Entropy (Borthwick, 1999) (Borthwick et al., 1998), CRF (Lafferty et al., 2001) and SVMs to unsupervised (Alfonseca and Manandhar, 2002), (Volker, 2005) and semi-supervised approaches (Li and Mccallum, 2005). However, these approaches do not perform well for Indian languages mainly due to lack of capitalization and unavailability of good gazetteer lists. The best F Score reported for Hindi NER using these approaches on a standard corpus (IJCNLP) is 65.13% ((Saha et al., 2008a)). Higher accuracies have been reported (81%) (Saha et al., 2008b), albeit, on a non-standard corpus using rules and comprehensive gazetteers.

Current state-of-the-art systems (Li and McCallum, 2003) (Saha et al., 2008b) use various language independent and language specific features, like, context word information, POS tags, suffix and prefix information, gazetteer lists, common preceding and following words, *etc.* The performance of these systems is significantly hampered when the test corpus is not similar to the training corpus. Few studies (Guo et al., 2009), (Poibeau and Kosseim, 2001) have been performed towards genre/domain adaptation. But this still remains an open area. Moreover, no work has been done towards this for Indian languages.

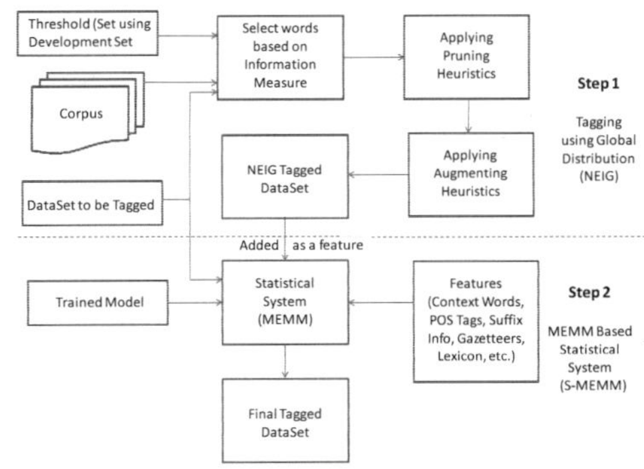

Figure 1: Block diagram of CLGIN Approach

One shortcoming of current approaches is that they do not leverage on global distributional characteristics of words (e.g., Information Content, Term Co-occurrence statistics, etc.) when a large corpus needs NEI. Rennie and Jaakkola (2005) introduced a new information measure and used it for NE detection. They used this approach only on uncapitalized and ungrammatical English text, like blogs where spellings and POS tags are not correct. Some semi-supervised approaches (Collins and Singer, 1999), (Riloff and Jones, 1999), (Paşca, 2007) have also used large available corpora to generate context patterns for named entities or for generating gazetteer lists and entity expansion using seed entities. Klementiev and Roth (2006) use cooccurrence of sets of terms within documents to boost the certainty (in a cross-lingual setting) that the terms in question were really transliterations of each other.

In this paper, we contend that using such global distributional characteristics improves the performance of Hindi NEI when applied to a large corpus. Further, we show that the performance of such systems which use global distribution characteristics is better than current state-of-the-art systems when the training and test corpus are not similar (different domain/genre) thereby being more suitable for domain adaptation.

3 MEMM based Statistical System (S-MEMM)

We implemented the Maximum Entropy Markov Model based system(Saha et al., 2008b) for NE Identification. We use this system as our Baseline and compare our approaches NGI and CLGIN with this baseline. We used various language dependent and independent features. An important

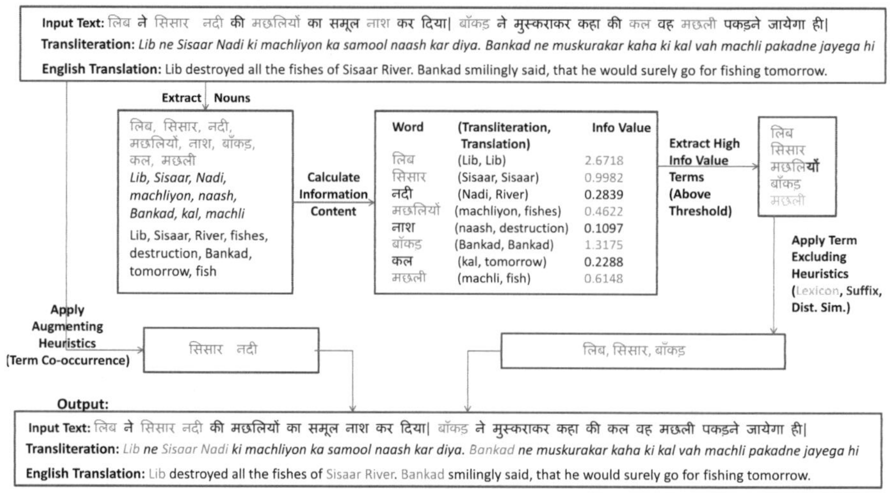

Figure 2: An Example explaining the NGI approach

modification was the use of **lexicon** along with traditionally used gazetteers. Gazetteers just improve the recall whereas including the lexicon improves the precision. The state-of-art Hindi NER systems do not use lexicon of general words but we found that using lexicons significantly improves the performance. Unlike English, NEs in Hindi are not capitalized and hence it becomes important to know, if a word is a common word or not.

Features used in S-MEMM were:

- Context Words: Preceding and succeeding two words of the current word
- Word suffix and prefix: Fixed length (size: 2) suffix information was used. Besides, suffix list of common location suffixes was created
- First word and last word information
- Previous NE Tag information
- Digit information
- Gazetteer Lists: Person and Location names, Frequent words after and before person, organization and location names, list of common initials, stopwords, *etc.*
- POS Tag Information
- Lexicons: If the stemmed word was present in the lexicon, this feature was true.

4 Our Approach-CLGIN

In this section, we describe our approach, CLGIN in detail. It combines the global information from the corpus with the local context. Figure 1 gives the block diagram of the system while tagging a corpus and Figure 2 explains the approach using an example. This approach involves two steps. Step 1 of CLGIN is NGI which creates a list of probable NEs (both uni-word and multi-word) from the given corpus and uses it to tag the whole corpus. Sections 4.1 and 4.2 explain this step in detail. Later, in step 2, it combines the tagging obtained from step 1, as a feature in the MEMM based statistical system. Output thus obtained from the MEMM system is the final output of the CLGIN approach. The creation of list in step 1, involves the following steps

- A list of all words which appeared as a noun at least once in the the corpus is extracted.
- List is ordered on the basis of the information content derived using the whole corpus. Words above the threshold (set during training using the development set) are selected as NEs.
- Heuristics are applied for pruning and augmenting the list.
- Multi-word NEs derived using term co-occurrence statistics along with language characteristics are added to the NE list.

The above process generates a list of NEs (uni-word and multi-word). In the second step, we provide this tagging to the S-MEMM along with other set of features described in Section 3

During training, the cutoff threshold is set for selecting NEs (in bullet 2) above. Also the tagging obtained from the step 1 is added as a feature to

S-MEMM and a model is trained during the training phase. The following sections describe this approach in detail.

4.1 Information Measures/Scoring Functions

Various measures have been introduced for determining the information content of the words. These include, IDF (Inverse Document Frequency) (Jones, 1972) , Residual IDF (Church and Gale, 1995), x^I- measure (Bookstein and Swanson, 1974), Gain (Papineni, 2001), *etc.* We introduced our own information measure, RF (Ratio of Frequencies).

4.1.1 RF (Ratio of Frequencies)

NEs are highly relevant words in a document (Clifton et al., 2002) and are expected to have high information content (Rennie and Jaakkola, 2005). It has been found that words that appear frequently in a set of documents and not so frequently in the rest of the documents are important with respect to that set of documents where they are frequent.

We expected the NEs to be concentrated in few documents. We defined a new criteria which measures the ratio of the total number of times the word appears in the corpus to the number of documents containing a word.

$RF(w) = \frac{cf(w)}{df(w)}$

where cf(w) is the total frequency of a word in the whole corpus and df(w) is the document frequency. This measure is different from the TF-IDF measure in terms of the term frequency. TF-IDF considers the frequency of the word in the document. RF considers it over the whole corpus.

We use the scoring function (information measure) to score all the words. During training, we fix a threshold using the development set. During testing, we pick words above the threshold as NEs. We then apply heuristics to augment this list as well as to exclude terms from the generated list.

4.2 Heuristics for Pruning and Augmenting NE List

Distributional Similarity: The underlying idea of Distributional Similarity is that a word is characterized by the company it keeps (Firth, 1957). Two words are said to be distributionally similar if they appear in similar contexts. From the previous step (Sect. 4.1), we get a list of words having high score. Say, top t, words were selected. In this step, we take t more words and then cluster together these words. The purpose at this phase is primarily to remove the false positives and to introduce more words which are expected to be NEs. For each distinct word, w in the corpus, we create a vector of the size of the number of distinct words in the corpus. Each term in the vector represents the frequency with which it appears in the context (context window: size 3) of word, w. It was observed that the NEs were clustered in some clusters and general words in other clusters. We tag a cluster as a NE cluster if most of the words in the cluster are good words. We define a word as good if it has high information content. If the sum of the ranks of 50% of the top ranked word is low, we tag the cluster as NE and add the words in that set as NEs. Also, if most of the words in the cluster have higher rank i.e. lower information content, we remove it from the NE set.

This heuristic is used for both **augmenting** the list as well to **exclude** terms from the list.

Lexicon: We used this as a list for **excluding** terms. Terms present in the lexicon have a high chance of not being NEs. When used alone, the lexicon is not very effective (explained in Section 5.2). But, when used with other approaches, it helps in improving the precision of the system significantly. State-of-art Hindi NER systems use lists of gazetteers for Person names, location names, organization names, *etc.* (Sangal et al., 2008), but lexicon of general words has not been used. Unlike English, for Indian languages, it is important to know, if a word is a general word or not. Lexicons as opposed to gazetteers are generic and can be applied to any domain. Unlike gazetteers, the words would be quite common and would appear in any text irrespective of the domain.

Suffixes: NEs in Hindi are open class words and appear as free morphemes. Unlike nouns, NEs, usually do not take any suffixes (attached to them). However, there are few exceptions like, लाल किले के बाहर (*laal kile ke baahar*, (outside Red Fort)) or when NEs are used as common nouns, देश को गांधियों की जरूरत है (*desh ko gandhiyon ki zaroorat hai*, The country needs Gandhis.) *etc.* We remove words appearing with common suffixes like एं (*ein*), ओं (*on*), येंगे (*yenge*), *etc.* from the NE list.

Term Co-occurrence: We use the term co-occurrence statistics to detect multi-word NEs. A word may be a NE in some context but not in another. E.g. महात्मा (*mahatma* "saint") when appearing with गांधी (*Gandhi* "Gandhi") is a NE, but may not be, otherwise. To identify such multi-words NEs, we use this heuristic. Such words can be identified using Term Co-occurrence. We use the given set of documents to find all word pairs. We then calculate Pointwise Mutual Information (PMI) (Church and Hanks, 1990) for each of these word pairs and order the pairs in descending order of their PMI values. Most of the word pairs belong to the following categories:

- Adjective Noun combination (Adjectives followed by noun): This was the most frequent combination. E.g. भीनी गंध (*bheeni gandh* "sweet smell")
- Noun Verb combination: दिल धड़कना (*dil dhadakna*, "heart beating")
- Adverb verb combination: खिलखिलाकर हंसना (*khilkhilakar hansna*, "merrily laugh")
- Cardinal/Ordinal Noun Combination: थोड़ी देर (*thodi der*, "some time")
- Named Entities
- Hindi Idioms: उल्लू सीधा (*ullu seedha*)
- Noun Noun Combination: ख्याती अर्जित (*khyati arjit*, "earn fame")
- Hindi Multiwords: जोश खरोश (*josh kharosh*)

We need to extract NEs from these word pairs. The first four combinations can be easily excluded because of the presence of a verb, cardinals and adjectives. Sometimes both words in the NEs appear as nouns. So, we cannot reject the Noun Noun combination. We handle rest of the cases by looking at the neighbours (context) of the word pairs.

We noticed three important things here:

- Multiwords which are followed (alteast once) by में (*mein*), से (*se*), ने (*ne*), के (*ke*), को (*ko*) (Hindi Case Markers) are usually NEs. We did not include की (*ki*) in the list because many words in the noun-noun combination are frequently followed by *ki* in the sense of किया/ करना (*kiya/karna*, "do/did") e.g. ख्याती अर्जित की (*khyati arjit ki*, "earned fame"), परीक्षा उत्तीर्ण की (*pariksha uttirand ki*, "cleared the exam"), *etc*.
- There were word pairs which were followed by a single word most of the time. E.g ईस्ट इंडिया (*East India*, "East India") was followed by कंपनी (*Company*, "Company") in almost all the cases. When *Company* appears alone, it may not be a NE, but when it appears with *East India*, it appears as a NE. Other examples of such word pairs were: खाँ इब्नू (*Khan Ibnu*, "Khan Ibnu") followed by अलीसम (*Alisam*, "Alisam")
- There were word pairs which were followed by uncommon words were not common words but were different words each time, it appeared. i.e. Most of the words following the word pair were not part of lexicon. गवर्नर जनरल (*governor general*, "Governor General") followed by [दलहौसी, बहदुर, सोलबरी, मैटकाफ़, लौर्ड ((*dalhousie, bahadur, solbari, metkaf, lord*), "Dalhousie, Bahadur, Solbari, Metkaf, Lord")] Such words are multi word NEs.

Corpus	No. of Tagged Documents	No. of Words	No. of NEs	Source Genre
Gyaan Nidhi	1570	569K	21K	Essay, Biography, History and Story

Table 2: Corpus Statistics

4.3 Step 2: Combining NGI with S-MEMM

The tagging obtained as the result of the step 1 (NGI), is given as input to the MEMM based statistical system (S-MEMM). This feature is introduced as a binary feature *OldTag=NE*. If a word is tagged as NE in the previous step, this feature is turned on, otherwise *OldTag=O* is turned on.

5 Experiments and Results

We have used *Gyaan Nidhi* Corpus for evaluation which is a collection of various books in Hindi. It contains about 75000 documents. The details of the corpus are given in Table 2. Names of persons, locations, organizations, books, plays, *etc*. were tagged as *NE* and other general words were tagged as *O* (others). The tagged documents are publicly made available at `http://www.cfilt.iitb.ac.in/ner.tar.gz`.

We use the following metrics for evaluation: Precision, Recall and F-Score. Precision is the ratio of the number of words correctly tagged as NEs to the total number of words tagged as NEs. Recall is the ratio of the number of words correctly tagged as NEs to the total number of NEs present in the data set. F Score is defined as $(F = 2 * P * R/(P + R))$

5.1 Comparison of Information Measures

We compare the performance of the various term informativeness measures for NEI which are Residual IDF[1], IDF [2], Gain[3] and x' measure [4] and the measure defined in Section 4.1.1. Table 3 shows the results averaged after five-fold cross validation. The graphs in the Figure 3 to Figure 7 show the distribution of words (nouns) over the range of values of each information measure.

Scoring Function	Prec.	Recall	F Score
Residual IDF	**0.476**	**0.537**	**0.504**
IDF	0.321	0.488	0.387
x-dash Measure	0.125	0.969	0.217
RF (Our Measure)	**0.624**	**0.396**	**0.484**
Gain	0.12	0.887	0.211

Table 3: Comparison of performance of various information measures

The best results were obtained using Residual IDF followed by Ratio of Frequencies (RF).

Method	Prec	Recall	F Score
S -MEMM (Baseline)	**0.871**	**0.762**	**0.812**
Res. IDF	0.476	0.537	0.504
Res. IDF + Dist Sim (DS)	0.588	0.522	0.553
Res. IDF + Lexicon (Lex)	0.586	0.569	0.572
Res. IDF + DS + Suffix	0.611	0.524	0.563
Res. IDF + Lex + Suffix	0.752	0.576	0.65
Res. IDF + Lex + Suffix + Term Cooccur (NGI)	**0.757**	**0.62**	**0.68**
CLGIN	**0.879**	**0.784**	**0.829**

Table 4: Performance of various Approaches (Here, train and test are similar)

5.2 NGI and CLGIN Approaches (Training and Test Set from Similar Genre)

Table 4 compares the results of S-MEMM, NGI approach and CLGIN. Besides, it also shows the step wise improvement of NGI approach. The final F-Score achieved using NGI approach was 68%. The F-Score of the Baseline system implemented using the MaxEnt package[1] from the OpenNLP community was 81.2%.

Using the lexicon alone gives an F-Score of only 11% (Precision: 5.97 Recall: 59.7 F-Score: 10.8562). But, when used with Residual IDF, the

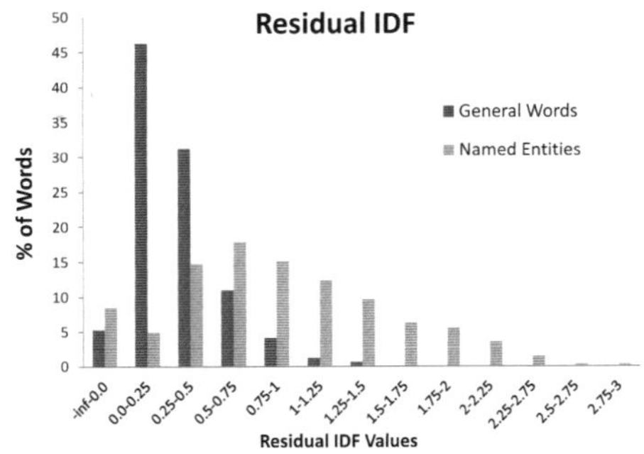

Figure 3: Distribution of Residual IDF values over the nouns in the corpus

performance of the overall system improves significantly to about 57%. Note that, the use of lexicon resulted in an increase in precision (0.5860) which was accompanied by improvement in recall (0.5693) also. The cutoff thresholds in both cases (Rows 2 and 4 of Table 4) were different. Suffix information improved the systems performance to 65%. As words were removed, more words from the initial ordered list (ordered on the basis of score/information content) were added. Hence, there was a small improvement in recall, too. Improvement by distributional similarity was eclipsed after the pruning by lexicon and suffix information. But, in the absence of lexicon; distributional similarity and suffix information can be used as the pruning heuristics. Adding the multiword NEs to the list as explained in the section 4.2 using term co-occurrence statistics, improved the accuracy significantly by 3%. Word pairs were arranged in the decreasing order of their PMI values and a list was created. We found that 50% of the NE word pairs in the whole tagged corpus lied in the top 1% of this word pairs list and about 70% of NE word pairs were covered in just top 2% of the list.

CLGIN which combines the global information obtained through NGI with the Baseline S-MEMM system gives an improvement of about 2%. After including this feature, the F-Score increased to 82.8%.

5.3 Performance Comparison of Baseline, NGI and CLGIN (Training and Test Data from different genre)

In the above experiments, documents were randomly placed into different splits. Gyaan Nidhi is a collection of various books on several top-

[1]Observed IDF - Expected IDF

[2]IDF = $-log\frac{df(w)}{D}$

[3]Gain = $\frac{d_w}{D}(\frac{d_w}{D} - 1 - log\frac{d_w}{D})$

[4]$x'(w) = df(w) - cf(w)$

[1]http://maxent.sourceforge.net/index.html

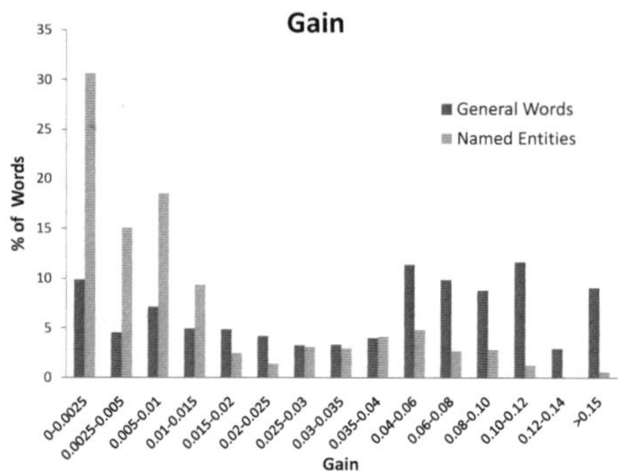

Figure 4: Distribution of Gain values over the nouns in the corpus

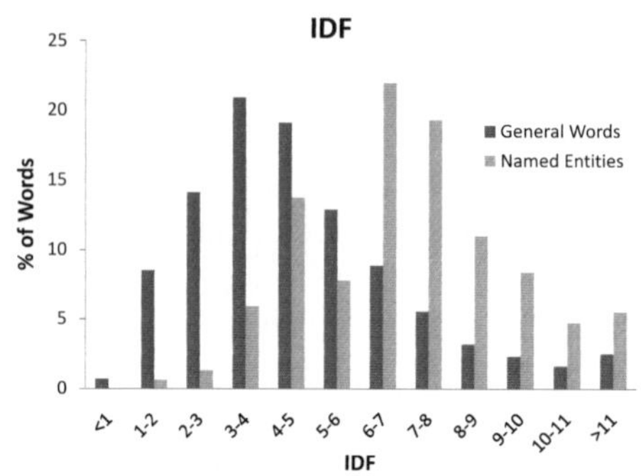

Figure 5: Distribution of IDF values over the nouns in the corpus

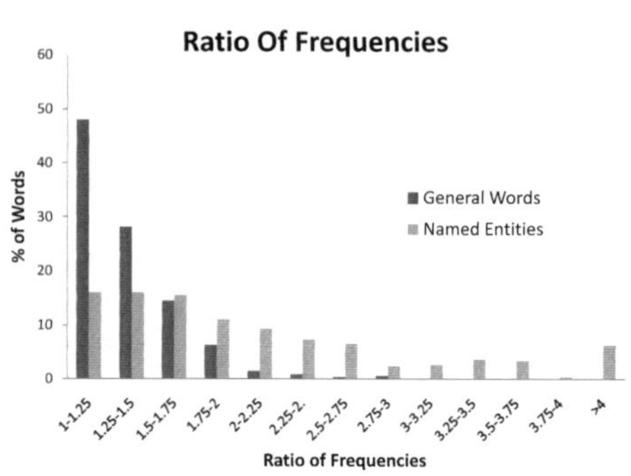

Figure 6: Distribution of Ratio of Frequencies(RF) values over the nouns in the corpus

ics. Random picking resulted into the mixing of the documents, with each split containing documents from all books. But, in this experiment, we divided documents into two groups such that documents from few books (genre: Story and History) were placed into one group and rest into another group (Genre: Biography and Essay). Table 5 compares the NGI and CLGIN approaches with

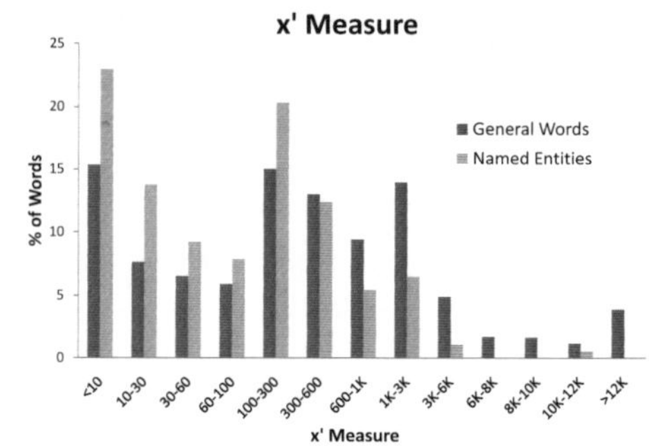

Figure 7: Distribution of x^I measure values over the nouns in the corpus

S-MEMM and shows that the **CLGIN results are significantly better than the Baseline System**, when the training and test sets belong to different genre. The results were obtained after 2-fold cross validation.

Method	Prec.	Recall	F Score
S-MEMM	0.842	0.479	0.610
NGI	0.744	0.609	0.67
CLGIN	**0.867**	**0.622**	**0.723**

Table 5: Performance of various Approaches (Here, train and test are from different genre)

Similar improvements were seen when the sets were divided into (Story and Biography) and (Essay and History) (The proportions of train and test sets in this division were uneven). The F Score of NGI system was 0.6576 and S-MEMM was 0.4766. The F Score of the combined system (CLGIN) was 0.6524.

6 Discussion and Error Analysis

6.1 RF and other information measures

As can be seen from the graphs in Figures 3 to 7, Residual IDF best separates the NEs from the general words. The measure introduced by us, Ratio of Frequencies is also a good measure, although not as good as Residual IDF but performs better than other measures. The words having RF value greater than 2.5 can be picked up as NEs, giving a high recall and precision. It is evident that IDF is better than both, Gain and x^I measure, as most of the general words have low IDF and NEs lie in the high IDF zone. But, the general words and NEs are not very clearly separated. As the number of nouns is about 7-8 times the number of NEs, the words having high IDF cannot be picked up. This would result in a low precision, as a large number of non-NEs would get mixed with the general words. Gain and x^I measure do not demarcate the NEs from the general words clearly. We observed that they are not good scoring functions for NEs.

Information Gain doesn't consider the frequency of the terms within the document itself. It only takes into account the document frequency for each word. x^I measure considers the frequency within document but it is highly biased towards high frequency words and hence doesn't perform well. Hence, common words like समय (*samay*, "time"), घर (*ghar*, "home"), etc. have higher scores compared to NEs like भारत(*bharat*, "India"), कलकत्ता (*kalkatta*, "Calcutta"), *etc.* Our measure on the other hand, overcomes this drawback, by considering the ratio. We could have combined the measures, instead of using only the best measure "Residual IDF", but the performance of "Gain", "IDF" and "x'-measure" was not good. Also, results of "RF" and "Residual IDF" were quite similar. Hence, we did not see any gain in combining the measures.

6.2 S-MEMM, NGI and CLGIN

The results in Section 5 show that adding the global information with the local context helps improve the tagging accuracy especially when the train and test data are from different genre. Several times, the local context is not sufficient to determine the word as a NE. For example, when the NEs are not followed by post positions or case markers, it becomes difficult for S-MEMM to identify NEs, *e.g.*, टैगोर एक अपवाद हैं, (*tagore ek apvaad hain*,"Tagore is an exception") or when the NEs are separated by commas, e.g. सुकुमारी दत्त, चुन्नीलाल.. (*Sukumari Dutt, Chunnilal ...* "Sukumari Dutt, Chunnilal .."). In such cases, because of the frequency statistics, the NGI approach is able to detect the words टैगोर (*Tagore*, "Tagore"), दत्त (*Dutt*, "Dutt"), *etc.* as NEs and frequently the CLGIN approach is able to detect such words as NEs.

The false positives in NEIG are words which are not present in the lexicon (uncommon words, words absent due to spelling variations *e.g.* सांप/साँप (*sanp* "snake")) but have high informativeness. Using the context words of these words is a possible way of eliminating these false positives. Many of the organization names having common words (मंडल (*mandal*, "board")) and person names (like प्रकाश (*prakash*,"light")) are present in the lexicon are not tagged by NEIG. Some errors were introduced because of the removal of morphed words. NEs like गुल्बानों, टोपे (*Gulbano, Tope*) were excluded.

Many of the errors using CLGIN are because of the presence of the words in the lexicon. This effect also gets passed on to the neighbouring words. But, the precision of CLGIN is significantly high compared to NGI because CLGIN uses context, as well.

The statistical system (S-MEMM) provides the context and the global system(NGI) provides a strong indication that the word is a NE and the performance of the combined approach(CLGIN) improves significantly.

7 Conclusion and Future Work

We presented an novel approach for Hindi NEI which combines the global distributional characteristics with local context. Results show that the proposed approach improves performance of NEI significantly, especially, when the train and test corpus belong to different genres. We also proposed a new measure for NEI which is based on term informativeness. The proposed measure performs quite competitively with the best known information measure in literature.

Future direction of the work will be to study the distributional characteristics of individual tags and move towards classification of identified entities. We also plan to extend the above approach to other Indian languages and other domains. We also expect further improvements in accuracy by replacing the MEMM model by CRF. Currently, we use a tagged corpus as development set to tune the cut-off threshold in NGI. To overcome this dependence and to make the approach unsupervised, a way out can be to find an approximation to the ratio of the number of nouns which are NEs to the number of nouns and then use this to decide the cut-off threshold.

Acknowledgments

We would like to acknowledge the efforts of Mr. Prabhakar Pandey and Mr. Devendra Kairwan for tagging the data with NE tags.

References

Enrique Alfonseca and Suresh Manandhar. 2002. An Unsupervised Method For General Named Entity Recognition and Automated Concept Discovery. In *Proceedings of the 1 st International Conference on General WordNet*.

Daniel M. Bikel, Richard Schwartz, and Ralph M. Weischedel. 1999. An Algorithm that Learns What's In A Name.

A. Bookstein and D. R. Swanson. 1974. Probabilistic Models for Automatic Indexing. *Journal of the American Society for Information Science*, 25:312–318.

Andrew Borthwick, John Sterling, Eugene Agichtein, and Ralph Grishman. 1998. Nyu: Description of the MENE Named Entity System as used in MUC-7. In *In Proceedings of the Seventh Message Understanding Conference (MUC-7*.

Andrew Eliot Borthwick. 1999. *A Maximum Entropy Approach to Named Entity Recognition*. Ph.D. thesis, New York, NY, USA. Adviser-Grishman, Ralph.

Kenneth Church and William Gale. 1995. Inverse Document Frequency (IDF): A Measure of Deviations from Poisson. In *Third Workshop on Very Large Corpora*, pages 121–130.

Kenneth Ward Church and Patrick Hanks. 1990. Word Association Norms, Mutual Information, and Lexicography.

Chris Clifton, Robert Cooley, and Jason Rennie. 2002. Topcat: Data mining for Topic Identification in a Text Corpus.

Michael Collins and Yoram Singer. 1999. Unsupervised Models for Named Entity Classification. In *In Proceedings of the Joint SIGDAT Conference on Empirical Methods in Natural Language Processing and Very Large Corpora*, pages 100–110.

J.R. Firth. 1957. A Synopsis of Linguistic Theory 1930-1955. In *In Studies in Linguistic Analysis*, pages 1–32.

Honglei Guo, Huijia Zhu, Zhili Guo, Xiaoxun Zhang, Xian Wu, and Zhong Su. 2009. Domain Adaptation with Latent Semantic Association for Named Entity Recognition. In *NAACL '09*, pages 281–289, Morristown, NJ, USA. Association for Computational Linguistics.

Karen Sprck Jones. 1972. A Statistical Interpretation of Term Specificity and its Application in Retrieval. *Journal of Documentation*, 28:11–21.

Alexandre Klementiev and Dan Roth. 2006. Named Entity Transliteration and Discovery from Multilingual Comparable Corpora. In *Proceedings of the main conference on Human Language Technology Conference of the North American Chapter of the Association of Computational Linguistics*, pages 82–88, Morristown, NJ, USA. Association for Computational Linguistics.

John D. Lafferty, Andrew McCallum, and Fernando C. N. Pereira. 2001. Conditional Random Fields: Probabilistic Models for Segmenting and Labeling Sequence Data. In *ICML '01: Proceedings of the Eighteenth International Conference on Machine Learning*, pages 282–289, San Francisco, CA, USA. Morgan Kaufmann Publishers Inc.

Wei Li and Andrew McCallum. 2003. Rapid Development of Hindi Named Entity Recognition using Conditional Random Fields and Feature Induction. *ACM Transactions on Asian Language Information Processing (TALIP)*, 2(3):290–294.

Wei Li and Andrew Mccallum. 2005. Semi-supervised Sequence Modeling with Syntactic Topic Models. In *AAAI-05, The Twentieth National Conference on Artificial Intelligence*.

Marius Paşca. 2007. Organizing and Searching the World Wide Web of facts – Step Two: Harnessing the Wisdom of the Crowds. In *WWW '07: Proceedings of the 16th international conference on World Wide Web*, pages 101–110, New York, NY, USA. ACM.

Kishore Papineni. 2001. Why Inverse Document Frequency? In *NAACL '01: Second meeting of the North American Chapter of the Association for Computational Linguistics on Language technologies 2001*, pages 1–8, Morristown, NJ, USA. Association for Computational Linguistics.

Thierry Poibeau and Leila Kosseim. 2001. Proper Name Extraction from Non-Journalistic Texts. In *In Computational Linguistics in the Netherlands*, pages 144–157.

Jason D. M. Rennie and Tommi Jaakkola. 2005. Using Term Informativeness for Named Entity Detection. In *SIGIR '05: Proceedings of the 28th annual international ACM SIGIR conference on Research and development in information retrieval*, pages 353–360, New York, NY, USA. ACM.

Ellen Riloff and Rosie Jones. 1999. Learning Dictionaries for Information Extraction by Multi-Level Bootstrapping. In *AAAI '99/IAAI '99: Proceedings of the sixteenth national conference on Artificial intelligence and the eleventh Innovative applications of artificial intelligence conference innovative applications of artificial intelligence*, pages 474–479, Menlo Park, CA, USA. American Association for Artificial Intelligence.

Sujan Kumar Saha, Sanjay Chatterji, Sandipan Dandapat, Sudeshna Sarkar, and Pabitra Mitra. 2008a. A Hybrid Named Entity Recognition System for South and South East Asian Languages. In *Proceedings of the IJCNLP-08 Workshop on Named Entity Recognition for South and South East Asian Languages*, pages 17–24, Hyderabad, India, January. Asian Federation of Natural Language Processing.

Sujan Kumar Saha, Sudeshna Sarkar, and Pabitra Mitra. 2008b. A Hybrid Feature Set Based Maximum Entropy Hindi Named Entity Recognition. In *Proceedings of the Third International Joint Conference on Natural Language Processing*, Kharagpur, India.

Rajeev Sangal, Dipti Sharma, and Anil Singh, editors. 2008. *Proceedings of the IJCNLP-08 Workshop on Named Entity Recognition for South and South East Asian Languages*. Asian Federation of Natural Language Processing, Hyderabad, India, January.

Johanna Volker. 2005. Towards Large-Scale, Open-Domain and Ontology-Based Named Entity Classification. In *Proceedings of the International Conference on Recent Advances in Natural Language Processing (RANLP'05*, pages 166–172. INCOMA Ltd.

Rule-based Named Entity Recognition in Urdu

Kashif Riaz
University of Minnesota
Department of Computer Science
Minneapolis, MN, USA
riaz@cs.umn.edu

Abstract

Named Entity Recognition or Extraction (NER) is an important task for automated text processing for industries and academia engaged in the field of language processing, intelligence gathering and Bioinformatics. In this paper we discuss the general problem of Named Entity Recognition, more specifically the challenges in NER in languages that do not have language resources e.g. large annotated corpora. We specifically address the challenges for Urdu NER and differentiate it from other South Asian (Indic) languages. We discuss the differences between Hindi and Urdu and conclude that the NER computational models for Hindi cannot be applied to Urdu. A rule-based Urdu NER algorithm is presented that outperforms the models that use statistical learning.

1. Introduction

Text processing applications, such as machine translation, information extraction, information retrieval or natural language understanding systems need to recognize multiple word expressions that refer to people names, organizational names, geographical locations, and other named entities. Proper Names play a crucial role in information management, both in specific applications and in underlying technologies that drive the application. Name Recognition becomes important in situations when the person or the organization is more important than the action it performed, for example, bankruptcy of the corner shop John & Sons is not as interesting as the bankruptcy of General Motors, an American car manufacturer. In this particular example, latter event will be of much interest for the financial markets and investors to track.

The proper name identification depends upon the domain, and the applications in that domain. For the purpose of this study we have limited the scope of names to entities proposed by Palmer and Day (1996), i.e. times, numbers, personal names, organizations, and geographical areas. The goal of a named entity finder is to find these entities.

In this paper we study the challenges of named entity recognition for resource scarce languages among South Asian languages. Urdu is used as an example language because of its large number of speakers, the only language in the region with Arabic script orthography, and interesting assumptions about its similarity with Hindi. Section 2 describes the characteristics and computational processing for Urdu. Section 3 motivates the named entity recognition task by outlining the challenges in NER in any language along with some of the approaches that have been used by well known NER systems. Section 4 discusses some previous work related to NER in South Asian languages. Section 5 describes challenges of NER in Urdu. Section 6 describes the complex relationship between Hindi and Urdu and asserts that NER computation models for Hindi cannot be used for Urdu NER. Section 7 presents a rule-based NER algorithm for Urdu NER. Section 8 presents the conclusion and future work. It is assumed that the reader knows the history, orthography and some characteristics of Urdu in general. We give a brief introduction to Urdu and Urdu processing in section 1.1. For a detailed explanation refer to Riaz (2008) that describe computational challenges for Urdu processing.

As a convention, Urdu words written in Arabic orthography are followed by English translation in parenthesis and are italicized.

2. Characteristics of Urdu

This section briefly introduces some right to left languages and a few characteristics of Urdu. Urdu is the national language of Pakistan, and one of the major languages of India. It is estimated that there are about 300 million speakers of Urdu. Most of the Urdu speakers live in Pakistan, India, UAE, U.K and USA. Recently, there has been a lot of interest in

Proceedings of the 2010 Named Entities Workshop, ACL 2010, pages 126–135,
Uppsala, Sweden, 16 July 2010.

computational processing of right to left languages. Most of the interest has been focused toward Arabic. There are other right to left languages like Urdu, Persian (Farsi), Dari, Punjabi, and Pashto that are mostly spoken in South Asia. Arabic is a Semitic language and the other languages belong to the Proto Indo Iranian languages. Arabic and these other languages only share script and some vocabulary. Therefore, the language specific task done for Arabic is not applicable to these languages. For example, stemming algorithms generated for Arabic will not work for a language like Urdu.

Unlike other languages in South Asia, Urdu shares its grammar with Hindi. The difference is vocabulary, and writing style. Hindi is written in Devanagri script whereas Urdu is written in Arabic script. Because of these similarities, Hindi and Urdu are considered one language for linguistic purposes but current Hindi resources cannot be used for Urdu processing (Riaz, 2009). Urdu is quite complex language because Urdu's grammar and morphology is a combination of many languages: Sanskrit, Arabic, Farsi, English and Turkish to name a few. Urdu's descriptive power is quite high. This means that there could be many different ways in which a concept can be expressed in Urdu. For example, in Urdu the words *Pachem* and *Maghreb* both are used for the direction *West*. In the previous example *Pachem* has its ancestry in Sanskrit and *Maghreb* has its roots in Arabic. Urdu is considered the *lingua franca* of business in Pakistan, and the South Asian community in the U.K (Baker et. al, 2003).

Urdu has a property of accepting lexical features and vocabulary from other languages, most notably English. This is called code-switching in linguistics e.g. it is not uncommon to see a right to left flow interrupted by a word written in English (left to right) and then continuation of the flow right to left. For example,وہ میرا laptop ہے *(That is my laptop)*. In the above example, Microsoft Word did not support English embedding within the Urdu sentence and displayed it improperly. But while electronically processing, the tokenization will be done correctly (Becker and Riaz, 2002). In order to process Urdu and other right to left languages Unicode encoding and proper font usage is necessary. Becker and Riaz (2002) discuss Urdu Unicode encoding in detail.

3. Challenges in NER

Named Entity Recognition was first introduced as part of Message Understanding Conference (MUC-6) in 1995 and a related conference MET-1 in 1996 introduced named entity recognition in non-English text. In spite of the recognized importance of names in applications, most text processing applications such as search systems, spelling checkers, and document management systems, do not treat proper names correctly. This suggests proper names are difficult to identify and interpret in unstructured text. Generally, names can have innumerable structure in and across languages. Names can overlap with other names and other words. Simple clues like capitalization can be misleading for English and mostly not present in non western languages like Urdu.

The goal of NER is first to recognize the potential named entities and then resolve the ambiguity in the name. There are two types of ambiguities in names, structural ambiguity and semantic ambiguity. Wacholder et al. (1997) describes these ambiguities in detail. Non-English names pose another dimension of problems in NER e.g. the most common first name in the world is Muhammad, which can be transliterated as Mohmmed, Muhammad, Mohammad, Mohamed, Mohd and many other variations. These variations make it difficult to find the intended named entity. This transliteration problem can be solved if the name Muhammad is written in Arabic script as محمد.

3.1 General Approaches to NER

Over the years many systems have been crafted to find names in different domains. Some are quite general and work in all domains, while others are domain specific. The domain specific systems do much better in their domains and perform poorly on foreign domains. On the other hand the systems that claim generality do not work as well as the best domain specific systems but do not fare poorly when the domain is changed.

Nymble (Bikel et al, 1996) is a purely statistical model where named entities are found using a generative statistical model using a variant of HMM (Hidden Markov Model). Recently, statistical discriminative models like Condition Random Fields (CRF) (Wallah, 2002) are used consistently for segmenting and labeling the sequence data as a graphical model (Lafferty et al. 2009). Nominator (Wacholder et al, 1997) is a fully implemented module for proper name recognition. It applies a set of heuristics to a list of words based on patterns of capitalization, punctuation and location within the sentence. Dr. Hermansen at Linguistic Analysis Systems Inc. has a well known system that recognizes names based on regional names (Erickson, 2005).

4. NER for South Asian languages and Related Work

Although over the years there has been considerable work done for NER in English and other European languages, the interest in the South Asian languages has been quite low until recently. One of the major reasons for the lack of research is the lack of enabling technologies like, parts of speech taggers, gazetteers, and most importantly, corpora and annotated training and test sets. One of the first NER study of South Asian languages and specifically on Urdu was done by Becker and Riaz (2002) who studied the challenges of NER in Urdu text without any available resources at the time. The by-product of that study was the creation of Becker-Riaz Urdu Corpus (2002). Another notable example of NER in South Asian language is DARPA's TIDES surprise language challenge where a new language is announced by the agency to build language processing tools in a short period of time. In 2003 the language chosen was Hindi. Li and McCallum (2003) tried conditional random fields on Hindi data and reported *f-measure* ranging from 56 to 71 with different boosting methods. Mukund et al. (2009) used CRF for Urdu NER and showed *f-measure* of 68.9%.

By far the most comprehensive attempt made to study NER for South Asian and South East Asian languages was by the NER workshop of International Joint Conference of Natural Language Processing in 2008. The workshop attempted to do Named Entity Recognition in Hindi, Bengali, Telugu, Oriya, and Urdu. Among all these languages Urdu is the only one that has Arabic script. Test and training data was provided for each language by different organizations therefore the quantity of the annotated data varied among different languages. Hindi and Bengali led the way with the most amounts of data; Urdu and Oriya were at the bottom with the least amount of data. Urdu had about 36,000 thousand tokens available. A shared task was defined to find named entities in the languages chosen by the researcher. There are 15 papers in the final proceedings of NER workshop at IJCNLP 2008, all cited in the references section, a significant number of those papers tried to address all languages in general, but resorted to Hindi, where the most number of resources were available. Some papers only addressed specific languages like Hindi, Bengali, Telugu and one paper addressed Tamil. There was not a single paper that focused on only Urdu named entity recognition. The papers that tried to address all languages, the computational model showed the lowest performance on Urdu. Among the experiments performed at Named Entity Workshop on various Indic languages and Urdu, almost all experiments used CFR with limited success.

4. NER challenges for Urdu

In general NER is a difficult task and a number of challenges need to be addressed in all languages. South Asian languages have some additional challenges. We will focus on language characteristics and some practical problems of language processing focusing on Urdu for examples. It is important to note that the following characteristics are not unique to Urdu nor to the South Asian languages.

5.1 No Capitalization

Capitalization, when available, is the most important feature for named entity extraction. English and many other European languages use it to recognize proper names. Orthography of Urdu does not support capitalization. English systems easily recognize acronyms by using capitalization, but in Urdu they are quite difficult to recognize. For example, بی بی سی *(transcribed BBC)* in Urdu cannot be recognized as an acronym.

5.2 Agglutinative nature

Agglutinative property means that some additional features can be added to the word to add more complex meaning. Agglutinative languages form sentences by adding a suffix to the root forms of the word. This feature was mentioned in relation to Telugu only in the NER literature of IJCNLP 2008 presuming unfamiliarity to Urdu by the authors. A deeper study shows that agglutinative nature of Urdu comes from Persian, Turkish and Dravidian languages. In Urdu *Hyderabad + i = Hyderabadi* حیدرآبادی; the root word is *Hyderabad* and the suffix is *i*. Here *Hyderabadi* should not be recognized as a named entity whereas *Hyderabad (city in India)* should be recognized as a location named entity.

5.3 Ambiguity

Ambiguity in proper name names is present in South Asian languages as in English. The names like Brown are ambiguous in English – name or color. Similarly, سحر *(Sahar)* is ambiguous in Urdu – name or morning dawn. In Urdu this gets more complicated because سحر *(Sahar)* also means a spell.

Common nouns can be used as proper names in South Asian languages. An example in Urdu is کریم *(generosity)* which is also a man's name.

5.4 Word Order

A number of South Asian languages have a different word-order than English and some have a free word-order. Urdu mostly has a word order but depending upon the domain the word order is not respected. e.g. *Jamal ne paani ka pura glass piya* and *Panni ka glass Jamal ne pura piya* both translates to *Jamal drank a whole glass of water.*

5.5 Spelling Variations

A number of situations occur in news articles where different authors or reporters scribe the name in different spellings even for native Urdu names. In English, this is recognized by capitalization and but in Urdu in the absence of capitalization this becomes a problem. An example is مسعود and مسود, where both strings represent the same person Masood. مسعود *(Masood)* represents the Arabic style of writing the name with an extra vowel and مسود *(Masood)* is written in the native Urdu form.

5.6 Ambiguity in Suffixes

A very common phenomenon in the proper names and common name in the South Asian languages is the use of a location suffix in a name. Sometimes the suffix is attached to the location name like a building or a road. A common practice is to append the location of person's origin in a name with a suffix *-i* or *-vi*. For example, if a person was from Batala (city in the Indian Punjab), *-vi* is added to the name to form *Batalvi*. This is observed in Urdu because most poets of Urdu use a name of their choosing, like an alias, at the end their name. This alias is called *takhalus* to refer themselves in their poetry. Almost always these names in absence of the poetic context are meaningful words that are not named entities.

5.7 Loan words in Urdu

Urdu has a number of loan words. Loan words are words that are not indigenous to Urdu. The named entity recognizer that is based on simple morphological cues will fail to recognize a large number of proper nouns. For example, گوانتاناموبے *(Guantanamo Bay)* is an English word with *Bay* as a cue for location. Similarly, for Osama Bin Laden, بن *(bin)* an Arabic cue needs to be used in the middle of the name for the person name.

5.8 Nested Entities

The named entities that are classified as nested contain two proper names that are nested together to form a new named entity. An example in Urdu is *Punjab University* where *Punjab* is the location name and *University* marks the whole entity as an organization.

5.9 Conjunction Ambiguity

Urdu text shows quite a few examples of conjunction ambiguities among proper nouns. That is, there is an ambiguity if the entity is one proper noun or two proper nouns e.g. *Toyota and Honda motor company* in English. Although, this phenomenon is present in most languages none of the papers in IJCNLP NER workshop mentioned them as a problem. An example of conjunction ambiguity is گوگل اور یاھو نے کھانا دیا *(Google and Yahoo offered banquet).*

5.10 Resource Challenges

NER approaches are either based on rule engine or inference engines. In each approach some type of corpus is required; lack of a large corpus for deriving rules is an issue for most South Asian languages, Urdu in particular. There are only two corpora available EMILLE corpus (Baker, et al., 2003) and Becker-Riaz (2002) corpus. The EMILLE corpus contains long running articles that do not have a lot of named entities. Becker-Riaz corpus contains short news articles and has a very rich content for named entity recognition. NER workshop at IJCNLP 2008 did not use either of them and contained only 36,000 Urdu tokens.

Recent experiments in NER in almost all aspects have been conducted through the use of inference engines using statistical machine learning. In the NER workshop at IJCNLP 2008, with one exception, all experiments used statistical machine learning for name recognition and conditional random fields (CRF) was favored by the majority. A good large annotated corpus is the pre-requisite to learn the rules. All experiments that used pure machine learning performed poorly and had to boost the performance of the system using gazetteers, online dictionaries and other hand crafted rules.

Urdu NER performed poorly and mostly at the bottom for each experiment and all researchers claimed the lack of the other resources to boost its performance. In summary, there is a dearth of annotated corpus for named entities for NER for South Asian languages. Urdu and Oriya are two languages where researchers could not find any gazetteers and online dictionaries for boosting the performance of the algorithms.

6. Analysis of Urdu and Hindi

Since Hindi NER was satisfactory in NER workshop at IJCNLP 2008 and Urdu and Hindi are closely related languages, a claim can be made that any computational model or algorithm that works for Hindi should work for Urdu also. This section describes in detail that this assertion is invalid for computational processing and sharing of resources. Extensive research has been done about the ancestry of Urdu and Hindi and their origins but no research study exists that compares and contrasts Urdu and Hindi in a scholarly fashion (Russell, 1996). Some rudimentary experiments for computationally recognizing names show that Hindi and Urdu behaved as two different languages. For example, while trying to recognize the capitol, the cues of recognition of locations are different e.g. *Dar-al-Khilafah* (Urdu) and *Rajdihani* (Hindi) are both used for the capitol of a city or a country. Therefore, we concluded that more research is warranted to understand the relationship between these two languages to understand if the computational models based one language can be used in some capacity for the other language.

The relationship between Hindi and Urdu is very complex, while analyzing the differences at high level they can be treated as the same language and play pivotal role in establishing the links between other South Asian communities across the world. At detailed levels they are separate languages and deserve to be studied and treated as separate languages. This is most apparent in the official documents produced by the Indian government in Hindi and news broadcasts that are not understandable by Urdu speakers (Matthews, 2002). The following example is borrowed from Russell (1996) to explain the growing divergence between Hindi and Urdu. Consider the sentence in English "*The eighteenth century was the period of the social, economic and political decline*". The Urdu translation of the sentence is "*Atharvin sadi samaji, iqtisadi aur siyasi zaval ka daur tha*" while the Hindi equivalent is "*Atharvin sadi samajik, arthik aur rajnitik girav ki sadi thi*". Russell points out that this example shows alone that Urdu speakers cannot understand the meaning of the Hindi equivalent and vice versa. Therefore, these two languages should not be treated as the same language in all circumstances.

We assert that that computational models built for one of the languages cannot be translated for the other language. A case in point is Hindi Wordnet (Jha et al., 2001), which is an excellent source for Hindi language processing but cannot be used for Urdu, because of the explanations given earlier. In addition, the following properties of the Hindi Wordnet make it unusable for Urdu processing without extra ordinary amount of work: The terminology used to describe parts of speech (POS) in Hindi Wordnet is completely foreign to Urdu speaker. Also, the POS names are Sanskrit-based whereas the Urdu POS are Persian and Arabic based. For example, in Hindi the word for noun is *sangya* and in Urdu it is called *ism.* The proper noun in Hindi is called *vyakti vachak sangy,* no Urdu speaker will know this unless they have studied Hindi grammar. In order to work through these differences, one has to be familiar with both languages at almost expert levels. In other words in order to use Hindi resources to do Urdu computational processing one has to know Hindi at detailed linguistic level. A detailed analysis of phonological differences between Hind and Urdu and the resource construction of Hindi using Highbrow formalisms is discussed in detail by Riaz (2009).

7. Rule-based Urdu NER

We used a hand crafted rule-based NER system for Urdu NER instead of using a machine learning approach for the following reasons:

- There are no good annotated corpora available. The only annotated corpus available is through the NER workshop of IJCNLP 2008 which is only 36000 words.
- At NER workshop IJCNLP 2008 Urdu data was available to all the researchers but none of the experiment fared well for Urdu using CRF.
- Conditional Random Fields (CRF) is the state of art for named entity extraction, in the absence of boosting methods like gazetteers, CRF performed poorly with only annotated text.

- There are no gazetteers and online dictionaries available for Urdu that are accessible through Web Services or for online consumption.
- Hindi resources cannot be used to bridge the lack of language resources for Urdu (Riaz, 2009).
- Creating a new set of tagged data set for modeling CRF or other new statistical algorithm on Urdu data is cost prohibitive at this time.

7.1 Experiment Setup

There are two corpora available for Urdu for research in NER; Becker-Riaz corpus and EMILLE corpus. Although EMILLE is a larger corpus, it contains articles that are long and deficient of named entities. Becker-Riaz corpus is a news article corpus and it contains abundant of named entities. We chose 2,262 documents from the Becker-Riaz corpus and removed a number of XML tags and their content for readability. A sample document from the reduced Becker-Riaz corpus is constructed by using XSLT is given below:

```
<cesDoc>
<doc-number>021003_uschinairaq_atif</doc-number>
<title>نئی عراق:نئی قرارداد روس کو قبول</title>
<para>امریکی ایوان
نمائندگان نے بدھ کو عراق سے متعلق صدر بش کی پالیسی کی سیاسی
حمایت کی ہے جس کے باعث بظاہر امریکہ کے لئے بغداد کے خلاف
عسکری قوت
استعمال کرنے کی راہ ہموار ہو جائے گی۔ تاہم امریکی سینیٹ اب اس
کرنے کی راہ ہموار ہو جائے گی۔ تاہم امریکی سینیٹ اب معاملے پر غور
اس معاملے
کرے گی۔</para>
</cesDoc>
```

The documents are not tagged with named entities so rules need to be constructed to find proper names. A number of proper noun cues are available in the text to generate those rules. About 200 documents were analyzed to construct the set of rules, while analyzing text a number of ambiguities were found – some of those are discussed in the earlier sections. The rules were constructed for the following named entities – examples are given in English for clarity.

- Person name e.g. George Bush
- Person of influence if proper name is identified e.g. President George Bush
- Location name e.g. Pakistan, Bharat, Punjab, America, Lahore
- Date: 1996
- Numbers: e.g. 31,000
- Organization e.g. Taliban, Al-Qaeda, B.B.C.

Although rules are designed to recognize the above named entities, the current implementation recognizes all of them as simple named-entities. While crafting rules for named entities a number of interesting rule patterns, heuristics and challenges were discovered that play important role when discovering a named entity. We mention some interesting ones below:

- Punctuation marks like ":" are useful but the position of their occurrence in text is important.
- Beginning of the sentence in title of news text has a different rule than beginning of the sentence in the paragraph text.
- Titles of the news text are not grammatically formed. A rudimentary POS tagger available from CRULP (Center for Research in Urdu language Processing) fails on marking the constituents of sentence. Moreover, POS tagger changed the order of words. This further complicated writing matching rules.
- Stemming reduces the precision of the system. It will conflate terms like *Pakistani* to *Pakistan.* Hence, marking *Pakistan* as named entity in the context of the *Pakistani* which is not a named entity.
- Suffix rules are very helpful in recognition of location names e.g. *–stan* for Pakistan, Afghanistan etc. But it does not find names like *Bharat, Iran* etc.
- Same suffix can identify location and organization e.g. *Taliban* and *Afghanistan.*
- String of names like *Rahid Latif, Shahid Afridi, and Muhammad Yousaf* are problematic for our NER system since there is no capitalization in Urdu and they occur without any prefix or suffix cues.
- Co-reference resolution for names will be non-trivial since they have multiple spellings, only context can be used to resolve them. For example, *Milosevic* is spelled at least with three different spellings.
- Honorific titles are very important but a title like *Sadr (President)* can occasionally lead to incorrect recognition because *Sadr* is the location of a well known neighborhood of *Karachi (largest city in Pakistan).*
- Honorific titles are sometimes transliterated into Urdu from English and other times they are scribed in indigenous from in another article to refer to the same person e.g. کیپٹن is the transliteration of *captain* and کپتانmeans *captain* in indigenous Urdu form.
- Anchoring around the named entities is a useful heuristic. The anchor text choice is one of the most challenging tasks for our system.

7.2 Algorithm for Urdu NER

In our rule-based system, the rules form a finite state automata (FSA) based on lexical cues. Some cues are at the start of the state, some are at the end of the state, sometimes the cues are found in the middle of the finite state machine. These rules are corpus-based, heuristic-based, and grammar-based. The rules are implicitly weighted in the order they are applied. For example, the most probable match is listed first and applied first on the text string. For example, one rule that has high chance of recognizing the person name is راہنما ----- نے. Here راہنما and نے are anchors. In English this rule will be represented as *Rahnuma* $[token_1, token_2]$ *post-position (Rahnuma* means leader in Urdu). In the example given $token_1, token_2$ will be tagged as a named entity. Each rule is represented as regular expressions since they are an ideal way to represent rules created as finite state automata. Instead of finding the named entities in each document in this version of the system the algorithm finds named entities in the given string of text regardless of the document. The input to the algorithm is a UTF-8 or UTF-16 Urdu text string. One document contains two input strings, the title of the document and the paragraph represented as long string without line breaks. There could be a number of named entities in the paragraph but our rules currently address on named-entity recognition per rule. An n-gram approach was used to limit the length of the input text. After a number of experiments, a 6-gram model was used for an input string. The bigram model was too small and trigram models showed it had no room for named-entities for multi word named entities, four gram and five gram models lacked adequate room for anchor texts and cues. 6-gram model was quite successful but sometimes the windows size was too big when a tri-gram would have worked e.g. two anchor tokens and a named-entity representing one token. The n-grams were constructed by using JDOM implementation to read in XML documents.

When a named entity is found with full confidence it is propagated to all 6-grams and if the matched named entity is found in other input strings (6-grams) it is tagged as a named-entity. Once the 6-gram is tagged it is not processed again. There are some named entities that are abundant in the text but sometimes their occurrences are ambiguous in a number of ways. The reason for these ambiguities is because these entities are so prevalent in the news articles and common in the South Asia that reporters and writers of news articles do not use cues to refer them in the news text. For example, cities like *Karachi, Lahore,* and countries like *America, Bharat, Pakistan* occur frequently with no cues. Instead of writing complicated regular expressions, a small authority file is created with these important names. This authority file serves like a mini gazetteer for our system. A lookup is done before the rules are applied if the name is found the entity is marked. Currently, the authority file contains 40 named entities after examining the 200 document rule-creation set. In the absence of the authority file, complicated rules will need to be crafted using morphological analysis for words like *Pakistan* and through some co-reference resolution for words like *Karachi*.

The complete algorithm is given below:

```
• Iterate over the input 6-grams
  a. Given the input text match the
     string's tokens with the tokens in
     the authority file.
  b. If the match occurs mark the
     named entity and iterate all
     other input strings and mark them
     with the matched entity if it is
     present.
     i. The strings that are tagged are
        removed from the pool to be
        matched
  c. If the match does not occur in
     the authority file iterate over
     the regular expressions to match
     the expression on the input
     string.
     i. If the match occurs on a
        regular expression, mark the
        name entity and iterate over
        all other input strings and
        mark them with the matched
        entity if it is present.
```

It is important to note that the algorithm presented above recognizes name entities in the exponential complexity for clarity but the actual implementation is done in linear time complexity.

In the algorithm, regular expressions that are the bottom of the list will be applied when the input string was not tagged with any previous regular expression and the input string did not have any token that is the authority file. The regular expressions that are towards the bottom of the list tend to have patterns that are mostly recognized by the readers who have background knowledge about the topic discussed in the document e.g. the string of names of cricket players without any reference to the *cricket* or *athlete*. English translation of the text would be *Rashid Latif and Shahid Afridi are in the field.* These names of Pakistani cricketers will be known to most South Asians who have followed cricket at any level.

Given an input 6-gram, there could be more than one entity in the input string but we are only finding one named entity and then not processing the string again. This might give the impression that other named entities will not be tagged. Our set up of n-grams prevents us from the missing the later named entity in the string because these entities will show up as one of subsequent 6-grams.

The rules at the top of the list could tie for importance e.g. The rules for جنرل فیصل *(General Faisal)* andفیصل شاھراہ *(Shahrah-e-Faisal or Faisal Boulevard)* have very consistent previous token cues. Our strategy of looping through all the 6-grams to tag the named entities is going to tag both strings as named entities but it will not classify فیصل شاھراہ as the location if the *"general"* rule was applied first. This has the side-effect of low recall for nested-entities.

7.3 Evaluation & Results

The rule sets were created from 200 documents of Becker-Riaz corpus and the experiment were run on 2,262 documents. Each of these documents is evaluated to create relevance judgments. The relevance judgments are created by two native speakers of Urdu who are avid news readers. The results of experiment runs were hard to grade on such a large set of documents so we chose 600 documents for evaluation. Two judges were chosen who are fluent in Urdu but required some coaching to recognize the named entities. At first judges were expecting terms like *Palestinian* and *elections* to be named entities but after some coaching all evaluation was done correctly. There were very few disagreements among the judges after coaching. A third native speaker was used to address instances of disagreements between the two initial judges. The evaluation set was chosen where all the judges agreed upon the named entities. The results are measured by $f-measure$ that is defined in terms of well known Information Retrieval measures of precision $P$and recall$R$. $f-measure$ is defined by the following equation: $f-measure = \frac{2PR}{P+R}$

Since our algorithm does not support named entity recognition at a document level, the total number of unique named entities in the evaluation set are found. The total numbers of unique named entities are 206. The algorithm matched about 2819 total named entities. While creating the rules and the evaluation set it looked as the number of documents grows the unique named-entities will level out gradually, but we found a lot of repetitions as the number of documents increased but new names consistently were added to the unique list but at a very low rate. Although, the corpus domain is news text, the genre of the documents spans over almost any news worthy information in South Asia, this results in increase of non-unique names. The algorithm execution resulted in 187 named-entities and 171 of those were true named entities. The results show the recall of 90.7% and precision of 91.5%. This gives the $f_1-measure$ value of 91.1%. We found that, suffixes cues and anchor text features were very useful feature but at the same time anchor text feature was the cause of most false positives. Almost all false positives were noun phrases. We ran our rule set on the 36,000 token Urdu data provided for IJCNLP 2008 NER Workshop. Without tuning any of the rules $f_1-measure$ was 72.4% and after adding a few rules after looking at the training set $f_1-measure$ was increased to 81.6% on the test set. A close analysis of this data showed considerable lack of named entities in contrast to the Becker-Riaz corpus. Therefore major results are drawn from the Becker-Riaz corpus. The results of rule execution on IJCNLP 2008 data for Urdu are better than any of the results reported in IJCNLP 2008 NER workshop for Urdu data.

7.3.1 Discussion

Although our results are very encouraging some discussion is warranted about the experience in creating and refining the rules for named entity recognition.

- The 6-gram is processed a number of times to see the performance with stemming and noise words. Both stemming and removal of stop words lowers the precision of the system.
- We mostly used Urdu postpositions as suffix anchor texts. This rule sometimes gave a high recall but very low precision e.g. the postposition conflicted with the transcribed English words in Urdu.
- We removed a rule where the entity is preceded by the punctuation mark colon in the title filed. This rule gave 100% recall but the precision was about 30%.

- Some of the cue words gave 100% recall but the precision was quite low e.g. the rule that identifies name entity through the cue word of transcribed English word of leader gave perfect recall but 56% precision.
- The phrases that could contain more than one token are sometimes written with the blank space between tokens and sometimes as one token e.g. وزیراعظم *(prime minister)*. In this case the rules are modified to recognize both occurrences.

8. Conclusion and Future work.

NER in Urdu is a challenging problem for language processing. In the absence of a learning training set, rule-based approach for NER in Urdu shows promising results. Also, we argue that Hindi resources like gazetteers etc. cannot be used Urdu NER models. Our results are an improvement on all other approaches that are used for Urdu NER. It also shows that our rule-based approach is superior to Conditional Random Fields approach used in IJCNLP 2008 NER workshop by the majority of the papers. In future we plan to use online dictionaries from CRULP through Web Services framework, if available instead of the manually created authority file. Finally, we want to change our regular expressions to accommodate already named entity tagged texts and also to identify names at document level.

9. References

D. Bikel, S. Miller, R. Schwartz, R. Weischedel *Nymble: A High Performance Learning Name-Finder,* Proceedings of 5th Conference on Applied Natural Language Processing. 1996

D. Becker, B. Bennett, E. Davis, D. Panton, and K. Riaz. *Named Entity Recognition in Urdu: A Progress Report.* Proceedings of the 2002 International Conference on Internet Computing. June 2002.

D. Becker, K. Riaz. *A Study in Urdu Corpus Construction.* Proceedings of the 3rd Workshop on Asian Language Resources and International Standardization at the 19th International Conference on Computational Linguistics. August 2002.

P. Baker, A. Hardie, T. McEnery, and B.D. Jayaram. *Corpus Data for South Asian Language Processing.* Proceedings of the 10th Annual Workshop for South Asian Language Processing, EACL 2003.

CRULP http://www.crulp.org/software/langproc/POS_tagger.htm (February 2010)

D. Palmer, D. Day, *A Statistical Profile of the Named Entity Task,* Proceedings of 5th Conference on Applied Natural Language Processing. 1996

D. Matthews, *Urdu in India*, Annual of Urdu Studies vol. 17 (2002).

J. Erickson, *Jack Hermansen on Mulit-culatural Name Recognition Software*, Dr. Dobbb's Journal July 2005.

J. Lafferty, A. McCallum, F. Pereira, *Conditional random fields: probabilistic models for segmenting and labeling sequence data*, International Conference on Machine Learning, 2001.

L. Wei ; A. McCallum, *Rapid development of Hindi named entity recognition using conditional random fields and feature induction*, ACM Transactions on Asian Language Information Processing (TALIP), volume 2, issue 3. 2003

Mukund, S., Srihari, R., *NE Tagging for Urdu based on Bootstrap POS Learning,* Third International Workshop on Information Access, Addressing the Information Need of Multilingual Societies (CLIAWS3), 2009

Ijaz, M., Hussain, S., *Corpus Based Lexicon Development,* in the Proccedings of Conference on Language Technology. 2007

Goyal, *Named Entity Recognition for South Asian Languages,* Workshop on NER for South and South East Asian Languages, IJCNLP 2008

Ekbal, S. Bandyopadhyay, *Bengali Named Entity Recognition Using Support Vector Machine,* Workshop on NER for South and South East Asian Languages, IJCNLP 2008

P. Srikanth, K. Murthy, *Named Entity Recognition for Telugu*, Workshop on NER for South and South East Asian Languages, IJCNLP 2008

Ekbal, R. Haque, A. Das, V. Poka, S. Bandyopadhyay, *Language Independent Named Entity Recognition in Indian Languages*, Workshop on NER for South and South East Asian Languages, IJCNLP 2008

K. Gali, H. Surana, A. Vaidya, P. Shishtla, D. Sharma, *Aggregating Machine Learning and Rule Based Heuristics for Named Entity Recognition,* Workshop on NER for South and South East Asian Languages, IJCNLP 2008

S. Kumar, S. Chatterji, S. Dandapat, S. Sarkar, *A Hybrid Named Entity Recognition System for South and South East Asian Languages,* Workshop on NER for South and South East Asian Languages, IJCNLP 2008

P. Shishtla, K. Gali, P. Pingali, V. Varma, *Experiments in Telugu NER: A Conditional Random Field Approach,* Workshop on NER for South and South East Asian Languages, IJCNLP 2008

Nayan, B. Ravi, K. Rao, P. Singh, S. Sanyal, R. Sanyal, *Named Entity Recognition for Indian Languages*, Workshop on NER for South and South East Asian Languages, IJCNLP 2008

P. Praveen, R. Kiran, *Hybrid Named Entity Recognition System for South and South East Asian Languages*, Workshop on NER for South and South East Asian Languages, IJCNLP 2008

Chaudhuri, S. Bhattacharya, *An Experiment on Automatic Detection of Named Entities in Bangla*, Workshop on NER for South and South East Asian Languages, IJCNLP 2008

P. Shishtla, P. Pingali, V. Varma, *A Character n-gram Based Approach for Improved Recall in Indian Language,* NER Workshop on NER for South and South East Asian Languages, IJCNLP 2008

R. Vijayakrishna, L. Sobha, *Domain Focused Named Entity Recognizer for Tamil Using Conditional Random Fields*, Workshop on NER for South and South East Asian Languages, IJCNLP 2008

P. Thompson, C. Dozier, *Name Searching and Information Retrieval*, Proceedings of Second Conference on Empirical Methods in Natural Language Processing. 1996

N. Wacholder, Y. Ravin, M. Choi, *Disambiguation of Proper Names in Text,* Proceedings of 5th Conference on Applied Natural Language Processing. 1997.

S. Martynuk, *Statistical Approach to the Debate on Hindi and Urdu*, Annual of Urdu Studies vol. 18 (2003)

R. Russell, *Some Notes on Hindi and Urdu*, Annual of Urdu Studies vol. 11 (1996).

K. Riaz, *Concept Search in Urdu*, Proceedings of the 2nd PhD workshop on Information and Knowledge Management, 2008

K. Riaz, *Urdu is not Hindi for Information Access,* Workshop on Multilingual Information Access, SIGIR 2009

S. Jha, D. Narayan, P. Pande, P. Bhattacharyya, *A WordNet for Hindi,* International Workshop on Lexical Resources in Natural Language Processing, Hyderabad, India, January 2001

H. Wallah, *Conditional Random Fields: An Introduction*, University of Pennsylvania CIS Technical Report MS-CIS-04-21, 2004.

CONE: Metrics for Automatic Evaluation of Named Entity Co-reference Resolution

Bo Lin, Rushin Shah, Robert Frederking, Anatole Gershman
Language Technologies Institute, School of Computer Science
Carnegie Mellon University
5000 Forbes Ave., PA 15213, USA
{bolin,rnshah,ref,anatoleg}@cs.cmu.edu

Abstract

Human annotation for Co-reference Resolution (CRR) is labor intensive and costly, and only a handful of annotated corpora are currently available. However, corpora with Named Entity (NE) annotations are widely available. Also, unlike current CRR systems, state-of-the-art NER systems have very high accuracy and can generate NE labels that are very close to the gold standard for unlabeled corpora. We propose a new set of metrics collectively called CONE for Named Entity Co-reference Resolution (NE-CRR) that use a subset of gold standard annotations, with the advantage that this subset can be easily approximated using NE labels when gold standard CRR annotations are absent. We define CONE B^3 and CONE CEAF metrics based on the traditional B^3 and CEAF metrics and show that CONE B^3 and CONE CEAF scores of any CRR system on any dataset are highly correlated with its B^3 and CEAF scores respectively. We obtain correlation factors greater than 0.6 for all CRR systems across all datasets, and a best-case correlation factor of 0.8. We also present a baseline method to estimate the gold standard required by CONE metrics, and show that CONE B^3 and CONE CEAF scores using this estimated gold standard are also correlated with B^3 and CEAF scores respectively. We thus demonstrate the suitability of CONE $B^3$and CONE CEAF for automatic evaluation of NE-CRR.

1 Introduction

Co-reference resolution (CRR) is the problem of determining whether two entity mentions in a text refer to the same entity in real world or not. Noun Phrase CRR (NP-CRR) considers all noun phrases as entities, while Named Entity CRR restricts itself to noun phrases that describe a Named Entity. In this paper, we consider the task of Named Entity CRR (NE-CRR) only. Most, if not all, recent efforts in the field of CRR have concentrated on machine-learning based approaches. Many of them formulate the problem as a pair-wise binary classification task, in which possible co-reference between every pair of mentions is considered, and produce chains of co-referring mentions for each entity as their output. One of the most important problems in CRR is the evaluation of CRR results. Different evaluation metrics have been proposed for this task. B-cubed (Bagga and Baldwin, 1998) and CEAF (Luo, 2005) are the two most popular metrics; they compute Precision, Recall and F1 measure between matched equivalent classes and use weighted sums of Precision, Recall and F1 to produce a global score. Like all metrics, B^3 and CEAF require gold standard annotations; however, gold standard CRR annotations are scarce, because producing such annotations involves a substantial amount of human effort since it requires an in-depth knowledge of linguistics and a high level of understanding of the particular text. Consequently, very few corpora with gold standard CRR annotations are available (NIST, 2003; MUC-6, 1995; Agirre, 2007). By contrast, gold standard Named Entity (NE) annotations are easy to produce; indeed, there are many NE annotated corpora of different sizes and genres. Similarly, there are few CRR systems and even the best scores obtained by them are only in the region of F1 = 0.5 - 0.6. There are only four such CRR systems freely available, to the best of our knowledge (Bengston and Roth, 2007; Versley et al., 2008; Baldridge and Torton, 2004; Baldwin and Carpenter, 2003). In comparison, there are numerous Named Entity recognition (NER) systems, both general-purpose and specialized, and many of them achieve scores better than F1 = 0.95 (Ratinov and Roth, 2009; Finkel et al.,

Proceedings of the 2010 Named Entities Workshop, ACL 2010, pages 136–144,
Uppsala, Sweden, 16 July 2010.

2005). Although these facts can be partly attributed to the 'hardness' of CRR compared to NER, they also reflect the substantial gap between NER and CRR research. In this paper, we present a set of metrics, collectively called CONE, that leverage widely available NER systems and resources and tools for the task of evaluating co-reference resolution systems. The basic idea behind CONE is to predict a CRR system's performance for the task of full NE-CRR on some dataset using its performance for the subtask of named mentions extraction and grouping (NMEG) on that dataset. The advantage of doing so is that measuring NE-CRR performance requires the co-reference information of all mentions of a Named Entity, including named mentions, nominal and pronominal references, while measuring the NMEG performance only requires co-reference information of named mentions of a NE, and this information is relatively easy to obtain automatically even in the absence of gold standard annotations. We compute correlation between CONE B^3, B^3, CONE CEAF and CEAF scores for various CRR systems on various gold-standard annotated datasets and show that the CONE B^3 and B^3 scores are highly correlated for all such combinations of CRR systems and datasets, as are CONE CEAF and CEAF scores, with a best-case correlation of 0.8. We produce estimated gold standard annotations for the Enron email corpus, since no actual gold standard CRR annotations exist for it, and then use CONE B^3 and CONE CEAF with these estimated gold standard annotations to compare the performance of various NE-CRR systems on this corpus. No such comparison has been previously performed for the Enron corpus.

We adopt the same terminology as in (Luo, 2005): a *mention* refers to each individual phrase and an *entity* refers to the *equivalence class* or *co-reference chain* with several mentions. This allows us to note some differences between NE-CRR and NP-CRR. NE-CRR involves indentifying named entities and extracting their co-referring mentions; equivalences classes without any NEs are not considered. NE-CRR is thus clearly a subset of NP-CRR, where all co-referring mentions and equivalence classes are considered. However, we focus on NE-CRR because it is currently a more active research area than NP-CRR and a better fit for target applications such as text forensics and web mining, and also because it is more amenable to the automatic evaluation approach that we propose.

The research questions that motivate our work are:

(1) Is it possible to use only NER resources to evaluate NE-CRR systems? If so, how is this problem formulated?

(2) How does one perform evaluation in a way that is accurate and automatic with least human intervention?

(3) How does one perform evaluation on large unlabeled datasets?

We show that our CONE metrics achieve good results and represent a promising first step toward answering these questions.

The rest of the paper is organized as follows. We present related work in the field of automatic evaluation methods for natural language processing tasks in Section 2. In Section 3, we give an overview of the standard metrics currently used for evaluating co-reference resolution. We define our new metrics CONE B^3 and CONE CEAF in Section 4. In section 5, we provide experimental results that illustrate the performance of CONE B^3 and CONE CEAF compared to B^3 and CEAF respectively. In Section 6, we give an example of the application of CONE metrics by evaluating NE-CRR systems on an unlabeled dataset, and discuss possible drawbacks and extensions of these metrics. Finally, in section 7 we present our conclusions and ideas for future work.

2 Related Work

There has been a substantial amount of research devoted to automatic evaluation for natural language processing, especially tasks involving language generation. The BLEU score (Papineni et al., 2002) proposed for evaluating machine translation results is the best known example of this. It uses n-gram statistics between machine generated results and references. It inspired the ROUGE metric (Lin and Hovy, 2003) and other methods (Louis and Nenkova, 2009) to perform automatic evaluation of text summarization. Both these metrics have show strong correlation between automatic evaluation results and human judgments. The two metrics successfully reduce the need for human judgment and help speed up research by allowing large-scale evaluation. Another example is the alignment entropy (Pervouchine et al., 2009) for evaluating transliteration alignment. It reduces the need for alignment gold standard and highly correlates with transliteration system performance. Thus it is able to serve as a good metric for transliteration alignment. We contrast our work with (Stoyanov et al., 2009), who show that the co-reference resolution problem can be separated into different parts according to the type of the mention. Some parts are relatively easy to solve. The resolver performs equally well in each part across datasets. They use the statistics of mentions in different parts with test results on other datasets as a predictor for unseen datasets, and obtain promising results with good correlations. We approach the problem from a different perspective. In our work, we show the correlation between the scores on traditional metrics and scores on our CONE metrics, and show how to automatically estimate the gold standard required by CONE metrics. Thus our method is able to predict the co-reference resolution performance without gold standard at all. We base our new metrics on the standard B^3 and CEAF metrics used for computing CRR scores. (Vilian et al., 1995; Bagga and Baldwin, 1998; Luo, 2005). B^3 and CEAF are believed to be more discriminative and interpretable than earlier metrics and are widely adopted especially for machine-learning based approaches.

3 Standard Metrics: B^3 and CEAF

We now provide an overview of the standard B^3 and CEAF metrics used to evaluate CRR systems. Both metrics assume that a CRR system produces a set of equivalence classes $\{O\}$ and assigns each mention to only one class. Let O_i be the class to which the ith mention was assigned by the system. We also assume that we have a set of correct equivalence classes $\{G\}$ (the gold standard). Let G_i be the gold standard class to which the ith mention should belong. Let N_i denote the number of mentions in O_i which are also in G_i – the correct mentions. B^3 computes the presence rate of correct mentions in the same equivalent classes. The individual precision and recall score is defined as follows:

$$P_i = \frac{N_i}{|O_i|} \qquad R_i = \frac{N_i}{|G_i|}$$

Here $|O_i|$ and $|G_i|$ are the cardinalities of sets O_i and G_i.

The final precision and recall scores are:

$$P = \sum_{i=1}^{n} w_i P_i \qquad R = \sum_{i=1}^{n} w_i R_i$$

Here, in the simplest case the weight w_i is set to 1/n, equal for all mentions.

CEAF (Luo, 2005) produces the optimal matching between output classes and true classes first, with the constraint that one true class, G_i, can be mapped to at most one output class, say $O_{f(i)}$ and vice versa. This can be solved by the KM algorithm (Kuhn, 1955; Munkres, 1957) for maximum matching in a bipartite graph. CEAF then computes the precision and recall score as follows:

$$P = \frac{\sum_i |M_{i,f(i)}|}{\sum_i |O_i|} \qquad R = \frac{\sum_i |M_{i,f(i)}|}{\sum_i |G_i|}$$

$$M_{i,j} = |O_i \cap G_j|$$

We use the terms $M_{i,j}$ from CEAF to re-write B^3, its formulas then reduce to:

$$P = \frac{1}{\sum_i |O_i|} \sum_i \sum_j \frac{|M_{i,j}|^2}{|O_i|}$$

$$R = \frac{1}{\sum_i |G_i|} \sum_i \sum_j \frac{|M_{i,j}|^2}{|G_i|}$$

We can see that B^3 simply iterates through all pairs of matchings instead of considering the one to one mappings as CEAF does. Thus, B^3 computes the weighted sum of the F-measures for each individual mention which helps alleviate the bias in the pure link-based F-measure, while CEAF computes the same as B^3 but enforces at most one matched equivalence class for every class in the system output and gold standard output.

4 CONE B^3 and CONE CEAF Metrics:

We now formally define the new CONE B^3 and CONE CEAF metrics that we propose for automatic evaluation of NE-CRR systems.

Let G denote the set of gold standard annotations and O denote the output of an NE-CRR system. Let G_i denote the equivalent class of entity i in the gold standard and O_j denote the equivalence class for entity j in the system output. Also let G_{ij} denote the jth mention in the equivalence class of entity i in the gold standard and O_{ij} denote the jth mention in the system output.

As described earlier, the standard B^3 and CEAF metrics evaluate scores using G and O and can be thought of as functions of the form $B^3(G, O)$. and $CEAF(G, O)$ respectively. Let us use $Score(G, O)$ to collectively refer to both these functions. An equivalence class G_i in G may contain three types of mentions: named mentions g^{NM}_{ij}, nominal mentions g^{NO}_{ij}, and pronominal mentions g^{PR}_{ij}. Similarly, we can define o^{NM}_{ij}, o^{NO}_{ij} and o^{PR}_{ij} for a class O_i in O. Now for each gold standard equivalence class G_i and system output equivalence class O_i, we define the following sets G^{NM}_i and O^{NM}_i:

$$\forall i, G^{NM}_i = \{g^{NM}_{ij}\}, g^{NM}_{ij} \subset G_i$$

$$\forall i, O^{NM}_i = \{o^{NM}_{ij}\}, o^{NM}_{ij} \subset O_i$$

In other words, G^{NM}_i and O^{NM}_i are the subsets of G_i and O_i containing all named mentions and no mentions of any other type.

Let G^{NM} denote the set of all such equivalance classes G^{NM}_i and O^{NM} denote the set of all equivalence classes O^{NM}_i. It is clear that G^{NM} and O^{NM} are pruned versions of the gold standard annotations and system output respectively.

We now define CONE B^3 and CONE CEAF as follows:

CONE $B^3 = B^3(G^{NM}, O^{NM})$

CONE CEAF = CEAF(G^{NM}, O^{NM})

Following our previous notation, we denote CONE B^3 and CONE CEAF collectively as Score(G^{NM}, O^{NM}). We observe that Score(G^{NM}, O^{NM}) measures a NE-CRR system's performance for the NE-CRR subtask of named mentions extraction and grouping (NMEG). We find that Score(G^{NM}, O^{NM}) is highly correlated with Score(G, O) for all the freely available NE-CRR systems over various datasets. This provides the neccessary justification for the use of Score(G^{NM}, O^{NM}).

We use SYNERGY (Shah et al., 2010), an ensemble NER system that combines the UIUC NER (Ritanov and Roth, 2009) and Stanford NER (Finkel et al., 2005) systems, to produce G^{NM} and O^{NM} from G and O by selecting named mentions. However, any other good NER system would serve the same purpose.

We see that while standard evaluation metrics require the use of G, i.e. the full set of NE-CRR gold standard annotations including named, nominal and pronimal mentions, CONE metrics require only G^{NM}, i.e. gold standard annotations consisting of named mentions only. The key advantage of using CONE metrics is that G^{NM} can be automatically approximated using an NER system with a good degree of accuracy. This is because state-of-the-art NER systems achieve near-optimal performance, exceeding F1 = 0.95 in many cases, and after obtaining their output, the task of estimating G^{NM} reduces to simply clustering it to seperate mentions of diffrerent real-world entities. This clustering can be thought of as a form of named entity matching, which is not a very hard problem. There exist systems that perform such matching in a sophisticated manner with a high degree of accuracy. We use simple heuristics such as exact matching, word matches, matches between initials, etc. to design such a matching system ourselves and use it to obtain estimates of G^{NM}, say $G^{NM\text{-}approx}$. We then calculate CONE B^3 and CONE CEAF scores using $G^{NM\text{-}approx}$ instead of G^{NM}; in other words, we perform fully automatic evaluation of NE-CRR systems by using Score($G^{NM\text{-}approx}$, O^{NM}) instead of Score(G^{NM}, O^{NM}). In order to show the validity of this evaluation, we calculate the correlation between the Score($G^{NM\text{-}approx}$, O^{NM}) and Score(G, O) for different NE-CRR systems across different datasets and find that they are indeed correlated. CONE thus makes automatic evaluation of NE-CRR systems possible. By leveraging the widely available named entity resources, it reduces the need for gold standard annotations in the evaluation process.

4.1 Analysis

There are two major kinds of errors that affect the performance of NE-CRR systems for the full NE-CRR task:

- Missing Named Entity (MNE): If a named mention is missing from the system output, it is very likely that its nearby nominal and anaphoric mentions will be lost, too
- Incorrectly grouped Named Entity (IGNE): Even if the named mention is correctly identified with its nearby nominal and anaphoric mentions to form a chain, it is still possible to misclassify the named mentions and its co-reference chain

Consider the following example of these two types of errors. Here, the alphabets represent the named mentions and numbers represent other type of mentions:

Gold standard, G: (A, B, C, 1, 2, 3, 4)
Output from System 1, $O1$: (A, B, 1, 2, 3)
Output from System 2, $O2$: (A, C, 1, 2, 4), (B, 3)
$O1$ shows an example of an MNE error, while $O2$ shows an example of an IGNE error.

Both these types of errors are in fact rooted in named mention extraction and grouping (NMEG). Therefore, we hypothesize that they must be preserved in a NE-CRR system's output for the subtask of named mentions extraction and grouping (NMEG) and will be reflected in the CONE B^3 and CONE CEAF metrics that evaluate scores for this subtask. Consider the following extension of the previous example:

G^{NM}: (A, B, C)
$O1^{NM}$: (A, B)
$O2^{NM}$: (A, C), (B)

We observe that the MNE error in *O1* is preserved in $O1^{NM}$, and the IGNE error in *O2* is preserved in $O2^{NM}$. Empirically we sample several output files in our experiments and observe the same phenomena. Therefore, we argue that it is possible to capture the two major kinds of errors described by considering only G^{NM} and O^{NM} instead of *G* and *O*.

We now provide a more detailed theoretical analysis of the CONE metrics. For a given NE-CRR system and dataset, consider the system output *O* and gold standard annotation *G*. Let P and R indicate precision and recall scores obtained by evaluating *O* against *G*, using CEAF. If we replace both *G* and *O* with their subsets G^{NM} and O^{NM} respectively, such that G^{NM} and O^{NM} contain only named mentions, we can modify the equations for precision and recall for CEAF to derive the following equations for precision P^{NM} and recall R^{NM} for CONE CEAF:

$$Sum\{O^{NM}\} = \sum_i \left|O^{NM}{}_i\right|$$

$$Sum\{G^{NM}\} = \sum_i \left|G^{NM}{}_i\right|$$

$$P^{NM} = \sum_i \frac{\left|M^{NM}{}_{i,f(i)}\right|}{Sum\{O^{NM}\}}$$

$$R^{NM} = \sum_i \frac{\left|M^{NM}{}_{i,f(i)}\right|}{Sum\{G^{NM}\}}$$

The corresponding equations for CONE B^3 Precision are:

$$P^{NM} = \sum_i \frac{\sum_j \left|M^{NM}{}_{i,j}\right|^2}{\left|O^{NM}{}_i\right| \times Sum\{O^{NM}\}}$$

$$R' = \sum_i \frac{\sum_j \left|M^{NM}{}_{i,j}\right|^2}{\left|R^{NM}{}_i\right| \times Sum\{R^{NM}\}}$$

In order to support the hypothesis that CONE metrics evaluated using (G^{NM}, O^{NM}) represent an effective substitute for standard metrics that use (*G*, *O*), we compute entity level correlation between the corresponding CONE and standard metrics. For example, in the case of CEAF / CONE CEAF Precision, we calculate correlation between the following quantities:

$$\vec{P}^{NM} = < \frac{\left|M^{NM}{}_{i,f(i)}\right|}{Sum\{S^{NM}\}} > \text{ and } \vec{P} = < \frac{\left|M_{i,f(i)}\right|}{Sum\{S\}} >$$

We perform this experiment with the LBJ and BART CRR systems on the ACE Phase 2 corpus. We illustrate the correlation results in Figure 1.

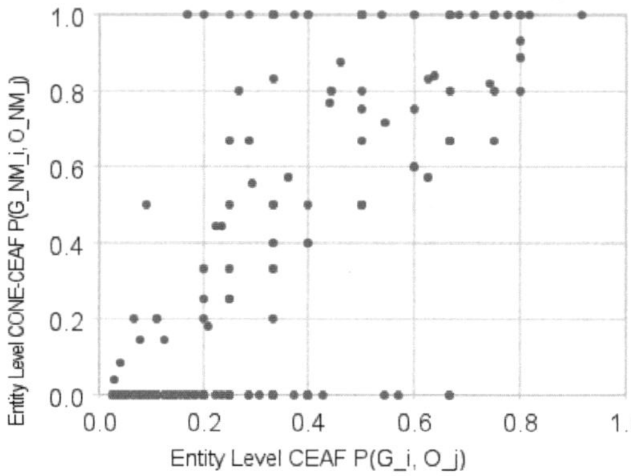

Figure 1. Correlation between $\vec{P}^{NM}$ and $\vec{P}$ - Entity Level CEAF Precision

From Figure 1, we can see that the two measures are highly correlated. In fact, we find that the Pearson's correlation coefficient (Soper et al., 1917; Cohen, 1988) is 0.73. The points lining up on the x-axis and y=1.0 represent very small equivalence classes and are a form of noise; their removal doesn't affect this coefficient. To show that this strong correlation is not a statistical anomaly, we also compute entity-level correlation using (G_i - $G^{NM}{}_i$, O_j - $O^{NM}{}_j$) and (G_i, O_j) instead of ($G^{NM}{}_i$, $O^{NM}{}_j$) and (G_i, O_j) and find that the coefficient drops to 0.03, which is obviously not correlated at all.

We now know $\vec{P}^{NM}$ and $\vec{P}$ are highly correlated. Assume the correlation is linear, with the following equation:

$$P_i = \alpha P^{NM}{}_i + \beta$$

where α and β are the linear regression parameters.

Thus

$$P = \sum_i P_i = \sum_i \left(\alpha P^{NM}{}_i + \beta\right) = n\alpha P^{NM} + n\beta$$

Here, *n* is the number of equivalence classes.

We conclude that the overall CEAF Precision and CONE CEAF Precision should be highly correlated too. We repeat this experiment with CEAF / CONE CEAF Recall, B^3 / CONE B^3 Precision and B^3 / CONE B^3 Recall and obtain similar results, allowing us to conclude that these sets of measures should also be highly correlated. We note here some generally accepted terminology regarding correlation: If two quantities have a Pearson's correlation coefficient greater than 0.7, they are considered "strongly correlated", if their correlation is between 0.5 and 0.7, they are considered "highly correlated", if it is between 0.3 and 0.5, they are considered "correlated", and otherwise they are considered "not correlated".

It is important to note that like all automatic evaluation metrics, CONE B^3 and CONE CEAF too can be easily 'cheated', e.g. a NE-CRR system that performs NER and named entity matching well but does not even detect and classify anaphora or nominal mentions would nonetheless score highly on these metrics. A possible solution to this problem would be to create gold standard annotations for a small subset of the data, call these annotations *G'*, and report two scores: B^3 / CEAF (*G'*), and CONE B^3 / CONE CEAF ($G^{NM\text{-}approx}$). Discrepancies between these two scores would enable the detection of such 'cheating'. A related point is that designers of NE-CRR systems should not optimize for CONE metrics alone, since by using $G^{NM\text{-}approx}$ (or G^{NM} where gold standard annotations are available), these metrics are obviously biased towards named mentions. This issue can also be addressed by having gold standard annotations *G'* for a small subset. One could then train a system by optimizing both B^3 / CEAF (*G'*) and CONE B^3 / CONE CEAF ($G^{NM\text{-}approx}$). This can be thought of as a form of semi-supervised learning, and may be useful in areas such as domain adaptation, where we could use some annotated test-set in a standard domain, e.g. newswire as the smaller set and an unlabeled large testset from some other domain, such as e-mail or biomedical documents. An interesting future direction is to monitor the effectiveness of our metrics over time. As co-reference resolution systems evolve in strength, our metrics might be less effective, however this could be a good indicator to discriminate on different subtasks the improvements gained by the co-reference resolution systems.

5 Experimental Results

We present experimental results in support of the validity and effectiveness of CONE metrics. As mentioned earlier, we used the following four publicly available CRR systems: UIUC's LBJ system (L), BART from JHU Summer Workshop (B), LingPipe from Alias-i (LP), and OpenNLP (OP) (Bengston and Roth, 2007; Versley et al., 2008; Baldridge and Torton, 2004; Baldwin and Carpenter, 2003). All these CRR systems perform Noun Phrase co-reference resolution (NP-CRR), not NE-CRR. So, we must first eliminate all equivalences classes that do not contain any named mentions. We do so using the SYNERGY NER system to separate named mentions from unnamed ones. Note that this must not be confused with the use of SYNERGY to produce G^{NM} and O^{NM} from *G* and *O* respectively. For that task, all equivalence classes in *G* and *O* already contain at least one named mention and we remove all unnamed mentions from each class. This process effectively converts the NP-CRR results of these systems into NE-CRR ones. We use the ACE Phase 2 NWIRE and ACE 2005 English datasets. We avoid using the ACE 2004 and MUC6 datasets because the UIUC LBJ system was trained on ACE 2004 (Bengston and Roth, 2008), while BART and LingPipe were trained on MUC6. There are 29 files in the test set of ACE Phrase 2 and 81 files in ACE 2005, summing up to 120 files with around 50,000 tokens with 5000 valid co-reference mentions. Tables 1 and 2 show the Pearson's correlation coefficients between CONE metric scores of the type Score(G^{NM}, O^{NM}) and standard metric scores of the type Score(*G*, *O*) for combinations of various CRR systems and datasets.

	B3/CONE B3			CEAF/CONE CEAF		
	P	R	F1	P	R	F1
L	0.82	0.71	0.7	0.81	0.71	0.77
B	0.85	0.5	0.66	0.71	0.61	0.68
LP	0.84	0.66	0.67	0.74	0.71	0.73
OP	0.31	0.57	0.61	0.79	0.72	0.79

Table 1. G^{NM}: Correlation on ACE Phase 2

	B3/CONE B3			CEAF/CONE CEAF		
	P	R	F1	P	R	F1
L	0.6	0.62	0.62	0.75	0.61	0.68
B	0.74	0.82	0.84	0.72	0.68	0.67
LP	0.91	0.65	0.73	0.44	0.57	0.53
OP	0.48	0.77	0.8	0.54	0.67	0.65

Table 2. G^{NM}: Correlation on ACE 2005

We observe from Tables 1 and 2 that CONE B^3 and CONE CEAF scores are highly correlated with B^3 and CEAF scores respectively, and this holds true for Precision, Recall and F1 scores, for all combinations of CRR systems and datasets. This justifies our assumption that a system's performance for the subtask of NMEG is a good predictor of its performance for the full task of NE-CRR. These correlation coefficients are graphically illustrated in Figures 2 and 3.

We now use our baseline named entity matching method to automatically generate estimated gold standard annotations $G^{NM\text{-}approx}$ and recalculate CONE CEAF and CONE B^3 scores using $G^{NM\text{-}approx}$ instead of G^{NM}. Tables 3 and 4 show the correlation coefficients between the new CONE scores and the standard metric scores.

	B3/CONE B3			CEAF/CONE CEAF		
	P	R	F1	P	R	F1
L	0.31	0.23	0.22	0.33	0.55	0.56
B	0.71	0.44	0.43	0.61	0.63	0.71
LP	0.57	0.43	0.49	0.36	0.25	0.31
OP	0.1	0.6	0.64	0.35	0.53	0.53

Table 3. $G^{NM\text{-}approx}$: Correlation on ACE Phase 2

	B3/CONE B3			CEAF/CONE CEAF		
	P	R	F1	P	R	F1
L	0.33	0.32	0.42	0.22	0.34	0.36
B	0.25	0.66	0.65	0.2	0.45	0.37
LP	0.19	0.33	0.34	0.77	0.68	0.72
OP	0.26	0.66	0.67	0.28	0.42	0.38

Table 4. $G^{NM\text{-}approx}$: Correlation on ACE Phase 2

We observe from Tables 3 and 4 that these correlation factors are encouraging, but not as good as those in Tables 1 and 2. All the corresponding CONE B^3 and CONE CEAF scores are correlated, but very few are highly correlated. We should note however that our baseline system to create $G^{NM\text{-}approx}$ uses relatively simple clustering methods and heuristics. It is easy to observe that a sophisticated named entity matching system would produce a $G^{NM\text{-}approx}$ that better approximates G^{NM} than our baseline method, and CONE B^3 and CONE CEAF scores calculated using this $G^{NM\text{-}approx}$ would be more correlated with standard B^3 and CEAF scores.

We note from the above results that correlations scores are very similar across different systems and datasets. In order to formalize this assertion, we calculate correlation scores in a system-independent and data-independent manner. We combine all the data points across all four different systems and plot them in Figure 2 and 3 for ACE Phase 2 NWIRE corpus and in Figure 4 and 5 for ACE 2005 corpus respectively. We illustrate only F1 scores; the results for precision and recall are similar.

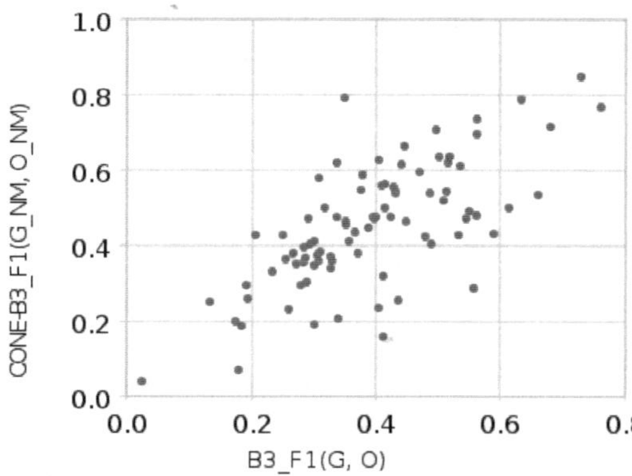

Figure 2. Correlation between B^3 F1 and CONE B^3 F1 for all systems on ACE 2

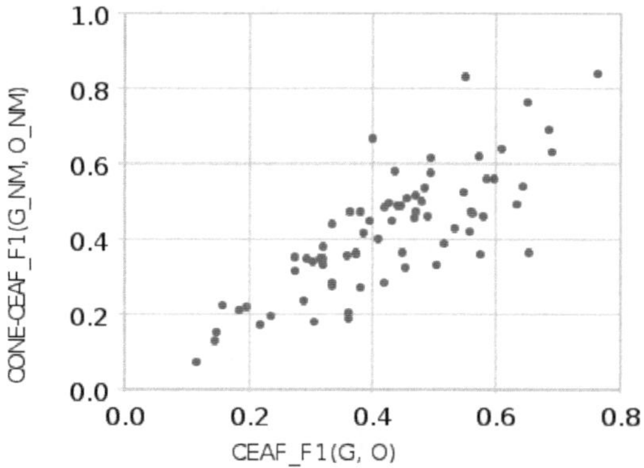

Figure 3. Correlation between CEAF F1 and CONE CEAF F1 for all systems on ACE 2

Figure 2 reflects a Pearson's correlation coefficient of 0.70, suggesting that all the B^3 F1 and CONE B^3 F1 scores for different systems are highly correlated and that CONE B^3 F1 does not bias towards any particular system. Figure 3 reflects a Pearson's correlation coefficient of 0.83, providing similar evidence for the system-independence of correlation between CEAF F1 and CONE CEAF F1 scores. Figures 4 and 5 corresponding to ACE 2005 reflect similar correlation coefficients of 0.89 and 0.82, and thus support the idea that the correlations between B^3 F1 and CONE B^3 F1, as well as between CEAF F1and CONE CEAF F1, are dataset-independent in addition to being system-independent.

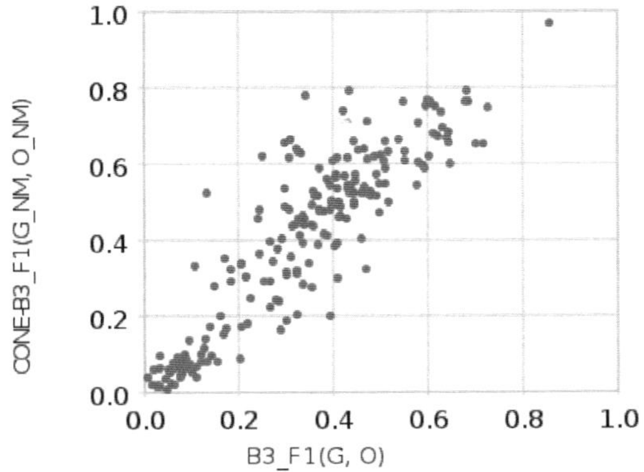

Figure 4. Correlation between B^3 F1 and CONE B^3 F1 for all systems on ACE 2005

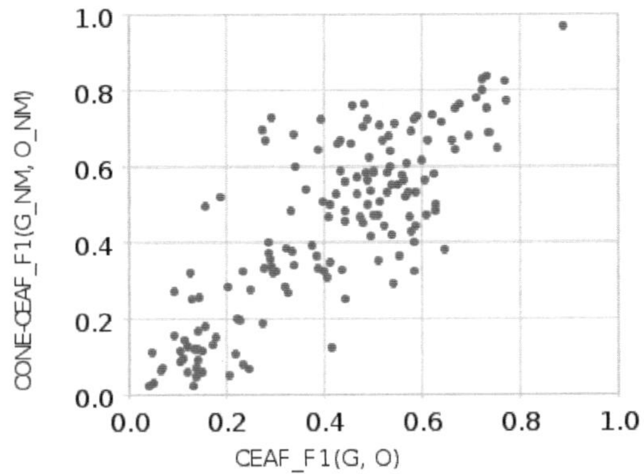

Figure 5. Correlation between CEAF F1 and CONE CEAF F1 for all systems on ACE 2005

6 Application and Discussion

To illustrate the applicability of CONE metrics, we consider the Enron e-mail corpus. It is of a different genre than the newswire corpora that CRR systems are usually trained on, and no CRR gold standard annotations exist for it. Consequently, no CRR systems have been evaluated on it so far. We used CONE B^3 and CONE CEAF to evaluate and compare the NE-CRR performance of various CRR systems on a subset of the Enron e-mail corpus (Klimt and Yang, 2004) that was cleaned and stripped of spam messages. We report the results in Table 5.

	CONE B^3			CONE CEAF		
	P	**R**	**F1**	**P**	**R**	**F1**
L	0.43	0.21	0.23	0.31	0.17	0.21
B	0.26	0.18	0.2	0.26	0.16	0.2
LP	0.61	0.51	0.53	0.58	0.53	0.54
OP	0.19	0.03	0.05	0.11	0.02	0.04

Table 5. $G^{NM\text{-}approx}$ Scores on Enron corpus

We find that LingPipe is the best of all the systems we considered, and LBJ is slightly ahead of BART in all measures. We suspect that since LingPipe is a commercial system, it may have extra training resources in the form of non-traditional corpora. Nevertheless, we believe our method is robust and scalable for large corpora without NE-CRR gold standard annotations.

7 Conclusion and Future Work

We propose the CONE B^3 and CONE CEAF metrics for automatic evaluation of Named Entity Co-reference Resolution (NE-CRR). These metrics measures a NE-CRR system's performance on the subtask of named mentions extraction and grouping (NMEG) and use it to estimate the system's performance on the full task of NE-CRR. We show that CONE B^3 and CONE CEAF scores of various systems across different datasets are strongly correlated with their standard B^3 and CEAF scores respectively. The advantage of CONE metrics compared to standard ones is that instead of the full gold standard data *G*, they only require a subset G^{NM} of named mentions which even if not available can be closely approximated by using a state-of-the-art NER system and clustering its results. Although we use a simple baseline algorithm for producing the approximate gold standard $G^{NM\text{-}approx}$, CONE B^3 and CONE CEAF scores of various systems obtained using this $G^{NM\text{-}approx}$ still prove to be correlated with their standard B^3 and CEAF scores obtained using the full gold standard *G*. CONE metrics thus reduce the need of expensive labeled corpora. We use CONE B^3 and CONE CEAF to evaluate the NE-CRR performance of various CRR systems on a subset of the Enron email corpus, for which no gold standard annotations exist and no such evaluations have been performed so far. In the future, we intend to use more sophisticated named entity matching schemes to produce better approximate gold standards $G^{NM\text{-}approx}$. We also intend to use the CONE metrics to evaluate NE-CRR systems on new datasets in domains such as chat, email, biomedical literature, etc. where very few corpora with gold standard annotations exist.

Acknowledgments

We would like to thank Prof. Ani Nenkova from the University of Pennsylvania for her talk about automatic evaluation for text summarization at the spring 2010 CMU LTI Colloquium and anonymous reviewers for insightful comments.

References

E. Agirre, L. Màrquez and R. Wicentowski, Eds. 2007. *Proceedings of the Fourth International Workshop on Semantic Evaluations (SemEval).*

A. Bagga and B. Baldwin. 1998. Algorithms for Scoring Coreference Chains. *Proceedings of LREC Workshop on Linguistic Coreference.*

J. Baldridge and T. Morton. 2004. OpenNLP. http://opennlp.sourceforge.net/.

B. Baldwin and B. Carpenter. 2003. LingPipe. Alias-i.

E. Bengtson and D. Roth. 2008. Understanding the Value of Features for Coreference Resolution. *Proceedings of EMNLP.*

J. Cohen. 1988. *Statistical power analysis for the behavioral sciences.* (2nd ed.)

A.K. Elmagarmid, P.G. Ipeirotis and V.S. Verykios. 2007. Duplicate Record Detection: A Survey. *IEEE Transactions on Knowledge and Data Engineering*, v.19 n.1, 2007.

J.R. Finkel, T. Grenager, and C. Manning. 2005. Incorporating Non-local Information into Information Extraction Systems by Gibbs Sampling. *Proceedings of ACL.*

B. Klimt and Y. Yang. 2004. The Enron corpus: A new dataset for email classification research. *Proceedings of ECML.*

H.W. Kuhn. 1955. The Hungarian method for the assignment problem. *Naval Research Logistics Quarterly*, 2(83).

C. Lin and E. Hovy. 2003. Automatic evaluation of summaries using n-gram co-occurrence statistics. *Proceedings of HLT-NAACL.*

C. Lin and F.J. Och. 2004. Automatic evaluation of machine translation quality using longest common subsequence and skip-bigram statistics. *Proceedings of ACL.*

A. Louis and A. Nenkova. 2009. Automatically Evaluating Content Selection in Summarization without Human Models. *Proceedings of EMNLP*, pages 306–314, Singapore, 6-7 August 2009.

X. Luo. 2005. On coreference resolution performance metrics. *Proceedings of EMNLP.*

MUC-6. 1995. *Proceedings of the Sixth Understanding Conference (MUC-6).*

J. Munkres. 1957. Algorithms for the assignment and transportation problems. *Journal of SIAM*, 5:32-38.

NIST. 2003. The ACE evaluation plan. www.nist.gov/speech/tests/ace/index.htm.

K Papineni, S Roukos, T Ward and W.J. Zhu. 2002. BLEU: a method for automatic evaluation of machine translation. *Proceedings of ACL.*

V. Pervouchine, H. Li and B. Lin. 2009. Transliteration alignment. *Proceedings of ACL.*

L. Ratinov and D. Roth. 2009. Design Challenges and Misconceptions in Named Entity Recognition. *Proceedings of CoNLL.*

R. Shah, B. Lin, A. Gershman and R. Frederking. 2010. SYNERGY: a named entity recognition system for resource-scarce languages such as Swahili using online machine translation. *Proceedings of LREC Workshop on African Language Technology.*

H.E. Soper, A.W. Young, B.M. Cave, A. Lee and K. Pearson. 1917. On the distribution of the correlation coefficient in small samples. Appendix II to the papers of "Student" and R. A. Fisher. A co-operative study. *Biometrika*, 11, 328-413.

V. Stoyanov, N. Gilbert, C. Cardie and E. Riloff. 2009. Conundrums in Noun Phrase Coreference Resolution: Making Sense of the State-of-the-Art. *Proceedings of ACL.*

Y. Versley, S.P. Ponzetto, M. Poesio, V. Eidelman, A. Jern, J. Smith, X. Yang and A. Moschitti. 2008. BART: A Modular Toolkit for Coreference Resolution. *Proceedings of EMNLP.*

M. Vilain, J. Burger, J. Aberdeen, D. Connolly and L. Hirschman. 1995. A model-theoretic coreference scoring scheme. *Proceedings of MUC 6.*

Author Index